CENTAUR of the NORTH

Rockford Public Library
Rockford, Illinois

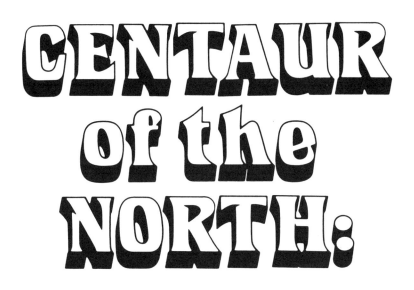

CENTAUR of the NORTH:

Francisco Villa, the Mexican Revolution, and Northern Mexico

Manuel A. Machado, Jr.

EAKIN PRESS ★ Austin, Texas

FIRST EDITION

Copyright © 1988
By Manuel A. Machado, Jr.

Published in the United States of America
By Eakin Press, P.O. Box 23069, Austin, Texas 78735

ISBN 0-89015-641-7

Library of Congress Cataloging-in-Publication Data

Machado, Manuel A.
    Centaur of the north.

    Bibliography: p.
    Includes index.
    1. Villa, Pancho, 1878-1923.   2. Mexico — History — Revolution, 1910-1920.
3. Revolutionists — Mexico — Biography.   I. Title.
F1234.V63M33   1988   972.08'1'0924   [B]   87-32966
ISBN 0-89015-641-7

*This work is affectionately dedicated to Cliff and
Sylvia Ashby and the original cast of* Pancho!

Contents

Foreword

Among the primary participants in Mexico's modern revolution, Pancho Villa has garnered the most acclaim and notoriety from both admirers and detractors. Born in 1878 at an *hacienda* in the state of Durango and baptized Doroteo Arango, the future revolutionist rapidly mastered the skills of horsemanship for which he became renowned in adulthood. Following a confrontation with *hacienda* owners in defense of his sister's honor, Doroteo fled the state and changed his name to Francisco Villa. In 1910, in support of the presidential ascendancy of Francisco Ignacio Madero, Villa flamboyantly entered the stage of national politics.

Like any tumultuous upheaval, Mexico's 20th century revolution promptly attracted the attention of serious scholars, most of whom endeavored to separate the violence from the social significance of the event. Inevitably not a few historians succumbed to the temptation of categorizing the principal revolutionaries in terms of ideologies. Madero, Carranza, Obregón, and even Zapata neatly filled ideological cubicles. Pancho Villa, seemingly devoid of ideology except insofar as an innate sense of justice guided his behavior toward opponents, eluded the net of revisionist historians.

In recent years, Manuel A. Machado, Jr., admittedly a sympathetic admirer of Pancho Villa, devoted countless hours of meticulous research in domestic and foreign archives to compile abundant documentation for an insightful biography of the Chihuahua revolutionary who styled himself the Centaur of the North. In pursuit of the enigmatic Villa, Dr. Machado wrote with strength and passion, tempered by the canon of historiography that truth and objectivity must be served. Casting aside doctrinaire constraints that characterize the writings of leading Mexicanist historians, Machado carefully avoided the pitfalls of philosophical polemics. Utilizing the talents of a humanities scholar, he reconstructed Villa's cultural landscape in varied colorful swatches.

While at times during the turbulent periods of the revolution Villa acted ruthlessly toward avowed enemies, in some situations he manifested genuine sorrow for the suffering of his loyal compatriots. As Machado interpreted the supporting evidence Villa was not a cardboard *caudillo*. Always controversial, seldom inactive, occasionally complex, Pancho Villa emerges in this biography as a rustic natural leader for whom the revolution provided a timely outlet for an unusually restless energy. With or without ideas, Villa's dynamic presence in northern Mexico gravely affected the careers of other ambitious revolutionary chieftains.

Despite the vast amount of scholarship on the Mexican Revolution that has been published in the last twenty years, the average American's awareness of this momentous event is limited to a nodding acquaintance with a triumvirate of charismatic generals whose reputations transcended the international boundary — Obregón, Villa, and Zapata. Of the three hierarchs, Villa definitely left an enduring legacy in borderlands history that now Dr. Manuel A. Machado, Jr., in *Centaur of the North*, places in perspective for a new generation of scholars and *aficionados* of Mexican history.

Félix D. Almaráz, Jr.
The University of Texas at San Antonio

Preface

An early spring sun shone through the iron bars on the window of the fetid sickroom, and the morning rays illuminated the frail figure on the bed. A faint smell of medication, urine, and general debility permeated the air of the small cubicle. On the spare iron bed lay a gray-haired woman obviously advanced in years and surrounded by attendants. Tourists gawked through the window of the sickroom, and an occasional camera flashed to obtain a picture of the fragile woman.

The rest of the house, converted into a museum, featured a bullet-riddled automobile, pictures and other memorabilia, and military artifacts from the early twentieth century. Large rooms and parlors had characterized this once opulent house. The house fronted a fairly busy street, and though it was only mid-March the promise of heat was already apparent in the air.

It was March 1979, and Cliff Ashby and I had taken a group of drama students from Texas Tech University south of the border. Our principal mission was to visit the occupant of the house. Ashby, a drama professor at Tech and a fine playwright, wanted to present publicity material to the elderly lady. As our group approached the large adobe structure, we saw over the large doorway that led to the vestibule a wrought-iron legend — "Quinta Luz."

The house was a gift from the woman's husband. The couple made their home there in Chihuahua City, Chihuahua, after their marriage in 1911, but the exigencies of political and social turmoil forced the husband to resume the mantle of hero and legend and set aside the mundane considerations of domesticity. The woman, Doña Luz Corral de Villa, was the wife of Francisco Villa, born Doroteo Arango and known more familiarly as Pancho Villa.

Cliff Ashby had written a play entitled *Pancho!*, based on the life of Pancho Villa, and we and some members of the cast went to

Chihuahua to interview her and present her with posters announcing the production of *Pancho!* The show was scheduled to open in the first week of April, but spring break intervened and allowed us to make the trip to northern Mexico. By taking some of the cast with us, we were able to give them an introduction to northern Mexico and to the lady who was the first wife of one of the most celebrated and simultaneously maligned heroes of the Mexican Revolution (1910–1920).

Doña Luz Corral Vda. de Villa had suffered a broken hip and was bedridden. When I first met her in 1962, vigor and tenacity had characterized her approach to life. She defended her late husband against the calumny and defamation hurled against him by those who came to dominate the fratricidal struggle of the Mexican Revolution. The seventeen-year interval between my first meeting with Señora de Villa and the 1979 meeting demonstrated the ravages of age and infirmity. Yet she remained sufficiently lucid to permit a taped interview that afternoon. Like her husband, Doña Luz Corral Vda. de Villa epitomized the toughness and independence of northern Mexico.

Acknowledgments

Work of this sort requires support, both fiscal and moral. Colleagues have read and criticized parts of the manuscript. Secretaries have labored over the preparation of the final product. Special thanks goes to Ms. Julie McVay, secretary of the Department of History at the University of Montana, who patiently worked on the final manuscript. As in so many other things, she has been a rock of support.

My family also merits mention. Often millstones around the necks of writers, the family still remains the basis of support. They endured the incessant clacking of a typewriter while I steadfastly ignored them.

The Research Advisory Council of the University of Montana funded research in Mexico City, Chihuahua, and Texas for this project. Additionally, the Department of History at Texas Tech University, Lubbock, Texas, where I served as a visiting professor in Spring 1979, provided secretarial service and sufficient time for initial phases of research and writing. The Fulbright Program on the International Exchange of Scholars provided me with a lectureship in Chihuahua where, once teaching duties were completed, I could roam around *villista* territory, poking my head in libraries, archives, and bookstores. All of the above receive my thanks.

Graduate students often provide the sounding board upon which a historian can try his material. Over the years many have provided legwork, editorial comments, and acted as foils for my views about Villa. Especially helpful were Tom Fulton, now of the U.S. Department of Agriculture, Scott Long, Connie Flaherty Erickson, and Christopher Stewart. Above all I must thank Joseph O'Dell, Jr., for his assistance, for we argued for hours about Villa and his role in Mexican history. Additionally, his own graduate research sharpened my perceptions of Villa immensely. Ronald

xi

Craig, one of my current graduate students, used his computer wizardry to supply pertinent maps.

Additionally, the staffs at the Centro de Estudios de Historia de México, CONDUMEX, S. A., the Biblioteca Nacional, the Archivo General de la Nación, the National Archives, Washington, D.C., the Bancroft Library, University of California, Berkeley, and the Benson Latin American Collection, University of Texas, Austin, provided invaluable assistance in the procurement of information. In Chihuahua, the Secretaría del Gobierno opened its records to me for the period during which the *villistas* controlled Chihuahua. The Centro de Información del Estado de Chihuahua (CIDECH) made the Francisco R. Almada Collection available. The El Paso Public Library's Southwest Collection also provided essential newspaper sources for the period, as well as photographic materials.

None of the above mentioned can be held responsible for what has been written. If their advice, for one reason or another, was not taken, it falls on my shoulders. This has been a project that has evolved over a period of about twenty-five years, always being sandwiched in between other, more immediate research. In a sense this is a project that will never end. Villa is too elusive a personality. More will continue to be written about him long after future generations of historians have rendered their judgments. I imagine that when Mexico celebrates the centennial of the revolution in 2010, Villa will remain the center of controversy.

Introduction

Mexico's northern tier of states demonstrates vast geographic and climatic diversity, ranging from arid deserts to coastal fishing ports and lumber-producing mountains in the Sierra Madre Occidental. Fertile land sprouts forth an abundance of crops if water reaches an area. Yet it is a region devoted in great part to pastoral concerns that must serve as year-round pasturage for cattle, sheep, goats, horses, mules, and donkeys. The average range requirement for the area consists of seventy-five acres per cow/calf unit, but this figure occasionally reaches 125 acres per cow/calf unit.

The land strikes the observer as hard, and it produces a breed of men who are rugged and individualistic. In great part the character of northern Mexico grew from the settlement patterns that in the seventeenth and eighteenth centuries injected Hispanic civilization into the nomadic tribes of the area. Settlement of Chihuahua did not occur in any concerted form until the eighteenth century. By that time, Spanish attitudes had undergone substantial changes. The War of Spanish Succession (1701–1713) introduced a Bourbon prince onto the Spanish throne and replaced the fierce religiosity of the Habsburgs with the rationalism of the Enlightenment. Thus, the corporatism of the Habsburg State gave way to the more individualistic temperament of the eighteenth century and helped nurture the fierce separatism and regionalism of the north.

Moreover, the Indian tribes of northern Mexico roamed freely, engaging in internecine warfare with each other and later with the Spanish and Creole settlers of the region. Domination of these indigenous peoples failed to destroy their essentially individualistic character. Unlike their Indian brethren to the south, the Indians of northern Mexico did not suffer from excessive centralization and too much reliance on a single authority. While these people ultimately blended, in the main, with the Spanish and Creole newcomers, it was, in many ways, a more workable relationship than the dichotomized relations between Indian and Hispanic civilizations in central and southern Mexico.

Northern Mexico gave rise to huge *latifundia* or *haciendas* dominated by the Creole minority and worked by an Indian and *mestizo* labor pool. On these semiautonomous holdings, some of them ranging into the millions of acres, debt peonage bound the workers to the *haciendas* and the mines. At the same time, the workers became increasingly adept at their various trades: miners, cowhands (*vaqueros*), wheelwrights, horse wranglers, hunters, builders. The turmoil and confusion of an independent Mexico failed to daunt the steady growth of the *hacienda* by the mid-nineteenth century. The advent of Porfirio Díaz (1876–1911) forced Mexico into modernity at one level while maintaining and expanding traditional institutions and privilege on another.

Throughout the long regime of Díaz (the *porfiriato*), Mexico began her leap into the modern world. Foreign capital flooded Mexico as the country slowly achieved economic stability. Lands in the north quickly came into the control of foreign and Mexican entrepreneurs. Holdings increased as did abuses of the *peones* that worked these lands. Discontent smoldered; grievances — real or imagined — increased.

From the northern crucible of disaffection came the majority of the bigger-than-life figures of the Mexican Revolution. They represented the inchoate desires of inarticulate peoples but at the same time looked to the satisfaction of their own interests. These men demanded recognition.

Heroes no longer occupy the fashionable position they once did in the writing of history. Instead, mass movements impelled by purported ideological underpinnings dominate historical writing. Historians of late have attempted to find ideological bases for revolutionary chaos begun by essentially unlettered peasants and to elevate their action to a loftier plane. As a consequence the heroes of these movements became pasteboard figures, acting inexorably within the context of their ideological parameters.

The Mexican Revolution of 1910–1920 produced a plethora of heroes and a mass of often conflicting ideas that eventually molded into the Constitution of 1917 and post-revolution programs. Anarchy and chaos, though, became the dominant factors of that decade of fratricidal strife. Factions united for limited objectives and then fell into internecine conflict that prolonged the bloodletting and forced the nation to suffer political instability, economic dislocation, and societal disruption.

Mexico's revolution of 1910 began as an essentially political movement aimed at the ouster of Porfirio Díaz. But within the nucleus of the revolutionary *côterie* the potential of political dissent and personal antipathies already germinated. The expulsion of Díaz in 1911 failed to produce the stability hoped for by Francisco Madero and his followers. Already disaffection — primarily from Pascual Orozco and Emiliano Zapata — manifested itself against the Madero government. By late 1912, Bernardo Reyes and Félix Díaz, nephew of the deposed dictator, conspired and ultimately succeeded, with the leadership of General of the Army Victoriano Huerta and the connivance of United States Ambassador Henry Lane Wilson, to overthrow Mexico. Ultimately, all of these men shared responsibility for Madero's assassination.

The counterrevolution of February 1913 against Madero led other Mexican revolutionary figures to join together against the dictator. Tenuously uniting under the banner of the Plan de Guadalupe, Venustiano Carranza, Alvaro Obregón, Francisco Villa, and Pablo González, among others, made common cause against the putative assassin of Francisco Madero.

In the period between 1913 and approximately 1917, major figures of the revolution dominated the scene. Brilliant battles and bold pronouncements punctuated the spectacle of a country in the throes of bloody revolutionary strife.

To ignore the role of personality in the Mexican Revolution is to render that movement sterile and colorless. Personalities so dominated the Mexican political and military scene that their personal struggles with each other overrode whatever philosophical foundations their different movements may have had.

Biography in the context of the Mexican Revolution provides the putative biographer with an exercise in intellectual terror. It seems as if none of the usual rules exist. Instead we see a society whose bounds have been rendered, where people normally destined for the lower rungs of the social ladder suddenly find themselves projected into prominence by the forces that wittingly or unwittingly unleashed violence in the name of orderly reform.

Like so many heroes of the revolution, Pancho Villa came from these recently unmanacled origins. Consequently, his barely literate facade and the nature of his activities did not allow for the collection and preservation of a corpus of papers upon which future biographers might draw. Instead of being able to implant ourselves firmly in Pancho's psyche, we find ourselves looking at Villa through the eyes of those who best knew him — supporters and detractors alike. Silvestre Terrazas, Lázaro de la Garza, various State Department officials, newspapers — all provide glimpses of Villa. We have had, in effect, to see him often through the eyes of the enemy, for the Archivo Carranza at CONDUMEX, S.A., has proved invaluable. Villa's *Memorias*, compiled by Martín Luis Guzmán, require considerable care in their use, for again is it Villa or is it Guzmán's perception of Villa? Still, Villa remains the most towering figure of Mexico's earth-shaking revolution, though in the end he was reduced to local influence and ultimately was bought off by the government.

In dealing with the Mexican Revolution, the force of personality inevitably becomes manifest. Imposing figures made their charisma felt and helped shape the course of Mexican history. Not all of them were winners.

The triumph of the Constitutionalist cause under Carranza meant that some of these powerful figures were suddenly made outlaws and/or opponents to the triumphant government. The choices faced by those disaffected from Carranza ranged from outright resistance, organization of factional interests outside the country, or boring exile, usually in the United States or Cuba. But these personalities generally chose to oppose the triumphant faction rather than submit and face execution or, worse, ignominious exile and rejection. Given the powerful and conflicting characters that dominated the Mexican Revolution, the choice seemed inescapable: resistance and continued struggle.

Moreover, the Mexican Revolution did not become a singular movement overnight. Rather, regional variations came into play. Northerners, southerners, and rebels from the east and west of Mexico pursued particular, often localized, objectives in the name of an amorphous political precept. To attempt to homogenize the Mexican Revolution is, ultimately, to disregard the regional character and the regional personalities that impelled that movement.

Each region of Mexico contributed its greats to the revolution, but none was nearly as significant as northern Mexico. From the north came Venustiano Carranza, Alvaro Obregón, Francisco Villa, Tomás Urbina, Benjamín Hill, and Plutarco Elías Calles. Each in his own way made a significant impact on the direction of the revolution, and each ultimately dominated a sector of the revolutionary movement through the force of his personality or skillful political manipulation.

Unfortunately, Mexican historiography and the dominant line in Mexico tends to ignore those forceful figures that ultimately found themselves at odds with the Constitutionalist cause. The most dominant figure of the revolution and, in fact, the man responsible for the military triumphs of *constitucionalismo,* was a bandit-cattle rustler-cowboy turned revolutionary who put together one of the most efficient military machines in Mexico. Francisco Villa, born Doroteo Arango, a barrel-chested, 180-pound man standing at five feet ten inches, came to dominate northern Mexico. But until 1967, he was considered by official circles as nothing more than an ungrateful bandit who turned against those who had given him the opportunity to better himself through service and submission to his betters.

Revolutions all create their own mythologies, and Mexico's major revolution certainly is no exception. Unfortunately, Villa, until recently, has not received the fair recognition commensurate with his contribution to the cause of the Mexican Revolution. Instead, he has been vilified and deprecated as a revolutionary who was intent upon the destruction of long-sought goals by the Mexican people.

An interesting facet of most revolutionary mythology lies in that it is usually created after the fact. Once ensconced, the triumphant revolutionaries attempt to justify their actions — often as barbaric as those of their opponents — by systematically degrading those who ran counter to the faction in power. Villa's fate at the hands of the mythologizers of the revolution is certainly no different.

Pancho Villa performed the most valuable services for the Constitutionalist cause. His control of the major railways on the north-south line to Mexico City from Chihuahua and the military machine that was his División del Norte (welded from disparate peasant, *vaquero,* and middle-sector elements) drove the supporters of Victoriano Huerta farther south until the petty jealousies of Venustiano Carranza brought the División del Norte to a halt.

Villa and Carranza's ultimate split came as no surprise. To Carranza, Villa personified the unlettered, unsophisticated, rude peasant. Villa in turn described Carranza as *un chocolatero perfumado,* a "perfumed chocolate drinker." Inexorably, their personality differences brought them into conflict — a conflict that prolonged the revolution even more.

But because Villa finally lost the struggle with Carranza he has, until recently, received the opprobrium of the ruling revolutionary cadres. The necessity of building a revolutionary hagiography in order to justify the revolution has forced the creation of good guys and bad guys. Villa became a bad guy, a counterrevolutionary intent upon the destruction of the sacred cause of *constitucionalismo*. It should be noted, parenthetically, that none of the major figures of the revolution could ever qualify as candidates for canonization, for they were all profoundly human, manifesting the weaknesses and strengths of the human condition.

Despite the near-satanic characteristics Villa's detractors have given him, the inescapable fact remains that the *villista* impact on the revolution cannot be ignored. Villa finally represented those elements of northern Mexico that found themselves in a constant struggle against the impositions of a more sophisticated and antipathetic Mexico City, for first and foremost Francisco Villa was a *norteño*, a denizen of the arid and semi-arid areas of Durango and Chihuahua.

This brief biography of Villa will deal more with the man and his personality than with the purported ideologies that impelled him to act as he did. Vibrancy and sheer human dynamism expressed through personality became the major factor of the revolution. We shall look at Villa as a representative of a northern tradition, as a military man, as a man with concern for the betterment of his people. At the same time, the impact of Villa on the culture of Mexico needs examination, for no one figure contributed so much, though indirectly, to the culture of the country. In song and literature the figure of Francisco Villa dominates the history of the revolution.

However, in no way will this biography attempt to obscure the atrocities committed either by Villa himself or in his name. For the barbarism that was so much a part of the Mexican Revolution is best represented in Francisco Villa. Killing, rapine, and a seeming lack of concern for human life characterized all of the major revolutionary groups. Villa's flamboyancy, however, singled him out for special consideration by both his supporters and enemies.

CHAPTER I

Death as Beginning

The revolutionary hydra, after devouring Zapata and Carranza, engulfed another of the highest heads of the primitive revolutionary family.
Jorge Vera Estañol

By 7:00 A.M., most of the cocks in and around Parral, Chihuahua, had stopped crowing. An occasional scruffy dog wandered through the morning heat on July 20, 1923. A spitting, sputtering automobile headed down the Calle Gabino Barreda. Though relatively new, the Dodge already showed the strain of being driven on the wretched roads common in southern Chihuahua and Durango at that time. Its rattles and creaks accompanied the complaints of its cold engine that early morning.

As the car approached the corner of Gabino Barreda and the Calle de San Juan de Dios, it became apparent that the driver and his party were out on a lark. The chauffeur, Rosalío Rosales, rode on the running board because his employer, a dangerous dilettante behind the wheel, wanted to do his own driving. In the car, accompanying the driver, were his secretary, Miguel Trillo, three bodyguards — Rafael Medrano, Claro Hurtado, and Ramón Contreras — and an assistant, Daniel Tamayo. Trillo, ever cautious, sensed possible danger, but ebullience from the night before cheered the occupants of the vehicle and made Trillo less feral in his precautions.

The car chugged and wove down the street though its driver, a nondrinker and therefore *en su juicio,* haplessly attempted to drive in

1

a straight line. At the Callejón de Meza, a peanut and sweets vendor ostentatiously saluted the driver, a not unusual occurrence in Parral, Chihuahua. Following its wobbly route, the car slowed in order to negotiate a corner. Because of the driver's lack of skill, the Dodge almost stopped as it turned from Gabino Barreda to San Juan de Dios. Suddenly, a door opened on Gabino Barreda 7–9, four black bores appeared at the ends of four new, army-issue rifles, and volleys of gunshots ripped into the nearly immobile Dodge. A second door opened, and four more rifles discharged their deadly projectiles toward the car. The driver and chauffeur received the first volleys of dum-dum shells. Francisco "Pancho" Villa, Centaur of the North, leader of the División del Norte during the 1910–1920 revolution, lay dead, the victim of cowardly assassination.

Even as death engulfed him, Francisco Villa had time to draw his gun and, relying on his legendary marksmanship, dropped one of the assassins. His secretary, Trillo, drew his weapon, but eleven deadly dum-dums claimed his life. Poor Rosalío Rosales died with his chief. The small group of bodyguards fought like the *villistas* they were, but death soon claimed them all. The wounded Ramón Contreras and Claro Hurtado left the car and headed for the Puente Guanajuato, where they later died on the riverbank. Rafael Medrano lived for eight agonizing days after receiving wounds in his belly.

Dum-dum shells had performed the grisly task well. Villa and his escort were practically eviscerated. Villa's death photo, a macabre exercise in the use of celluloid, shows him lying in the foyer of the Hidalgo Hotel in Parral with his left side blown away, his internal organs on view for the curious and the diabolical.

The death of Francisco Villa, born Doroteo Arango in 1878, resulted from political expediency at both state and federal levels and from the desire for personal vengeance by Melitón Lozoya. Indeterminate plotters worked behind the scenes, laid meticulous plans, and accomplished the murder.

Despite his uneasy truce with the government, Villa, after his retirement in July 1920, continued to frighten the ruling claques in Mexico City and in both Chihuahua and Durango. In the spring of 1922, rumors abounded that Villa planned to launch his candidacy for the governorship of Durango, a prospect that disgusted and caused apprehension in President Alvaro Obregón and his crony, Plutarco Elías Calles, Mexico's secretary of *gobernación*. In June

1922, Villa granted an interview to a reporter for the Mexico City daily *El Universal*. In that interview, Villa declared that he had given his word to "Fito [Adolfo de la Huerta] to retire from politics during Obregón's presidency and not spill any more Mexican blood. And Francisco Villa always keeps his word!"

Throughout most of 1922, *El Universal* had run a straw vote of presidential possibilities. Figuring prominently on the list, though certainly not at the head of it, stood the name of Francisco Villa. Villa's reaction to the poll was humorous. He declared to Regino Hernández Llergo: "that would be good! Francisco Villa, who can barely read, wanting to be president of the Republic . . . ." Then, wistfully, "I have partisans . . . . I could pull in more men than anybody because the people know why I fought and . . . who knows if someday I might have to take to the hills again."

Villa's interview with Hernández Llergo served to harden the political power structure against a possible *villista* resurgence. While denying his desire to run for the governorship of Durango, Villa continued to dangle the threat of his potential involvement in Mexico's political life. On June 14, in *El Universal*, Villa reportedly declared that the matter of the governorship should wait awhile. He further stated that "I have lots of partisans! I have friends in every social stratum . . . . Yes Sir, I believe that no one has today the following that Francisco Villa has! For that reason they [Obregón *et al.*] fear me; they fear me because they know that the day in which I throw myself into the struggle, I will, Sir, overwhelm them."

Three days later, *El Universal* continued to publish comments that Villa had made to Hernández Llergo. Villa, disillusioned by the United States, admonished all Mexicans to keep an eye on the *gringos*, for they posited a constant threat to Mexico. "To you who are young," he said, "and as good Mexicans which you must be, I ask you not to forget the great danger and that you always remind your friends and children of it, so that when the day comes, the gringos will not catch us napping." Mexico, he observed painfully, continued to suffer from disunity, a factor that could ultimately lead to Mexico's defeat.

In great part, Villa attributed the dissension in Mexican ranks to the radicalism of the administration. He criticized Calles for his radicalism because the radicals constantly strove for an equality of classes. To Villa, society was a ladder, with some who made it to the top and others who must content themselves with a lower rung.

Political activity in Mexico intensified throughout 1922 and early 1923. Who would be the successor to Obregón? Calles? Secretary of the Treasury De la Huerta, provisional president of Mexico from May to the end of November 1920, disclaimed any ambition for the presidency; straw votes in *El Universal* showed that great numbers of individuals saw him as the ideal choice for that office. Certainly, he needed a power base, and that base busied himself cultivating roses, building schools, raising cotton, wheat, and cattle, and caching arms at Canutillo. Throughout Obregón's presidency, a constant irritant had been the good relations between De la Huerta and Villa.

Even before assuming the presidency, Obregón, vengeful and desirous of destroying Villa, was cautioned by Calles. Calles observed that Canutillo could not be taken by surprise, for Villa, with 200 men, would wreak havoc on any federal force that might attempt to dislodge him from the place. Furthermore, Villa's knowledge of the terrain could prove disastrous to any attempted invasion. According to essayist Roberto Blanco Moheno, Calles observed: " 'Villa knows that terrain better than anyone. If you don't believe it, ask General Pershing.' " Calles further noted that Obregón should be patient, for " 'if Villa threatens with another barbarity later on, you can organize things for what we know must be done.' "

Obregón continued to fear the possible alliance between Villa and De la Huerta. From 1921 to mid-1923, Obregón carefully watched the relations between his secretary of the treasury and his northern enemy. In early 1923, De la Huerta, returning from conferences in the United States, stopped in Jiménez, Chihuahua, to talk with Villa. Villa boarded the train and continued on to Torreón with De la Huerta. As Villa climbed aboard De la Huerta's car, he further aggravated Obregón and Calles by stating: "See, now the bandits and soldiers are together."

Political and personal animosities thus ran at high levels. The hatred that Melitón Lozoya bore Villa stemmed from Villa's bringing Lozoya face to face with his own weak character. Additionally, Lozoya's uncle wanted to be governor of Durango. Villa, thoroughly contemptuous of the whole Lozoya clan, let it be known that the election of the elder Lozoya would not meet with favor at Canutillo. A new candidate was found. Lozoya, moreover, was a thief. When Villa made his peace with De la Huerta in July 1920, he asked for and received the *hacienda* at Canutillo. Previous to that time, Lozoya took the stock and equipment from the *hacienda*. In a rather frightening interview, Villa told Lozoya that he had one month in which to return the stolen goods. A month came and went; Villa took no action. His mercurial temper, flaring at the sight of Lozoya, subsided as he turned to other pursuits.

Lozoya, however, felt uncomfortable about the entire affair. The humiliating interview with Villa had hardened Lozoya in his resolve to rid the region of its unofficial chieftain. He soon gathered about him some of Villa's enemies in and around Parral. Lozoya felt self-satisfied as Crisóstomo, Juan, and José Barraza, Juan and José Sáenz Pardo, Librado Martínez, José and Ramón Guerra, and Juventino Ruiz joined the move to eliminate Francisco Villa. However, even Juan and José Barraza could not bring themselves to participate in an assassination plot despite their grudges against Villa.

The loss of the Barraza brothers did not deter the plotters, for the money man, Jesús Salas Barraza, proved ample compensation for the loss of two rifles. This man, a Durango politician, claimed that he wanted to rid the nation of Villa for "social vengeance." Salas Barraza capitalized on the availability of private money that was offered to do away with Villa. Rumors abounded that the State of New Mexico wanted to contribute $50,000 for Villa, dead or alive, as revenge for the raid on Columbus, New Mexico, on March 9, 1916. The State of Chihuahua allegedly had 100,000 pesos on hand for Villa. Salas Barraza, through a variety of sources, collected approximately $50,000 in U.S. currency to carry out Villa's assassination.

The vengeful cadre rented the house on Gabino Barreda from Guillermo Gallardo and began to study the movements of their proposed target. Between May 10 and July 20, the killers kept a constant watch. Rumors circulated around Parral that a plot existed to kill Villa and that these warnings had reached him. One American living in Chihuahua, an admirer of Villa, claimed that he personally wrote to Villa warning of a plot, spearheaded by Calles, to assassinate the *jefe* of Canutillo. The American reportedly charged: "Now is the time for all decent Mexicans and their American friends to destroy Obregón and his bolsheviks."

Villa failed to heed the warnings. Arrogantly certain about his own position in the area, he failed to conceive that anyone either would or could attempt to stop him. In fact, he treated such warnings derisively. He occasionally left his stronghold and went relatively exposed to Parral, where he stayed at the Hidalgo Hotel which he owned. Villa had purchased the hotel as a means of ensuring lodging for his men when they made their occasional forays into Parral. Often his entire bodyguard of fifty men joined the Centaur of the North; at other times, merely a carload of men chugged and bounced along the road from Canutillo to Parral.

But the plotters continued to maintain their vigil. They observed Villa's every movement. To be sure, the triggermen were not in the affair on purely idealistic grounds. Money talks, and Salas Barraza bought many men. He promised each man 300 pesos after the assassination. In addition, they all received five pesos per day for food and fifteen pesos a week for rent. Additional sites for surveillance purposes were rented for forty pesos per month. Ostensibly, these men were in Parral to sell hay, which was bought and paid for by Salas Barraza. Since guns and ammunition are needed to kill a man from ambush, Salas Barraza again opened his purse. Provisions, alfalfa for the horses, guns, and ammunition for the assassination totaled only 10,000 pesos. Salas Barraza apparently pocketed the rest of the money that came to him through diverse sources.

The wait was long and dreary. That summer in Chihuahua was far from pleasant, and the men in the house on Gabino Barreda became edgy. On July 10, Villa came to town, providing the opportunity to complete their assignment. As men loaded rifles and took their positions, students from the Colegio Progreso appeared and stepped into the line of fire. Lozoya ordered that no shots be fired.

Tension continued to mount. Lozoya and his assassins began to lose their nerve. Despite careful arrangements, the cowardice of the assassins became clearly manifest. Col. Félix C. Lara, commander of the Parral garrison, conveniently left on maneuvers with his troops. Coincidentally, the weapons acquired for the job were of the latest military issue.

By July 19, Salas Barraza, Lozoya, José Guerra, and Librado Martínez became increasingly apprehensive. They paced the house on Gabino Barreda like "caged animals." Late that afternoon, Villa and his escort entered town. Fortuitously, Villa had to come for the Canutillo payroll. At the same time, he planned to attend the christening of the son of one of his former *dorados* that evening. Villa's escort was small because the Centaur of the North did not want to impose too much on his former comrade.

Then came the fateful morning of July 20. The peanut vendor, a goon hired by Salas Barraza, shouted *"¡Viva Villa!"* once to indicate that Villa rode in the front seat of the Dodge. This call to life announced his death. Villa was buried in a simple grave in Parral despite the fact that he constructed a mausoleum for himself in Chihuahua City. Two years after his death, someone raided his grave and stole his head. The Centaur of the North, in death, became a headless rider.

Protests over the death of Villa immediately appeared. Due to unusual pressure, the Chamber of Deputies formed a commission by August 1 to investigate the death of the feared guerrilla leader. On August 9, Salas Barraza wrote a confession to Obregón, claiming the plot to do away with Villa as his own. Salas Barraza's volubility led him to say that the 100,000 pesos offered by Chihuahua for Villa would be used for the benefit of the children of Villa's victims. A court quickly sentenced Salas Barraza to twenty years in the penitentiary. Six months later, Salas Barraza became a colonel in the regular Mexican army.

One United States consular official from Chihuahua noted that since Villa's death, Calles, holed up in an *hacienda* in Monterrey, surrounded himself with federal troops "guarding against any possible attempt at taking his life." This official continued that "the killing of General Villa was . . . a political move on the part of the present administration and it is firmly believed" that General Calles "plotted the assassination." The possibility also existed that "serious results may come from this move . . . . Calles has . . . some terrible enemies in the former villista chieftains and if an open revolution does not occur every other conceivable effort will be made to prohibit [Calles' candidacy]."

The United States consul in Chihuahua City, a former Villa stronghold, also saw the death of Villa essentially as a political expediency. Occupants of this city believed, according to the consul, that the federal government was privy to and even a prime mover in the assassination. Villa obviously had been preparing for a potential fight. War matériél had reached Canutillo in increasing quantities. Arms and ammunition came into Mexico surreptitiously through Ojinaga, Chihuahua, destined for Canutillo. At the time of his death, Villa possessed sufficient ordnance to equip 2,500 to 3,000 men, enough to give Calles pause about the presidency.

While disapproving the politics behind the death of Villa, the United States consul in Chihuahua wrote with relief that "a grave potential danger to the peace of Mexico has been removed by the death of Francisco Villa . . . . The prospects for a peaceful presidential election next year have been measurably increased by the passing of this man who always left bloodshed and terror in his wake . . . ."

Speculations about Villa's political maneuvering were rife shortly after his death. Reports in the *New York Times* as early as July 6 indicated that Villa leaned strongly toward Raúl Madero, former governor of Nuevo León, or Adolfo de la Huerta. The *New York Times* of July 22 reported that the assassinated Villa "considered Calles as far from fitted for the presidency." Additionally, the announced candidacy of Raúl Madero died with Francisco Villa. Villa's murder removed "the danger of another revolution when the elections are held and also removes the essential backing of one candidate who could give General Calles real opposition."

The *New York Times* advanced the idea that Villa held the balance of power in the presidential struggle. As long as Villa lived, neither Obregón nor Calles could feel secure. Villa's preference for De la Huerta was well known. Villa, a week before his death, declared that he would have something to say in the nomination and election of a president in 1924.

Nationally, Mexican folk opinion crystallized in *corridos* (folk songs) that sang of the death of the fabled guerrilla leader. Throughout these *corridos* ran the recurrent theme of the assassination as a political ploy by the government. One such *corrido* declared:

> *Traitorous politicians of venal instincts/ who feared Villa for his great heart/ joined to make their criminal plans/ that serve as a shame for the entire nation . . . .*

Another *corrido*, written on the occasion of Obregón's own assassination on July 20, 1928, reemphasized the theme of Obregón's involvement in the death of Francisco Villa. The song, entitled "A Telegram From Hell Upon the Death of Obregon," stated:

Villa, who was always ready/ to know of everything/ with great joy/ let Obregón know:/ 'Obregón, you are a witness/ that I never feared death/ but to tell you the truth/ I had better luck than you.' The whole Nation knows/ of the means that you used/ to remove me from your path/ because you feared me.

Mexico had lost one of its greatest heroes. Though defeated in battle, Villa projected the image of the undaunted battler for the rights of the Mexican people. According to Blanco Moheno, the Mexican people wept "over its enormous loss." Soon they erected "though only in [their] heart[s], the monument that Villa deserves." Above all, Villa represented the people. "He knew, even with his ignorance, how to dictate the eternal lesson of total and barbaric justice."

CHAPTER II

"... This f------ crazy world!"

T hroughout Mexico thousands of infants came unheralded into the world on June 5, 1878. Clarions failed to announce their arrival nor, in the majority of cases, was there much fuss made over so mundane an occurrence. On the Hacienda of Río Grande in the *municipio* of San Juan del Río, Durango, a boy child came to Agustín Arango and his wife, Micaéla Arámbula. The child, named Doroteo, would be the first of five children born to them. Doroteo, Hipólito, Antonio, Mariana, and Martinita would remain essentially unlettered and would work at *hacienda* tasks alongside their parents.

The Arango family had some mobility during the children's formative years. Unlike many *campesinos* in northern Mexico, the Arangos avoided peonage on the *haciendas* but rather worked as sharecroppers. When Agustín Arango died in 1893, Doroteo was left as the oldest male in the family to provide the sole support of his mother, two sisters, and two brothers. As such, he continued the sharecropping that had begun with his father, this time on the Hacienda de Gogojito owned by Agustín López Negrete. In the following year, the life of the adolescent Doroteo Arango underwent a major change.

According to his own recollection, on September 22, 1894, Doroteo had returned from the fields that he sharecropped with López

Negrete. As he neared his house he heard his mother's anguished pleading. Don Agustín López Negrete had cast lecherous eyes at Doroteo's sister, Martinita, and Micaéla Arámbula de Arango begged the *hacendado* to leave her daughter alone.

Without being seen, sixteen-year-old Doroteo slipped to the home of a cousin and there grabbed a pistol that customarily hung on a peg in the house. When he returned to his own house, López Negrete continued to threaten Martinita. Without much ado, Doroteo opened fire, placing three shots into the *hacendado*. When servants attempted to capture Doroteo, the *hacendado* called them off, asked to be placed in his coach, and returned to the *hacienda*. He demanded that the boy be brought to him alive. Doroteo, meanwhile, mounted his horse and headed into the hills.

The next day, September 23, Doroteo discovered that Agustín López Negrete still lived but was in serious condition. More importantly, authorities in Canatlán, Durango, were now forming a posse to bring down the obstreperous youth. Before escaping into the hills for the next year, young Arango sent word to his mother to return to the house in Río Grande.

From 1894 until he attained a modicum of legitimacy in 1910, Doroteo Arango lived a life of constant pursuit by law enforcement agencies in Mexico. Beginning with his first encounter with the system of privilege represented by Agustín López Negrete, evasion from prosecution or summary execution became a principal activity for young Arango. He spent months moving throughout the mountains near his home, surviving on broiled, unsalted meat, and becoming increasingly feral.

Early in 1895, through what he termed ignorance or inexperience, three men captured Arango and took him to jail in San Juan del Río. Since his summary execution had been decreed throughout the state of Durango, he planned to escape at the first opportunity. The morning after his capture, Arango was set to grinding corn for *tortillas* and *tamales*. He grasped the stone *metate* (grinder), killed one of his guards, and made for the hills. To his good fortune, Arango found a horse that had recently been rounded up and thus made good his escape, remaining in the vicinity of the Sierra de la Silla and the Sierra de Gamón for the next year.

At this juncture, changes began to occur in Doroteo Arango. His unwitting and instinctive challenge of the justice system under the *porfiriato* had made him an outlaw. To avoid constant chase, he needed to change identities. Finally, he struck upon Francisco Villa, a name that twenty years later would reverberate throughout Mexico as the symbol of violence, unbridled brigandage, and primitive justice for Mexico's *campesinos.*

Various authorities have wrangled over the origin of Villa's newly acquired name. There are those who claim that he was in fact a bastard son of a Creole aristocrat named Villa, or a descendant of a nineteenth-century bandit named Villa. Villa's own account, in the *Memorias* prepared by Martín Luis Guzmán, attributes the name to his paternal grandfather. According to Villa, Agustín Arango was the bastard son of Don Jesús Villa. Because of the illegitimacy of his birth, Agustín took his mother's maiden name — Arango. Doroteo Arango reverted to his natural grandfather's name as a means of changing identity.

From this point forward, the exploits of Francisco "Pancho" Villa became interwoven with legend. In general, the outline of his life between 1895 and 1910 can be traced, though without a great deal of chronological exactitude. Villa's own accounts, while occasionally questionable, still provide at least basic information for anyone attempting a biography of one of Mexico's most quixotic and enigmatic revolutionary heroes.

Throughout most of 1895, Villa spent his time in the hills near San Juan del Río. In October, seven men captured him. As they casually prepared lunch and discussed when to deliver him to the authorities, Villa, who kept a pistol tucked under his blanket, carefully inched the gun out. While waiting for the moment to make his escape, Villa's captors set about the task of roasting ears of corn. Two went for wood, two went to cut corn in a field, and three remained on guard. Amidst a furious burst of gunfire, Villa ran for his horse which stood about 400 yards away. The three guards took cover, and Villa headed toward his mother's house.

Three months later, *rurales* from Canatlán attempted to capture the elusive Villa. As the *rurales* prepared to charge his hiding place in the mountains, they formed a perfect target. Villa recalls killing three men and a number of horses, thus forcing the *rurales* to retreat.

Villa proceeded to change locales. He killed some beef animals, dried the meat, and earned some much needed cash by selling part of the meat to some timber workers in the mountains.

These same lumbermen also bought provisions for him as necessity arose.

In June 1896 Villa met Ignacio Parra and Refugio Alvarado, two locally known bandits. No other avenue seemed open to him, and he resolved to accept their invitation to join them. No longer would Villa ride alone. His solitary existence now became a part of the banditry of northern Mexico wherein he would gain a fearsome reputation before his aggressive talents would be put to more constructive use.

His first exploit with Parra and Alvarado involved the stealing of a mule train. Villa carried out his assignment with alacrity and netted 5,000 pesos after the trio sold the mules in Parral, Chihuahua. As a final step toward ultimate ingratiation with Alvarado and Parra, Villa stole a fine horse in Parral, and from there the trio returned to Durango.

Brigandage proved lucrative for Villa. He and his partners succeeded in robbing payrolls and shipments of money from mines around Durango and Chihuahua. In one haul they cleared 50,000 pesos apiece and returned to San Juan del Río. There Villa, according to his own account, spread the wealth around the area, helping family and friends who were in financial straits. Such bounty, however, could not go unnoticed. Late in 1896, *rurales* made another attempt to capture Villa, and he and his companions again sought refuge in the hills. The escape did not go without mishap. Villa received a flesh wound on the chest, and Alvarado took a slug in the leg.

By the next year, Parra, Alvarado, and Villa continued to rustle cattle, sell the meat, and split the proceeds. Unfortunately, Alvarado and Villa fell out. When Villa told Parra of the dispute, Parra and Alvarado met. Parra returned alone. According to Villa's account, "I don't know what words or difficulties passed between them . . . . Parra let me know that Refugio would no longer be with us." Thieves fall out, and Villa and Parra proved no exception. A disagreement over the killing of an old bread vendor led Villa to leave Parra.

Villa soon felt a need to settle down. Circumstances had forced his entry into outlawry; yet the life of a bandit proved quite insecure and risky. At various times between 1895 and 1910 Villa attempted to gain an honest living, establishing a butcher shop in Hidalgo del Parral, Chihuahua. Of course, his former occupation helped. He rustled whatever cattle he needed. If the cattle were un-branded, he could also sell the hides. Animals with brands made sale of the hides more difficult, though there were certainly buyers around who did not look too carefully at the origin of hides or cattle purchased from Villa.

Attempts to work also included a stint at mining and stone-masonry. Yet the relentless course of porfirian justice continued to pursue Villa, and the mountains provided his best escape from the *rurales*. By the turn of the century, Villa was already wanted in both Durango and Chihuahua.

Again he attempted to earn a living without resort to banditry; and again privilege and the discriminatory social system of Mexico kept Villa from a peaceful existence. By 1909, Villa and his *compadre* Eleuterio Soto had a butcher shop in Chihuahua. Unfortunately for Villa, powerful families that controlled the state — principally the Terrazases and the Creels — also controlled the public slaughter-house in Chihuahua City. Villa felt oppressed and squeezed by the domination of a few families in the state. By 1910, social disruption in Mexico would lead Villa into his principal role in the revolution in northern Mexico.

For all of the vaunted successes of the *porfiriato* in reducing the banditry in Mexico, northern Mexico, especially Chihuahua, con-tinued to suffer from some outlawry. While wealthy families such as the Terrazases, the Cuiltys, the Lujanes, and the Creels increased their holdings and their control of the state, restless elements — in-cluding some of the *peones* and *campesinos* — began to agitate for re-form, land redistribution, and admission to the mainstream of the social and economic life of the country.

The closed corporation that ran the state of Chihuahua re-fused to admit new blood that was not connected to it by alliance or marriage. Luis Terrazas, venerable patriarch of the largest *latifundio* in Mexico, successfully arranged marriages for his various offspring in order to enlarge the family holdings. While the combined family *haciendas* effectively covered 6.5 million acres of Chihuahua, bank-ing, mining, and lumbering also occupied the Terrazas clan. Such an effective hold on the economy successfully excluded many mid-dle- and upper-class individuals who sought *entrée* to the regional power structure.

This group of excluded yet intelligent, well-bred individuals were among the first to join in the agitation against the system of government under Porfirio Díaz. Francisco I. Madero of Coahuila rose to the leadership of this disaffected group. His espousal of politically liberal principles — "Effective suffrage, No reelection!" — drew adherents as Díaz prepared in 1909 and 1910 to succeed himself in office once again. Despite statements to the contrary, Díaz chose to impose himself upon the country again. As a consequence, he engendered opposition.

But opposition to Díaz required more than lofty phrases and great ideals. The very real possibility of armed revolt remained just beneath the surface of the minds of the political schemers who sought to unseat Díaz. Madero himself, a strong advocate of political processes, still recognized the probability of revolution. By 1910, Madero was the only viable candidate left to oppose Díaz. His incarceration in early summer and Díaz's rigged victory left revolution as the only alternative. By October, Madero had been transferred from one prison to another until he ended up in the federal penitentiary of San Luis Potosí. Allowed to escape, Madero made his way to San Antonio, Texas, where he made common cause with other dissidents. While in prison he penned his famous Plan de San Luis Potosí, which called upon Mexicans to engage in national uprising on November 20, 1910. He declared the presidential election null and void and argued that in a fair contest he would have won.

Madero's adherents joined him in San Antonio and began to plot the eventual overthrow of Díaz. From San Antonio the *maderistas* returned to Mexico in order to recruit an army to fight Don Porfirio. Appeals made to a variety of social sectors demonstrated how the ouster of Díaz and the installation of Madero would be of direct benefit to them. Thus, often contradictory promises were made to agrarians, excluded middle-class elements, and individuals like Francisco Villa.

Don Abraham González of Chihuahua undertook the task of recruiting an army in Mexico's largest state. Educated and of some financial means, González saw his career as a banker come to an abrupt halt when banks in Chihuahua were consolidated by the Terrazas-Creel combination. As a result, González became the representative of an El Paso company that dealt in land and cattle. In this way he had already met with Francisco Villa when he bought a few head of cattle from Villa without inquiring too closely about the original ownership of the stock.

Throughout October 1910, suspicious characters began appearing in and around Chihuahua City. A feeling of discontent and barely contained violence permeated the ambience of the area. Southern Chihuahua underwent a tremendous upsurge in cattle rustling, and brigandage increased. Respectable citizens became increasingly uneasy. Before the revolution formally began in November, Villa headed one of these groups that preyed upon the Terrazas-Creel cattle herds and sold the meat.

Villa's growing notoriety spread throughout the state in the fall of 1910. His putative appearance in all places simultaneously made him one of the most wanted men in Chihuahua. Local law enforcement agencies placed a reward on Villa, dead or alive. The threat of betrayal, however, did not deter Villa from his activities. He continued to steal cattle, rob payrolls, and generally leave the local law officers wondering where he would strike next.

Tentative feelers went out to Villa from Abraham González. An intermediary made contact with Villa in October and arranged a meeting between the bandit and the frustrated banker. Villa and González met at a house that Villa owned in Chihuahua City. While the threat of exposure remained very real, Villa felt a compulsion to meet this member of the so-called privileged class that sought to change things for the lower classes. González carefully and patiently explained to Villa that Madero, a member of a prominent family from Coahuila, sought to change the system of privilege and exclusion of the lower classes from active participation in Mexican life. González, according to Villa, invited the bandit to join the revolution "that was being made for the rights of people suppressed by tyranny and by the rich." Villa continued:

> There, one night, I understood how the battle that years before I had begun with those that exploited the poor, who pursued us, and who dishonored and broke our sisters and daughters could bring some good to the persecuted and humbled . . . .

It became difficult, however, for Villa to come to grips with what to him was an apparent contradiction: Madero and González, both educated men of means, sought to better the lot of the less fortunate by overthrowing a tyrannical system of government. In one of his initial interviews with González, Villa declared "My God, what is happening in this crazy world; it's crazy, this fucking crazy world!''

Villa retained a suspicion that he was being manipulated. In fact, he almost shot González when they met at an Anti-Reelectionist meeting. González had reached for a key; Villa thought he had reached for a gun. Too many years in the hills had conditioned Villa to shoot first and worry about the consequences later. González's apparent sincerity and his treatment of Villa as an equal ultimately convinced Villa that his future and that of Mexico lay with the *maderistas*.

Tight surveillance of the Anti-Reelectionists continued throughout the month of October. At one point Villa and his cohorts were forced to take extreme action against a former comrade, Claro Reza. Reza, incarcerated for a variety of felonies, promised to deliver Villa to the authorities in exchange for dropping the charges. Before his confinement, Reza had insinuated himself into the inner circle of the Anti-Reelectionists and became privy to many of their plans. Consequently, when Villa and his followers decided that Reza was a liability, they had a double motive. Not only was he selling out to the authorities, but he also posed a real danger to the Anti-Reelectionist cause. In broad daylight, Villa, Eleuterio Soto, and José Sánchez ambushed Reza. A crowd gathered, and Villa and his companions fled through the crowd and took to the hills. Troops from the local Chihuahua garrison gave only half-hearted chase. Ultimately, no arrests were made, but Anti-Reelectionist activity came under stricter surveillance.

Tension continued to build in and around Chihuahua City. By October 4, Villa and his men were situated at Villa's house, serving principally as bodyguards for Abraham González. On November 17, three days before the official outbreak of the revolution, González, accompanied by Cástulo Herrera, went to Villa's home. There González announced that Herrera would have overall command of the forces in Chihuahua. While Villa felt that he could carry out the overall direction of the campaign effectively, he still bowed to González's judgment. While both Villa and Herrera viewed each other suspiciously, Villa vowed to follow Herrera's command. González would head for Ojinaga in the north while Herrera and Villa would prepare to move to the southern part of Chihuahua.

Villa's recruitment and adherence to the revolutionary cause also carried with it a responsibility to enlist an army of irregulars. Shortages of money and ordnance conditioned the character of the army that Villa would recruit to Chihuahua. Each follower needed two major items: a horse and a gun. This was no peasant revolution. Men of some means were required because only they could afford horses and guns. At a later stage, peasants would join the movement, but in the beginning the irregular forces were constituted by men of at least modest property.

For six days, November 17–22, Herrera, Villa, and an irregular force of 375 men stayed in the mountains. On the sixth day, the forces moved onto the plain, and Villa, acting under Herrera's orders, took fifteen men to reconnoiter San Andrés. Villa and his men proceeded to ambush federal troops as they got off the train in San Andrés. These soldiers took refuge at the Hacienda de Bustillos. San Andrés was secured for the revolution, at least for the time being.

With the revolution officially launched on November 20, the Anti-Reelectionists throughout Mexico began to take form as active rebels against the established regime. Minor successes of forces under Villa in central Chihuahua demonstrated to federal authorities that the revolution was no mere exercise in social banditry. A diverse group composed the soldiers of the revolution, each individual having joined for his own altruistic or personal motives.

By the first of December, the revolution in Chihuahua still remained an essentially uncoordinated series of uprisings against the *ancién régime*. Supplies continued to be difficult to obtain. Villa and some of his men at one point entered Chihuahua City *incognito* and obtained foodstuffs in order to sustain the troops in the mountains.

At the time that Villa made his presence felt around Chihuahua City, Pascual Orozco, Jr., and his forces began a string of successes that would catapult Orozco to eventual leadership of all the revolutionary forces. From Ciudad Guerrero, Orozco telegraphed Villa to inform him that the city had fallen and that he could supply Villa's forces with ammunition.

The sporadic nature of the fighting in Chihuahua ultimately required some coordination. The immediate objective of a meeting between the leading revolutionary commanders proved to be the impending approach of federal forces under Gen. Juan J. Navarro. On the evening of December 10, the decision was reached that the various *caudillos* would march out to meet the enemy. The movement would occur in staggered order rather than *en masse*, and commanders would maintain constant communication with each other. Thus, on December 11, Villa and other leaders began their march.

Early in the morning, however, Navarro was already ensconced in Cerro Prieto. No sooner had Villa and his column taken positions than did Navarro open fire. Combat lasted for almost four hours. Rebel forces found themselves outgunned, especially in terms of federal artillery. Orozco's cavalry engaged federal cavalrymen under Gen. Trucy Aubert. Villa saw the cavalry battle on the plains below Cerro Prieto and despaired at being unable to render assistance to Orozco. He recounted that his own forces were essentially scattered as a result of the artillery barrages. Orozco, too, was forced to retreat, and Cerro Prieto remained in federal hands.

On the evening of December 11, Villa and Orozco finally rejoined forces. Both leaders were desolated by their loss to the *federales* and by the loss of so many good fighters. Tactical and logistical considerations became increasingly necessary. As a result, Villa and his men decided to ambush a supply train of ten mules and fifty soldiers that had left Chihuahua City for Navarro's forces.

Villa's forces reached San Andrés and received word that the ammunition was in Santa Isabel. Additionally, federal troops were on the way to San Andrés. Villa, unfortunately, confused the news. He thought the men heading for San Andrés were the same fifty who were escorting the mule train to Navarro's army. To Villa's dismay, the *federales* made their way into San Andrés before he discovered their presence. Gathering what men he could, Villa and his men made for the train station. The rest of his troops, many of them from San Andrés, were visiting family and friends. Consequently, many of the arms and ammunition carried by the mobile rebel army remained under rebel control. By dark, the *federales* failed to rout Villa and his men from the station. A rebel retreat and the ultimate regathering of forces, mainly on foot, taught Villa some valuable military lessons.

The retreat from San Andrés carried with it the loss of horses that needed replacement. Villa took the most natural expedient: he confiscated horses from a large *hacienda*. While Villa and his men awaited the arrival of the horses, they slaughtered cattle in order to sustain themselves. Horses were caught and ridden bareback. As Villa's makeshift cavalry began to move, they also acquired saddles and bridles for their mounts. In Satevó, Villa and his forces finally finished equipping their cavalry by taking weapons, horses, and saddlery from fifty *rurales* located there.

After eight days in Satevó, Villa's forces moved on. They occupied the Hacienda del Sauz, where Villa, through a combination of extortion and persuasion, obtained food for his men, feed for the horses, and 1,500 pesos for expenses from the owner. Already the pattern for maintenance of the revolutionary armies was established: forage from the land and force the enemies of the revolution to pay for the costs of liberating Mexico.

Though Orozco emerged as the principal tactician of the revolution, different revolutionary leaders continued to act independently. Although they maintained communications with each other, there existed great flexibility of action. Villa, for example, attacked Ciudad Camargo on February 7, 1911, but federal reinforcements from Chihuahua City forced him to abandon the city for which his troops had fought so valiantly. No coordination existed as yet for the movement of different troops and for an overall campaign strategy.

Revolutionary battle still entailed guerrilla activities against the *federales*. Shortages of arms, lack of rapid mobility, and disorganized general command kept revolutionary leaders operating within limited territorial areas. A major breakthrough for the revolutionaries under Villa and Orozco came when in early March they took possession of the Northwestern and Mexican Central Railway. In this way they could isolate Ciudad Juárez on the border from reinforcements coming directly from Chihuahua City. Some federal reinforcements did reach Juárez, but they came from the east rather than the south.

While sporadic encounters between rebels and *federales* occupied much of the time of commanders in Chihuahua, Francisco Madero reentered Mexico and summoned Villa to him at Bustillos. This time Villa effectively seized San Andrés and from there rode on to meet with Madero. The meeting proved a surprise to Villa. He found Madero to be an *hacendado* who was willing to fight for the poor and oppressed and who treated him with respect and even affection. In his *Memorias*, Villa recounted that if all the rich of Mexico were like Madero "no one would have to fight and the suffering of the poor would not exist." At no time, however, did Villa take an egalitarian position and call for the eradication of poverty. Rather he argued that while the poor always existed, they should suffer no exploitation.

After a brief meeting with Madero, Villa returned to San Andrés. The next day Madero went to San Andrés and was received with all military honors as befit the president of Mexico. Before returning to Bustillos, Madero asked that Villa join him there the next day in order to coordinate the campaign with Orozco.

The meeting at Bustillos proved to be different from the first two times that Madero and Villa had seen each other. Madero asked both men if an attack on Chihuahua City might be prudent. Both Villa and Orozco opposed such a move because of the chronic shortage of ammunition that faced the revolutionary troops. Madero seemed pleased that such unanimity existed. He ordered Villa back to San Andrés and promised to send troop trains for Villa to make a sweep around Chihuahua and toward Ciudad Juárez. Villa sent his horses and the majority of his men on the trains, and he set out for Bustillos. The railroads proved a difficulty. Heavily laden trains failed to make some of the passes. As a result, since rebels now controlled the northern tracks and trains, they telegraphed ahead for additional locomotives to be waiting at Temósachic. The arrival of more locomotives facilitated the movement of rebel troops. When they arrived at Estación Guzmán, trains were unloaded and troops and horses allowed to rest.

When Madero arrived, at least according to Villa, Orozco posed serious problems. He refused to disarm dissident troops under Salazar, García, and Alañiz. Orozco claimed that it would require too much bloodshed. Villa, instead, was assigned the task. Villa's men circled the dissidents, and in four minutes all of the dissidents were captured and disarmed. Villa delivered the recalcitrant chieftains to Madero and told him that "his order was accomplished with no dead or wounded, just a few bruised heads."

In many respects, Villa's bravado served him well. In March, Villa attempted to avoid bloodshed at Pilar de Conchos. He wrote the federal commander there that he should lay down his arms in order to avoid needless killing. Villa stated that

> if you ignore this order, we shall make use of our weapons. In that case you shall be responsible before history and the nation for fratricide, and you shall be judged militarily. If caprice blinds you, come out to the field of honor; but we do not wish, for highly

patriotic reasons, that the war should be effected where there are families.

While the rebels did not win decisive military victories, their activities proved sufficiently disruptive to force the *federales* to wonder where the next strike would be. A pattern, however, did begin to emerge. The suffocation of the north through the capture of Ciudad Juárez would, in fact, prove invaluable, for Juárez was Mexico's major port of entry and principal railhead. Control of the railways and the flow of commerce — both military and civilian — would give to the rebels an unprecedented advantage. By mid-April 1911, *villista* troops seized Estación Bauche after a long battle that lasted until dark. The personal intervention of Villa and his reinforcements in the conflict turned the tide in favor of the revolutionaries. The way was cleared for a rebel march directly at Ciudad Juárez.

As the push for the border intensified, foreign filibusters who had joined Madero, under the leadership of Giussepe Garibaldi, grandson of the Italian liberator, came into conflict with Villa. One of Villa's men, while walking through Garibaldi's camp, was disarmed by the foreign commander. When Villa requested return of the weapons, Garibaldi rudely refused. As a result, Villa and thirty men headed for the camp. Villa got the drop on Garibaldi and publicly forced him to return the weaponry as well as hand over his own guns. Villa enjoined Garibaldi to cease his posturing. He also told him that he should feel lucky that he remained alive in his own camp rather than being stood against an adobe wall and shot full of lead. Unfortunately, Madero heard of the altercation and summoned Villa to his headquarters. While Madero privately sympathized with Villa, he still forced both commanders to heal their breach publicly. Villa was asked to return the weapons to Garibaldi in order to minimize the humiliation worked upon the hapless Italian mercenary.

The seizure of Ciudad Juárez superseded most considerations. In Madero's view, the capture of Juárez remained a high-risk item. A Boer general, Viljoen, supported Madero's thinking. Villa and Orozco, however, insisted that Juárez would not be an insurmountable target. At the very least, they argued, their proximity to Juárez would dictate that they should at least give the capture a try.

Still, Madero refused to order the attack on Juárez. In part, he feared that stray shells would fall in El Paso and thus provoke problems with the United States. Villa and Orozco had other plans. Through a clever ruse, they provoked an attack on some of their troops by soldiers garrisoned in Juárez. Thus, on the evening of May 7, *federales* began firing at a squad commanded by José Orozco. Villa and Pascual Orozco had spent the night in El Paso. On May 8, shots brought them back across the border. While Madero ordered that the troops be forced to retreat, Villa and Orozco answered that they were under such heavy fire that conveying the order to the men would be impossible. Resigned, Madero allowed Orozco and Villa to position their troops for a full-fledged attack on Ciudad Juárez.

While Villa at least had a profound respect for Madero, he did not trust the president's military judgment. Villa summarized the situation:

> . . . Mr. Madero was the president of the Republic but not a military man. We put in motion the plans to reach a great victory or die in the trying.

Madero, who had hoped for a negotiated peace with Díaz, finally had to accept a military solution. Villa and Orozco hungered for a major victory, and through a ruse they finally obtained one.

The battle lasted from May 8 through May 10, 1911. Inexorably, Orozco and Villa squeezed the federal soldiers into the garrison as rebel forces occupied more and more of the city. Gen. Juan J. Navarro, a nemesis to both Villa and Orozco, commanded the garrison there. When he finally saw the futility of a prolonged struggle, he surrendered on May 10.

The capture of the Juárez garrison provided the revolutionaries with great quantities of arms, ammunition, and some artillery pieces. Additionally, rank and file soldiers chose to join the rebels. But federal officers were slated for firing squads, especially General Navarro. Fortunately, Navarro received a reprieve from Madero, an action that infuriated both Orozco and Villa.

Villa became reconciled to Navarro's continued existence. As a token of his submission, Villa took nine federal officers with him to El Paso for dinner. Predictions abounded that these men would not return alive. After paying for a splendid meal, Villa and the nine officers returned to Juárez. Villa asserted that "some of my companions had predicted that the Federal officers would not return. They looked at me with increased respect when they saw that they were wrong."

Orozco did not react to Navarro with the same grace. Rather, he attempted to manipulate Villa into disarming Madero's guards and seizing leadership of the revolution. Once Villa became cognizant of the maneuver, he retreated to his quarters for three days. Shamefaced, he finally approached Madero and resigned his commission as a colonel in the Liberating Army.

The Navarro incident, the abortive insubordination of Villa and Orozco, and the distribution of political posts finally drove both Villa and Orozco out of the army. In Chihuahua City, Madero began making cabinet appointments in the provisional government. He named Venustiano Carranza, former senator from Coahuila, as secretary of war, a post coveted by Orozco. Debate became acrimonious, and Abraham González was forced to intervene. While Villa calmed down, Orozco continued to nurse his indignation. Orozco retired with a bonus of 50,000 pesos. Villa, however, would accept only 10,000 pesos and a train ride to San Andrés. There he distributed his bonus to the widows and dependents of men who had followed him and died in battle.

While the revolution preoccupied Villa most of the time, his penchant for women did not abate during his early revolutionary years. In November 1910, he met his future wife, María Luz Corral, the daughter of a poor but respectable widow. When Luz Corral first saw Villa in her mother's store, she attempted to disguise her discomfiture by crocheting. Luz and her mother handed out merchandise to the revolutionaries, though Luz claimed that she "was so frightened that my hand trembled and made difficult writing a list of the goods my mother delivered to each rebel." Already Villa had dispatched Claro Reza in the streets of San Andrés, and his feral reputation kept apace with him.

Villa took note of the young lady and did not forget her. His repeated visits to San Andrés always included a stop at the home of María Luz Corral. Finally, he confessed his infatuation with the young lady. Luz Corral, in her autobiography, wrote that Villa "frankly confessed his love for me and told me of his lonely and errant life. Villa also admitted that he hoped that with the quick end of the Revolution he could settle down and have a home." Implicitly, Pancho Villa proposed. Luz Corral's mother told the rebel leader that when he returned again to San Andrés, he would have an answer to his proposal.

Luz decided she would marry the rebel leader. But, she wondered, would they have a house? Would she be forced to follow him to military encampments? Finally, Luz and her mother agreed that marriage to Villa would not be a bad thing.

The revolution, however, had yet to triumph. Throughout the winter and early spring of 1910–1911, Luz Corral wondered if Villa would return. Finally, on May 25, 1911, Villa returned to San Andrés. When the train whistle blew in San Andrés on that day, and Villa stepped from the coach, Luz saw her fantasies fulfilled. On May 29, Villa and Luz Corral were married.

Villa, true to his intention, opened a meat business in San Andrés. At the urging of Abraham González, he began to import equipment for a slaughterhouse in Juárez. At no time did anyone question where he obtained such a ready supply of cattle. His former profession, obviously, had stood him in good stead.

A society based on position rather than talent nurtured Doroteo Arango. The first thirty years of his life were, in fact, spent attempting to find a niche in a society increasingly dominated by a gerontocracy headed by an aging *caudillo* and becoming more and more exclusionary. Pancho Villa *née* Doroteo Arango saw that through a change of leadership from top to bottom of the sociopolitical structure he might be able to advance. His preconceptions about the aristocracy and the educated classes of Mexico received a pummeling when he encountered Abraham González and Francisco Madero.

Both of these men treated Villa with respect born of beneficent spirits rather than *noblesse oblige*. To Villa, conditioned to distrust most of the middle and upper classes, González and Madero personified all that was good. His career as a bandit and cattle rustler actually helped him make contact with González, himself excluded from banking because of the monopoly of the Terrazas-Creel family.

Throughout the *maderista* revolution, Villa attempted to be a good subordinate. Yet his anarchistic instincts occasionally took hold, and he would act impulsively though with unusual success. Villa's anger over Madero's treatment of Navarro and some of his political appointments flashed and then subsided into shame. His retirement to private life and family concerns would not, however, last. Forces gathered that would eventually drag Francisco Villa back into battle.

CHAPTER III

Reluctant Maderista?

Francisco I. Madero's ascension to the presidency in November 1911 failed to bring peace to Mexico. Emiliano Zapata in the south had already denounced the new president in the Plan de Ayala. Other revolutionaries who at first supported the new president looked askance as only token acknowledgment was made of revolutionary contribution to the new government. Nepotism and a reliance on disgruntled upper- and middle-class elements characterized the Madero cabinet. In the north, Pascual Orozco, Jr., nurtured his antagonism toward Madero, though he was made military commander of Chihuahua.

Francisco Villa, shamed by what he thought was his personal betrayal of Madero, attempted to tend to his own affairs during the period between June 1911 and January 1912. Villa strove to establish his meat-cutting business in San Andrés and then in Chihuahua City. Still, Villa felt obligations to help alleviate the suffering of the widows and orphans born of the revolution. In June 1911, for example, he went to Chihuahua City to organize a bullfight, the proceeds of which would be used for charitable purposes. In part, his agreement to retire from active military duty still carried with it social obligations, for Villa took it upon himself to render aid to those who had undergone familial loss.

In mid-July, Villa and his new bride went to Mexico City to meet with Madero. Since they had not had a honeymoon, the trip south proved to be both a wedding trip and a report to Madero on affairs in Chihuahua. Thus far, Madero remained as president-elect rather than president in fact. The interim presidency of Francisco León de la Barra continued to carry on the affairs of government until Madero was installed at the end of November.

The first six months of the marriage of Luz Corral and Pancho Villa passed "like a dream." Villa attended to his meat-cutting business. He would, with regularity, get up early in the morning, go to his ranch, La Boquilla, to select the cattle for slaughter, and tour his various shops to collect the monies and discuss business with his managers and bookkeeper. Ever cognizant of his responsibilities, both familial and revolutionary, Villa asked brother Antonio to live with them, as well as some of the dependents of Villa's men who had died in battle.

Political passions refused to subside. While on the surface the Madero presidency seemed to fulfill the majority of aspirations, there remained the disaffected elements. Zapata in the south already denounced Madero. Former revolutionaries viewed with suspicion the continuation of the predominantly *porfirista* bureaucracy and military establishment. Moreover, Madero drew upon the members of his own moneyed class to make up his government. By early 1912, it became apparent that Madero the peacemaker would in fact be faced with strife once again.

The president leaned rather heavily on Villa to maintain *maderista* support in northern Mexico. With Abraham González ensconced as governor of Chihuahua, Madero felt that Villa was controllable in the area. Villa did not supinely accept the abuse that he often received. He demanded payment for money and goods granted to the revolution. As early as August 1911, he asked that monies borrowed from him be repaid either in cash or in kind. By December, he listed his losses and asked payment for them. Though willing to work for the revolution, Villa insisted on remuneration for personal expenditures.

The bill presented to Madero included a long series of items that ultimately ended up in the hands of Pascual Orozco, Jr. Of 200 horses, for example, Orozco took 130; Orozco additionally grabbed 200 head of slaughter cattle and 115 mules, as well as money and foodstuffs. Villa asked that Madero relieve him of this burden so that he could support his family and other dependents. He further accused the government of its ingratitude for the social work he had performed and asked Madero that he "be just with the man who has suffered so much for you."

Despite differences with Madero, Villa continued to be a staunch supporter of the little man from Coahuila. At the end of December 1911, Villa traveled to Mexico City. Madero expressed concern about Orozco because of Orozco's festering antagonism about the cabinet appointments. Villa regretfully reported that Orozco was keeping strange company. Alberto Terrazas, son of Luis Terrazas, and Juan Creel were constant companions of Orozco. Madero hoped that Villa would serve as his eyes in Chihuahua with regard to Orozco. Villa, in his *Memorias,* stated that "Orozco, as head of the military department of Chihuahua, has converted himself into king of Chihuahua."

Winds of dissension continued to reach Mexico City from the north. Orozco, while continuing to pay lip service to Madero, carefully planned his moves against the government. In February 1912, Villa again visited Madero in Mexico City. He was asked to renew his pledge of loyalty and to prepare for military action. Villa replied that he would have "a lot of people ready when the necessity arises."

In Chihuahua, Governor González took steps to neutralize the discontent manifested by Orozco and his backers. Militia units were created. Villa, asked to organize such units in Satevó and Zaragosa, did so with alacrity and placed them under the control of former revolutionary officers. But the problem that faced González and through him Madero did not entail Orozco alone. Realignment of political allegiances ultimately brought about much of the difficulty as conservative *hacendados* gravitated toward Orozco.

Actual disruption occurred in early February. On February 2, shots rang out through Chihuahua City. A troop rebellion in the federal prison in Chihuahua led Villa to believe that the Orozco rebellion had begun. Pascual Orozco, Jr., however, was in the governor's palace with Interim Governor Aureliano González. These two summoned Villa to come to the gubernatorial headquarters. They asked that Villa take 100 men and prepare to fight against the rebellion. Villa impulsively began to organize his men when it dawned on him that once again Orozco attempted to manipulate him as he had done in Ciudad Juárez. Villa claimed later that the prison revolt constituted a set-up job whereby Orozco's men would have a pretext to seize the city, especially if Villa were out of the way.

When it became apparent that Villa would not lend his support to any sort of deceit, Orozco attempted to buy Villa's neutrality. He dispatched his father, Pascual, Sr., to Villa with an offer of 300,000 pesos if Villa would go to the United States. Villa, incensed, told the old man in no uncertain terms what he thought of traitors and declared that Orozco was lucky to be leaving Villa's home with his life.

Authorities in Chihuahua attempted to respond to the growing unrest. Demands for land forced the government to pass an agrarian law on February 16, 1912. In the legislation, the state government received authorization to seek a loan of six million pesos. Of that amount, two and one-half million aimed at irrigation projects while two million was earmarked for the purchase and distribution of land to villages. Another million pesos would be funneled into the capitalization of an agrarian bank. Finally, the remaining 500,000 pesos was dedicated to schools and the purchase of school supplies.

Such action failed to offset the discontent. On March 1, 1912, Pascual Orozco, Jr., proclaimed his disavowal of the Madero government. Despite attempts to win Villa to the Orozco camp, Villa remained faithful to Madero and González. By March 2, Villa neared Chihuahua City with some of his irregulars. Orozco's *colorados*, shouting the slogan of *tierra y justicia* (land and justice), met the *villistas* outside Chihuahua City. There, according to Villa's own account, he was forced to retreat because González had asked that he not enter into combat. Other accounts differ. In any event, Villa staged a retreat in his first encounter with the *orozquistas*. Luckily, González and Villa made their escape from Chihuahua City when Orozco captured the capital of the state. Mexican officials along the border asked that additional federal troops be dispatched to Chihuahua City in order to quell the uprising.

While Orozco received support from conservatives, the Plan Orozquista of March 25, 1912, did not promise to maintain the status quo. In many respects, the Plan Orozquista constituted a far more radical document than Madero's Plan de San Luis Potosí. Orozco called for abolition of *tiendas de raya* (company stores) on the *haciendas* and the payment of wages in legal tender, not scrip. Moreover, the plan also called for a ten-hour working day, nationalization of the railroads, and the use of Mexican laborers on the railroads instead of foreigners. Its most important provisions should have left conservative supporters a bit fearful for their properties. Agrarian reform provisions in the Plan Orozquista called for a cautious but thorough redistribution of lands. Lands seized illegally by *hacendados* would be returned to the *campesinos*. Land left fallow would be nationalized, and all nationalized and uncultivated lands would be distributed to the villages. Payments for these lands would be through the use of agricultural bonds that bore a four percent interest rate.

Conservatives in Chihuahua did not see the Plan Orozquista as a threat, for they felt that Orozco was bought and paid for by their money. The real threat, from the point of view of Chihuahua's landed aristocracy, came from Madero. Madero attempted to collect back taxes on properties in Chihuahua. Under Díaz, the failure to collect taxes proved a way to maintain *hacendado* support. Madero, however, saw this as a massive abuse and moved to recoup lost revenue. The United States consul in Chihuahua, Marion T. Letcher, reported that "it is easy to understand that such a measure would not win the support of people owning a million or more acres."

Conservative support and money alone could not lead Orozco to victory. The money supply was finite, after all, and Orozco was obligated to keep his army supplied. Thus, following a pattern established during the Madero revolution, Orozco and his supporters began rustling cattle and then selling them across the border as a means of purchasing arms and supplies.

But even additional sources of funds failed to maintain the flow of war matériél into Mexico. On March 14, 1912, both Houses of the United States Congress expressed their view to President William Howard Taft that no arms, munitions, or military ordnance could be sold to any faction in Mexico. Nonmilitary supplies could still cross the border, but disorder must cease. Such a move made the military situation difficult for both the Mexican government and the Orozco rebels. The government position, however, seemed not as bleak, for it could purchase armaments legitimately from Europe. Orozco, stuck in the middle of the Chihuahua desert, had only his smuggling resources for supplies.

Military organization by the Mexican government during the

Orozco rebellion required the blending of irregular militia units such as those commanded by Villa with the regular army. Thus, in April 1912, Gen. Victoriano Huerta, an old-line *porfirista* military man, became commander of the Federal Division of the North. Villa was asked to coordinate with Huerta and to place himself under Huerta's command. Although Huerta did not like the irregulars because of their lack of military discipline, he recognized the necessity of working with the likes of Villa if he was to prosecute a successful campaign against Orozco's *colorados*.

As a result, in mid-April, Huerta asked permission of Madero to elevate Villa to the rank of honorary brigadier general in the hope of building better working relations with the guerrilla leader. Huerta readily recognized the necessity of assuaging Villa's ego and saw that accumulation of rank and prestige might be one way of acquiring an ally in Villa. Permission was received, and Villa was elevated in early May.

Meanwhile, military reverses plagued Villa's irregular troops. An attempt to seize Parral in southern Chihuahua in mid-April failed. While Villa's men controlled the town for a while, superior forces under José Inez Salazar and later Emilio P. Campa drove the *villista* militia out of Parral. The military retreat, however, did not prove to be a total rout, for Villa at that time acquired another ally in Maclovio Herrera, who was attached to the federal garrison in Parral. While over half of the garrison supported Orozco, Herrera brought his men over to Villa and the government.

Initially, it seemed that Orozco would be successful. Braulio Hernández, former secretary of Abraham González and now an ardent *colorado*, approached Villa's wife with an offer of amnesty for her husband if she could induce him to turn in his arms. Luz Corral de Villa, a tough lady even then, repulsed Hernández, assuring him that she would prefer poverty with honor rather than live with a turncoat.

The Orozco rebellion took on the characteristics of civil war. Fighting was relentless. Armies moved quickly, taking few prisoners. Both armies used mercenaries. In mid-April, the forced retreat of Villa brought on by José Inez Salazar caused the death of an American machine gunner fighting for the *villistas*. The machine gunner, Thomas Fountain, was captured, tried by the *colorados*, and executed. Despite protests from the Department of State, Orozco maintained that Fountain was handling a machine gun without any thought as to its nationality. Villa, angered by the loss of one of his men, vowed to kill any Americans that might be working for Orozco if the *colorados* continued to execute mercenaries in the employ of the Mexican army.

Military mobility on both sides necessitated the use of railroads and horses. Also, the acquisition of foodstuffs fell not to a formal quartermaster corps but rather to *soldaderas,* women who accompanied individual soldiers on their missions. Thus, the women played a pivotal role in the well-being of military establishments throughout the Mexican Revolution. They effectively scrounged for food and occasionally fought with as much vigor and ruthlessness as their men. For them, the battles were exaggeratedly real, for the loss of their men would leave them without protectors. When Huerta's army arrived in Parral, it came complete with *soldaderas.*

Villa, however, left Luz Corral at home, though there were times that he could have used her ministrations. Throughout most of the spring, Villa suffered from intermittent fevers with symptoms suspiciously like malaria. Often he would be incapacitated for days at a time.

By Villa's own account, the recurrent fevers ultimately came close to costing him his life. The scenario began May 22, 1912, when Villa decisively defeated Orozco at Rellano. Villa kept an Arabian mare that his men had seized. Rather than return the horse to its owner, Villa, a keen judge of horseflesh, decided to keep her for himself. When Villa met with Huerta at Parral ten days later, Huerta ordered the return of the horse. Luz Corral, in her autobiography, claimed that Huerta's mind had been poisoned against Villa by the very conservatives who covertly supported Orozco. Already prejudiced against Villa, Huerta refused to tolerate even the slightest hint of insubordination. Villa, aware of Huerta's displeasure over the "liberation" of the mare, refused to answer a summons to appear before General Huerta. Fever racked his body, and he claimed that he could not possibly see Huerta until the following day. Huerta would not allow such insolence and ordered that Villa be placed under arrest. Troops arrived and took Villa to the military prison in Parral. Huerta followed the arrest with an order for the immediate execution of Villa.

Villa's refusal to return the horse and his unwillingness to see Huerta ultimately led to an order for his execution. The situation became tense. When Villa emerged from his house the next day, he was arrested and sent immediately to the firing squad. Villa continually asked the cause of his summary treatment, but the only answer he could get was that the order came from higher authority. Despite appeals and various time-killing devices, Huerta remained resolute in his desire to do away with Villa. Finally, the intervention of Emilio and Raúl Madero, brothers of the president, forced Huerta to stay the execution. At the last minute, Col. Rubio Navarrete appeared with a telegram from Mexico City. The order came from Madero that Villa was not to be executed but rather sent to the federal penitentiary in Mexico City. Villa had shed tears of frustration over the injustice. The reprieve from Madero came just before Huerta began the execution.

Huerta began to nurse serious indignation against Madero. The president, when he appointed Huerta to head the campaign against Orozco, promised not to interfere in military decisions. To Huerta, the summary execution of insubordinate officers constituted a military decision. Yet, Madero intervened and overrode Huerta's expressed instructions.

Madero's intervention in Villa's behalf prompted journalists to wonder if Huerta was finished as commander of the anti-Orozco campaign. The presidential office in Mexico City received inquiries about Huerta's status. Madero found himself categorically denying the role of Emilio and Raúl Madero in the salvation of Villa. The president expressed confidence in Huerta as commander of the campaign in the north. Villa, stated Madero, came under the jurisdiction of a competent judge, and neither Huerta nor Villa held personal animosity for each other. A deluded idealist, Madero refused to see his military commander in Chihuahua in other than the most favorable light.

Villa's departure for Mexico City from Parral brought about an emotional farewell to his troops. He exhorted them to continue fighting for the sake of the revolution and declared his boundless affection for them. To Col. Rubio Navarrete he gave his horse and sword. It was Navarrete who saved his life. Odd, Villa mused, that after so much fighting against federal soldiers that it was a *federal* who saved him instead of a revolutionary.

Villa thought that the reprieve would free him. Instead, it sent him to Lecumberri prison in Mexico City, where he would have to face charges before a military tribunal. Villa faced a multitude of charges including forceful extortion in Parral. Villa responded that the government of Chihuahua had authorized him to raise funds for maintenance of the state militias. He claimed that insubordination was nothing more than a ruse on the part of Huerta to get Villa out of the way in the Division of the North. While the robbery charge was dropped, it still took until October to disprove the charge; Villa was still sentenced to the federal prison at Santiago Tlatelolco.

For three months Villa remained in solitary confinement when he was not in hearings before the judge. He began to challenge the system. At one point he declared that he would only enter the solitary cell dead. Jailers became perplexed. Finally, an order came from the secretary of government, roughly the attorney general, that Villa could be taken from solitary. At this point Santiago Tlatelolco became his home. While technically not in solitary, Villa still could not have visitors. Only occasionally could someone prevail upon the director of the prison to allow a visit with Villa.

Part of the Villa legend revolves around the fact that he learned to read while in prison. In Guzmán's version of the *Memorias,* Villa improved his reading and writing skills. He did not, in effect, start from total illiteracy. Be that as it may, Villa made many valuable contacts in prison, one of which would eventually free him.

Carlos Jaúregui clerked for the court. He was a young man who saw in Villa much of the practical application of the idealism that young Jaúregui carried. He and Villa would have long conversations in prison. In time, Jaúregui convinced Villa that he should escape from Tlatelolco.

Villa felt abandoned by the Madero government. Letters to Madero went unheeded as Villa desperately sought to vindicate himself. The idea of escape became more and more appealing. At the same time, he wrote confidentially to his brother Hipólito, making provisions for the care of his family and for his dependents.

The date for Villa's escape was set. Arrangements with Hipólito and Carlos Jaúregui were finalized. Unfortunately, Villa suffered from excessive garrulousness. Former *porfirista* and presidential aspirant Bernardo Reyes, also a prisoner in Tlatelolco, became a Villa confidant. When Villa accidentally revealed some of his plans, the escape set for December 24 required readjustment for fear of exposure.

Reyes also talked too much. By the time Villa made his escape on December 27, he became privy to plans on the part of Félix Díaz, nephew of old Don Porfirio, and Reyes to overthrow Madero. All this time, Madero felt that he had the situation under control.

Madero continued to give comfort to his avowed enemies. In early December, he informed Abraham González that Luis Terrazas planned to return to Chihuahua and specifically ordered that Terrazas, who claimed no collusion with Orozco, should be protected from political passions.

Apparently, official connivance — whether ordered by Madero or not — facilitated the escape of Mexico's great guerrilla fighter. A new year rolled around as he headed north to the border. On January 2, 1913, traveling from Mazatlán, Villa arrived at Tucson, Arizona. On January 6 he made his way to El Paso, Texas, and on January 12 he informed Abraham González of the plans he had heard from Bernardo Reyes. Although González forwarded the intelligence to Madero, little heed was paid to Villa's warning.

Privy to the escape plans, Villa's wife made her way to El Paso and was there joined by her husband. For a long period of time Villa received visitors, both Mexican and others. News from Mexico City was getting worse. Abraham González through intermediaries urged Villa to remain in El Paso until the situation in the country could right itself. For almost another month Villa stayed on the border, hungering to return to Mexico.

Rumors abounded about the proposed coup led by Villa's nemesis, Victoriano Huerta. González, cognizant of what had occurred in Mexico City with the overthrow of Madero on February 19, dispatched 1,500 pesos to Villa in order for him to return to Mexico and take up the fight against Huerta. Villa, borrowing another 3,000 pesos from his brother Hipólito, began buying arms, ammunition, horses, and saddlery in order to effect a strike against Huerta. By this time, González himself had been overthrown and killed, following the death of Madero by less than two weeks.

Persecuted, ignored, viewed as a barbarian, Villa still retained his faith in Madero and Abraham González. The death of Madero on February 22, 1913, and the death of González, both of them at the hands of Huerta, galvanized Villa into action once again. In early March he crossed the Río Grande, accompanied by only eight men. He would avenge the death of the two men who had treated him with equity and respect.

CHAPTER IV

". . . Free men who conquer for liberty . . ."

Nine men crossed the Río Grande into Mexico at Isleta, Texas, on March 13, 1913. They crossed with little money, a few armaments, and a lot of determination to avenge the death of their martyred leaders. Victoriano Huerta, usurper of Mexico's presidency, was implicated in the deaths of Francisco Madero and Governor Abraham González of Chihuahua. The leader of the nine men who entered Mexico through Isleta felt a particular affection for Madero and González. On March 7, barely two weeks after the assassination of Madero on February 22, González met his death in Bachimba Canyon, where he was thrown under a train. Pancho Villa would avenge the death of his two idols.

Little ideological motive existed here. Villa set his course for a vendetta against Huerta and all who would support him. Villa and his men carefully made their way to San Andrés, where Villa's wife maintained their home. Once in San Andrés, Villa received word that Gen. Jesús Rábago wanted to speak to him about allying himself with Huerta. The offer was certainly attractive. Rábago promised Villa 100,000 pesos if he would publicly adhere to Huerta and sweetened the offer with a promise of promotion to brigadier general. Characteristically, Villa responded to Rábago's message by declaring: "Tell Huerta that with regard to the rank, I don't need it because I command as the Supreme Chief of all free men who conquer for liberty; with regard to the 100,000 pesos . . . let him drink it up in *aguardiente!"* His attack on Huerta's propensity for liquor underscored Villa's own abstention from spirits.

Villa could not help a bit of bravado. He still only had eight men with him in San Andrés. He had obtained money from his brother, from Abraham González before his death, and from José María Maytorena, governor of Sonora, and had begun a program of recruitment and purchase of ordnance. Well before he was ready to do battle with the *huertistas*, Villa told Rábago that he would personally bring 3,000 men to Chihuahua and there settle accounts with Huerta and all of his supporters.

Revolution against Huerta did not await the arrival of Pancho Villa. Even before Villa crossed at Isleta, Manuel Chao, a later Villa supporter, and others in Chihuahua began launching attacks on the *huertistas* throughout the state. The arrival of Villa, however, began to galvanize resistance in Chihuahua into a more cohesive movement against Huerta.

By the end of March 1913, Chihuahua joined the list of states in open revolt against Huerta. Sonora, then headed by Maytorena, and Coahuila, governed by Venustiano Carranza, led the fight against Huerta. On March 26, Venustiano Carranza issued the Plan de Guadalupe and in two days gained the adherence of principal revolutionary leaders. Villa, Obregón, Pablo González, and, tentatively, Emiliano Zapata joined Carranza in the declaration against Huerta.

The revolution, however, proved less than monolithic. Regional and personal disputes characterized it throughout its course. Varied segments of the population made up its armies and its various governments, and personalities that represented the differing aspirations of the revolutionaries often subsumed ideological issues. In many respects, the *villista* movement was peopled with malcontents who had few defined goals beyond the military destruction of the enemy.

Into this nexus of conflicting personalities and issues stepped the United States. Officially neutral vis-à-vis the different factions, the United States, now headed by Woodrow Wilson, hoped to guide the revolutionary factions into more liberal and democratic lines.

As Villa recruited men, it became apparent that the multifaceted nature of the revolution attracted adherents from all social strata. Some of Villa's followers came from moneyed stock. Others were laborers or came from peasant backgrounds. Professional military men also constituted a significant portion of Villa's forces. Intellectuals, including such men as Silvestre Terrazas (a distant cousin of Luis Terrazas though on opposite sides of the political fence), joined Villa. Some of Villa's followers, like revolutionaries throughout Mexico, joined for the sheer love of fighting and looting. The revolution caused unprecedented economic and social dislocation. The chaos provided a means for social mobility and economic aggrandizement.

The most notorious of Villa's followers was a former railroad engineer, Rodolfo Fierro. Fierro, who "could drive the girls crazy with his looks," proved incredibly cruel. According to Roberto Blanco Moheno, "He frightens Villa who fears such evil. Fierro kills for the sheer joy of killing, rapes women, impales prisoners, burns houses. He is bestiality liberated. War frees good and evil."

The sheer barbarism of Rodolfo Fierro horrified professional military men who had joined Villa. Eugenio Aguirre Benavides, for example, constantly remonstrated with Villa over Fierro's indiscriminate shooting of individuals who crossed him. In one instance, Aguirre Benavides complained about Fierro killing an officer who disagreed with him. While Villa agreed, he still saw Fierro as extremely useful. He told Aguirre Benavides that he was probably "right, but do you think I would have a useful fellow like Fierro shot for one death? When times change and I have to return to the *sierra,* Fierro and his *compañeros* will follow me while you and your officers abandon me." Villa, it seems, possessed certain prophetic gifts.

Then there was Toribio Ortega, a cattleman from Chihuahua. Known as *El Honrado,* the honorable, Ortega refused to execute prisoners, much to the disgust of Fierro, Tomás Urbina, and others, and also accepted only the paltry salary paid him by the revolution. Ortega fell among the more idealistic of Villa's followers.

Felipe Angeles, former commandant of the Military Academy at Chapultepec under Madero, at first joined Carranza as minister of war. In early 1914, however, Villa requested that Angeles be transferred to the División del Norte as an artillery specialist. Angeles provided much of the stability for the División del Norte and often acted as a brake on some of the *villista* excesses.

Tomás Urbina, probably second only to Fierro in ferocity, became a *villista*. He was Villa's *compadre*, so close as to ask Villa to be godfather to his children. Unfortunately, the revolution would also unleash unprecedented greed in Urbina, who would ultimately suffer execution at the hands of his *compadre* for stealing funds.

Col. Juan Medina, a former federal officer, also joined Villa. Like most professional soldiers, the excesses of nonprofessional military men like Fierro and even Villa made Medina and others recoil with horror. When a summary execution was ordered for Gen. Benjamín Yuriar in November 1913, Medina wanted to prepare a long indictment and hold a formal court-martial. Villa's position remained peasant-simple: "I have no time for such papers. If a soldier or an officer is insubordinate, I shoot him without delay. If you want to have a court martial, do so and decide whether or not I acted according to military policy." Even rebels have short memories. Villa essentially advocated the same thing that Huerta tried to do to him in June 1913.

Finally, there were Villa's *dorados*, a select group of fighters organized in late 1913 and early 1914. One hundred men superbly mounted with two horses and a rifle apiece constituted each of three squadrons. They formed the elite of the *villista* cavalry and refused to be encumbered by *soldaderas* who would slow them down. In many respects, Villa's *dorados* paved the way for some of Villa's most impressive victories, for they combined speed and surprise that characterized much of Villa's military prowess. Intensely loyal to Villa, the *dorados* also served as his bodyguards when he would be in residence somewhere.

The arrival of Villa in Chihuahua in March 1913 strengthened resistance to the Huerta dictatorship. Coupled to the antipathy felt toward Huerta, northern Mexicans viewed Pascual Orozco with equal distaste, for Orozco, after having fought against Huerta in 1912, callously joined forces with the murderer of Madero. By May 1913, United States consular officials in Chihuahua viewed federal control of the area as precarious. Villa, it was reported, would probably attack Chihuahua City given his control of the Northwestern Railroad south of Madera. Three hundred well-armed men comprised the *villista* force and had, on May 2, routed *huertista* irregulars.

Tenuous control of Chihuahua and the north generally forced Huerta to take a more aggressive posture toward United States citizens. While attempting to curry favor with the United States, Huerta felt no qualms about pressuring interests in the United States for support. Consequently, Huerta, the dictator, hoped for a *rapprochement* with the United States at the same time that he extorted support from United States interests.

Plans for eventual military control of the north continued to materialize. By the end of May, Villa proposed that he and Carranza meet in order to join forces and to coordinate plans for the siege of a major northern city. At this juncture, it appeared that Ciudad Juárez would prove the best target. Carranza, however, demurred, and nearly a year would elapse before the two leaders would meet.

Villa continued to accumulate men and arms. By July, *villista* troops amassed west of Ciudad Juárez under the command of Toribio Ortega. Within the United States consular district of Ciudad Juárez, the town was the only area still under federal control. As a result, local government showed signs of weakening as commerce ground to a standstill and the customs receipts from Mexico's largest port of entry dwindled. United States citizens in the area, moreover, left in droves, leaving few of their countrymen in the region.

Villista victories began to accumulate with increasing frequency. On August 26, 1913, *federales* at San Andrés were routed by forces personally under Villa's command. A troop train in Juárez failed to go south to reinforce the garrison at San Andrés, and it became apparent that Villa was applying pressure to government forces.

In large measure, Villa's ferocity at San Andrés grew out of personal vengeance. *Orozquista* sympathizers, at least according to Luz Corral, poisoned the daughter of Francisco Villa and Luz Corral. Villa, ever fond of children and especially one of his own, gave no quarter to the *federales* in San Andrés. He personally ordered the execution of 400 prisoners after the *federales* fled from San Andrés.

While in San Andrés, Villa, his brothers Hipólito and Antonio, and assorted men robbed a train of 122 silver bars and hid them for future use. Additionally, *villistas* routed some *colorados* under José Inez Salazar. With the capture of sixty *colorados*, Villa decided that prisoners were a liability. Consequently, he ordered the execution of forty of these unfortunates. The executions were carried out by standing the *orozquistas* three deep in order to conserve ammunition, a function presided over by Fierro.

Gradually, throughout the late summer and early autumn of 1913, Villa continued to gather men to his side and to undermine federal control of Chihuahua. Impressive victories and augmented armies moved Villa toward bigger game. By late September, it became apparent that Villa would move toward Torreón, a major cotton and railroad center in southern Coahuila. Plans were laid for a siege of the town.

At about 9:00 P.M. on October 1, *villistas* entered Torreón and began to sack many Spanish-owned enterprises and a few American-owned stores. Also, out of sheer curiosity and perversity, Villa's forces vandalized a French clothing store. As they entered the town, the *villistas* presented *vales* or vouchers for payment of goods seized. These vouchers could then be cashed in at General Headquarters. By the morning of October 2, Villa effectively controlled Torreón, and the *federales* wholly evacuated the area that evening.

Once in absolute control of the city, Villa imposed a rigid order on his men. Looting ceased. While indiscriminate as to who got hurt during the heat of battle, Villa offered, reported one U.S. official, "every consideration to our people who are uninjured." Villa did not, however, include Spaniards and other pro-*huertista* foreigners residing in Torreón in his guarantees.

Villa ensconced himself at Torreón and allowed his army to recuperate from the siege of that major town. By October 20, however, preparations were under way for a move against Chihuahua City with the intention of driving the *federales* completely out of the state. On that date Villa and 6,000 men left Torreón and moved toward Jiménez, where an additional 4,000 men joined them. By the end of October estimates of *villista* strength ranged as high as 16,000 well-armed, well-mounted, and well-supplied men.

Villista activity around Chihuahua increased. It became apparent that in a very short time the areas around Chihuahua City and throughout the state, for that matter, would come under *villista* control. Prominent Mexican families left towns such as Santa Rosalía and sought refuge in Chihuahua City. Indicative of the growing uncertainty in the area, silver coinage practically ceased circulation because of the unstable exchange rates for paper currency. Informed predictions held that Chihuahua City would fall with only a nominal defense, though troop concentrations in the Chihuahua garrison indicated the possibility of a protracted and energetic attempt to stave off the rebels.

Federal forces established a defense perimeter around Chihuahua City. On the evening of November 5, the *villista* insurgents launched their attacks principally with small-arms fire. On the next morning, both sides engaged in battle again, but this time both sides used heavy artillery. The fighting continued, but the rebels failed to make significant headway. Federal reinforcements arrived, and trains from Torreón dispatched 2,000 additional rebel troops, thus depleting the garrison there. By November 10, the rebels found that Chihuahua City was too heavily protected and withdrew to the south. While the *federales* claimed a victory, the rebel retreat was more a tactical one rather than the result of superior power on the part of the government forces.

During the siege of Chihuahua City, Villa recognized that as long as the northern artery from Juárez remained in federal control, Chihuahua City could still remain a government stronghold and negate *villista* control of the state. In a lightning strike, a detachment of 1,500 *villistas* seized a southbound train out of Ciudad Juárez. Reversing it, they mounted the train and moved into Juárez at 1:00 A.M. on November 15. Four hours of fighting left Mexico's major border town in rebel hands. Looting and pillage did not attend the capture of Ciudad Juárez; rather, Villa's forces policed the area and maintained order.

Meanwhile, the majority of *villista* forces remained concentrated around Chihuahua City. Villa and his staff deduced that in this way the *federales* would still see the major *villista* thrust as Chihuahua City and be caught unawares. In this, there remains no doubt as to the tactical success of the maneuver.

The capture of Ciudad Juárez proved the turning point of the northern campaign against Victoriano Huerta. *Villista* control of that border city allowed weapons to flow across the Río Bravo. Because of the arms embargo still in force against Mexico, weapons and ammunition came packed in unlikely cartons. Piano cases, wagon loads of coal, cases of tinned food, and other ruses transported weaponry to Villa's forces. The Constitutionalists willingly paid the exorbitant prices charged for this ordnance.

Control of Juárez allowed Villa to prepare for the final assault on Chihuahua City. On November 22, approximately 1,200 men from Juárez began moving south. The squeeze on Chihuahua led

United States officials to assume that Villa would triumph in northern Mexico. The United States consul in Ciudad Juárez believed that forced loans and expropriations of properties could be expected but hoped "that foreigners will not be called on." He further reported that to date no serious losses had occurred.

Two days after the *villista* departure from Ciudad Juárez, Villa's major troop strength engaged federal forces headed by Pascual Orozco and José Inez Salazar at Tierra Blanca, thirty kilometers from Chihuahua City. By 4:00 P.M. of November 24, both sides joined in pitched battle, and hostilities continued into the night. By noon of November 25, the *federales* retreated, overwhelmed by Villa's superior strength and tactics. In part, internecine conflict between Orozco and Governor Salvador Mercado kept Orozco from obtaining the best possible defensive positions. By the time Orozco moved against Villa, he walked into a well-prepared trap. The Battle of Tierra Blanca capped the campaign in the north. From Torreón, Villa in four weeks laid siege to Chihuahua, captured Juárez, and then drove out the rebels at Tierra Blanca.

Feeble attempts to reinforce federal troops at Tierra Blanca failed. Villa recalls that Rodolfo Fierro single-handedly stopped a train bearing troops for the battle. "In a rain of bullets," recalls Villa, "[Fierro] leaped from his horse to the train and, climbing from one car to another, reached the brake cylinder, released the air and stopped the train. A beautiful feat, Señor! Soldiers from the Corps of Scouts then fell on the train, and the slaughter was horrible."

Villa refused to allow the *federales* to enjoy an orderly retreat from Tierra Blanca and Chihuahua. *Villista* forces pursued the *federales* with a view toward their annihilation. In part, this ferocity on Villa's part grew out of the consuming hatred he felt toward Orozco. The rout of the *colorados* and the retreat of federal forces from Chihuahua left the town virtually ungarrisoned. Only 300 troops remained in the area to maintain order and attempt some sort of defense of the city.

Villa's victory at Tierra Blanca underscored the effectiveness brought to the rebel army through the control of Ciudad Juárez. Aid to the *villistas* came directly from Juárez. Arms, ammunition, fodder for the animals, and food came by train. Private cars brought medical assistance to wounded *villistas*. Additionally, many families in Juárez converted their homes and businesses into temporary hospitals in order to care for Villa's troops. Villa felt especially grateful to Zach Lamar Cobb, the collector of customs in El Paso, who expedited much of the assistance received by the *villistas*.

By the end of November, Gen. Salvador Mercado ordered his troops completely out of Chihuahua City with the exception of the small contingent to maintain order. Mercado personally accompanied the women and children and made for Ojinaga, across the border from Presidio, Texas, in an attempt to rebuild a countermove against Villa. Clearly, Mercado recognized that a defense of Chihuahua was untenable. He requested from Villa that his small garrison, left for the maintenance of order, be allowed to leave once the Constitutionalists took the city. Villa apparently accepted the proposition.

The capture of Chihuahua City forced many of its leading citizens to flee toward the United States border because of their *huertista* sympathies. Referred to as the "better class" by one United States official, the fear spread throughout Chihuahua that Villa would wreak a terrible vengeance on all who supported Huerta and Orozco. The utter isolation of Chihuahua City through a destruction of telegraph lines allowed Villa to operate in a vacuum and thus leave the country and the world at large wondering about his moves and plans.

Once Villa formally occupied Chihuahua City on December 8, he began to plan for the final battle with the *federales* in Chihuahua. Mercado had gone to Ojinaga; there Villa would attack again. Calling together his commanders, Villa gave the assignment for the seizure of Ojinaga to Pánfilo Natera. At the same time, Villa saw to it that order reigned in Chihuahua City, though some of the city's leading citizens were arrested for political reasons. Marion Letcher, United States consul in Chihuahua, reported that one of these luminaries was seized from the British Vice-Consulate, where he had sought refuge.

As a matter of revolutionary justice, Villa decreed confiscation of all properties belonging to the elder Terrazas, Enrique Creel, Juan Creel, and all members of that rather large clan. Even before Villa formally decreed the confiscation, Enrique C. Creel, son-in-law of Luis Terrazas, asked the United States *charge d' affaires* to seek guarantees from Villa. Creel, quite rightly, felt that a *villista* capture of Chihuahua would result in reprisals for his family.

Little time was required for Villa to drop his bombshell. On December 12, 1913, Villa took formal action. He recognized that he needed to provide for the widows and orphans of revolutionaries. As a consequence, the estates of the rich and powerful of Chihuahua became fair game. Villa decreed as confiscated the properties of those "who in a thousand ways had defrauded the public trust for over half a century of domination by trickery and force." Moreover, he declared, it is "just that the hour has arrived for these individuals to render accounts before public scrutiny."

Villa's December 12 decree named specifically the Terrazases as among the most prominent evildoers of Chihuahua. Confiscated were properties belonging to "Terrazas and sons, the Creel brothers, the Falomir brothers, the Luján brothers, J. Francisco Molina, and all of their relatives and other accomplices [such as the Spaniards and other Huerta supporters] who with them have become involved in the dirty business and in fraudulent combinations that in other times was called politics." This decree included banks, mines, land, cattle, houses, and personal effects. Through this action Villa merely confirmed his belief that the Terrazas clan, its collateral relations and allies, foreign and domestic, constituted the major evil for the state. In this way too he legitimized the *villista* sale of cattle to buyers in the United States.

Military matters, however, continued to preoccupy Villa. His capture of Chihuahua had greatly reduced the number of troops that he could leave garrisoned at Torreón, and as a result, the *federales* recaptured that city in early December. Immediate recapture of Torreón could not be carried out until *villista* forces finished driving the *federales* out of Ojinaga.

Villista commanders Ortega and Natera could not consummate the capture of Ojinaga. Throughout the first week of January 1914, the *federales* continued a fierce resistance to the *villistas*. Finally, Villa himself took command of the forces assigned to Ojinaga. In preparing to strike, Villa exhorted his men: "We are ready to take Ojinaga. Chiefs and soldiers of liberty, any man who turns his back will be shot then and there." On January 10, Villa and his men gained a decisive victory that probably guaranteed the annihilation of the *federales*, including Orozco and Salazar. Federal troops fled to Presidio, where they were captured and interned by the United States Army. Orozco and Salazar, however, escaped and would eventually return to cause more trouble.

Even before the victory at Ojinaga, Villa became the symbol of the revolution. Lionized by the press, this crude bandit knew well the uses of publicity and propaganda and played to effective coverage of his campaigns. Many liberal elements in the United States saw in Villa a sort of Mexican noble savage arising out of the oppression of the *porfiriato* and valiantly struggling to liberate his people from the tyranny of Huerta. Ambrose Pierce, by this time in his seventies and probably a bit senile, crossed into Ojinaga during the heat of battle and was never seen again. He left what seemed to be a suicide note in which he said:

> If you hear of my being stood up against a Mexican stone wall and shot to rags please know that it is a pretty good way to depart this life. It beats old age, disease or falling down the cellar stairs. To be a gringo in Mexico — ah, that is euthanasia.

The recapture of Torreón by the *federales* galled Villa. Yet his stunning victories at Juárez, Tierra Blanca, Chihuahua, and Ojinaga brought increasing numbers of adherents. His army began to grow. Former federal officers who had remained loyal to Madero joined the *villista* army.

By early March 1914, Villa began to formulate his plans for the capture of Torreón. By mid-March, *villistas* began moving out of Chihuahua City to the south. By this time, Villa controlled between ten and fifteen thousand troops. He did, however, note that he still needed more infantry and requested that Governor Manuel Chao have infantry in readiness in case they were needed.

The drive to the south took ten days. Accompanying Villa were some of the most famous names of the revolution: Felipe Angeles, José Trinidad Rodríguez, Maclovio Herrera, Eugenio Aguirre Benavides. The arrival of Angeles brought some changes to the Villa war machine. At Villa's request, Angeles came to Villa from Carranza's peripatetic cabinet and took over the artillery operations of the División del Norte.

On March 26, after successfully reducing federal outposts on the road to Torreón, Villa launched his attack on the city. For five days he relentlessly fought. It proved to be a house-by-house, street-by-street fight. Still, the *villistas* did not successfully control the city. On April 1, Villa ordered that Angeles use his artillery to reduce the city to rubble. Luckily for the *federales,* a duststorm began to blow on April 2, and they made their escape in the howling wind and swirling dust of the desert.

Losses were heavy for the *federales*. A thousand federal soldiers died, and 2,200 wounded escaped. Three hundred prisoners, however, fell into *villista* hands. Villa's forces sustained moderate losses. Of the 8,200 men used in the Battle of Torreón, only 550 were killed and 1,150 were wounded. Villa's victory at Torreón made public the internal weaknesses of the Huerta regime. Also, Villa came across a wealthy prize in Torreón: more than 150,000 bales of cotton were stored in Mexico's cotton capital. As a consequence, Villa found himself able to sell the cotton at his price and raise revenue for his growing and increasingly powerful army. Additionally, more artillery fell to the *villistas* and thus strengthened their already burgeoning force.

The fall of Torreón secured the north for the Constitutionalist cause. From Villa's capture of Chihuahua until the definitive fall of Torreón on April 2, 1914, other matters also preoccupied Villa. Since he controlled Chihuahua, he now had to run a government, an area in which he found himself woefully inadequate. He also had to treat with foreigners, many of whom were unfriendly and not sympathetic to the cause that Villa espoused. Moreover, the internecine struggles occurring within the revolutionary ranks were leading to alienation and a new wave of fratricide in Mexico.

CHAPTER V

"Disciplined and Orderly"

Clamor for land, cries for revenge, demands for payment — all of these and more inundated the *villistas* as they took control of Chihuahua after the successful ouster of the *federales*. The removal of legitimized authority created a vacuum and forced Francisco Villa and his supporters, most of them unschooled politically or otherwise, to establish some form of temporary government in Chihuahua. There exists no doubt that Villa himself had some idea as to how government should be established in the area. But practical application of his ideas often had to bend to military and political exigency dictated by a broader policy established by Carranza.

With the seizure of Ciudad Juárez in November 1913, *villista* authority began to assert itself. Villa and his followers recognized that municipal functions needed to continue if order was to prevail. Unlike his hero, Madero, Villa drove out all *huertista* functionaries, confiscated their properties, and, on occasion, ordered that some of them be shot. By November 17, Villa saw to it that municipal offices were manned and that the customshouse — a major source of revenue — continued to function. At the same time, he ordered the execution of some federal officers. Others, however, fled to El Paso, preferring internment at Fort Bliss.

Juan Medina's disenchantment with Villa over the execution

of General Yuriar had forced him to retire to El Paso. The *villista* victory at Juárez, however, brought Medina back. Importuned by Villa to become the administrator of Ciudad Juárez, Medina carefully watched all sources of revenue, especially that from the gambling houses. In that way water, sanitation, and other civic services could be maintained. Medina also ordered that there be no persecution of people coming back to Juárez from the United States. What rankled Medina was the rush of confiscations that occurred. Villa argued that it would be difficult to stop these since confiscation constituted a function of the revolution. When Medina threatened to resign, Villa backed down about the confiscated properties in Juárez.

Gambling halls provided early revenue to *villista* authorities in Juárez. No source of revenue escaped scrutiny. Juan Medina, Villa's disenchanted military advisor, became the overseer of Juárez and posted guards on the local banks to assure that money was not taken out in wholesale lots. Medina further ordered an audit of all gambling house books. In so doing, he found that he could seize 300,000 pesos of gold and silver from the gamblers.

Quiet prevailed in Juárez. Villa conferred with the mayor of El Paso and agreed to a resumption of common streetcar service. It seemed to U.S. government officials that relations between the two cities would remain normal. To assure order, Villa left a garrison in Juárez of approximately 2,500 men. By mid-December, Villa slowly began to reduce the size of his garrison at Juárez. He was obviously preparing to move toward Ojinaga.

The *villista* movement to the south and the ultimate victory over the *federales* at Tierra Blanca forced Villa to impose governance over the entire state. In Villa's *Memorias* he purportedly wrote that

> it was best we present a good appearance to the eyes observing
> from across the border. We now had international relations, and
> would be watched by newspapers from all over the world. They
> would see that we were not only victorious but disciplined and or-
> derly.

In large measure, Villa's early actions as military governor of Chihuahua reflected the sense of vendetta with which he entered the revolutionary fray. A strong antipathy against the landed classes of Chihuahua brought about decrees of confiscation that divested the Terrazases and the Creels of their properties. Villa ordered that these confiscations would go to the payment of pensions to widows and children of soldiers who fell in the struggle for Chihuahua. His decree also carried with it a general restoration of property to those people whose lands had been confiscated by the large landholders. While this action was anathema to men such as Carranza and later even Felipe Angeles, it still reflected Villa's attitude. He wanted to care for those who had fought to restore themselves to positions of equity within the state.

Under Juan Medina and with Villa's blessing, city government in Juárez underwent reorganization. Industries, transportation, and telegraph and postal service were in a state of chaos when the Constitutionalists moved into the area in November 1913. The railroad was in disrepair and no material with which to make repairs could be found. Fuel supplies became scarce, and food for man and beast was precious. Revenue from the gambling houses and the customshouse helped pay for these because the medium of trade was cash. Despite the difficulties, noted the United States consul in Juárez, there existed a "noticeable improvement" in conditions.

Villista government in Chihuahua showed little mercy toward those government workers who served during the terms of the "traitors" Rábago and Mercado. Villa refused to pay them for any back wages that might be owed. He decreed that new people would eventually take over government offices and that until that time, all but essential offices would be closed.

Ciudad Juárez did present some unique problems to the new administrators appointed by Villa. The head of immigration, Dr. Benjamín Castillo, for example, seemed unable to come to grips with the functions of his office and instead tried to expand his authority. Like many revolutionaries, Castillo possessed a rigid moralism about society. As a result, he constantly refused passage to prostitutes coming from El Paso to Ciudad Juárez. While perhaps a distasteful enterprise, the prostitutes, saloons, and gambling houses did generate revenue for local authorities.

In late December 1913, Carranza already was receiving negative reports about Villa's conduct in Chihuahua. Villa was pictured as an animal who tolerated excesses in order to assure his supremacy. Citizens of Chihuahua City, many of them *orozquistas,* feared Villa and hoped that Carranza would soon arrive to modify or negate the excesses of his strongest military arm.

Revenues and goods that came to the early *villista* government in Chihuahua often went for social purposes. Villa's predilection to help the poor, while haphazard, reflected his genuine concern for the people of the areas he controlled. In late December 1913, for example, Villa ordered his soldiers to give each person who made up a crowd around them a useful present such as cloth, a shovel, and other such items. This, of course, cost the *villista* government nothing, for most of these goods were "liberated" from mercantile establishments owned by Spaniards in Chihuahua City.

In the first few months of *villista* administration in Chihuahua, general order seemed to prevail. As early as late November 1913, the United States consul in Ciudad Juárez attempted to put to rest the unease that had been manifested in El Paso. He could see "no cause for anxiety by people on the north side of [the] Río Grande."

Seeds of discord among those revolutionaries charged with the administration of Chihuahua, however, presaged the open rupture that would occur in September 1914. Appointment of local officials occupied some of Villa's time, and he attempted to superintend even the most trivial appointment. In January 1914, the head of the Immigration Department in Juárez received summary expulsion from his job by Villa. The good Dr. Castillo, a Carranza appointee, had offended Villa with his bureaucratic ways. Villa in turn appointed a former federal telegrapher who was then promptly fired by L. Mora Gutiérrez, Carranza's representative in Juárez. This action gave Villa pause, and he began to view Carranza with greater suspicion.

Villista control of Chihuahua, even before the fall of Ojinaga, seemed assured. Revolutionary disruption had caused severe shortages to appear throughout Chihuahua, and Villa, acting both as military and civilian governor of the state, noted that commerce to Chihuahua from the United States had ceased. While the military necessity of isolating Torreón remained clear, daily needs of the populace deserved attention. As a consequence, Villa proposed that necessities — foodstuffs, petroleum, salt, soap, candies — enter duty-free. At the same time, Villa acknowledged the importance of customs revenues as a means of maintaining the solvency of the revolution. Villa wrote to Carranza that the "State is in ruins, and we shall all suffer alike. Neither my subordinates nor I have commercial interests. I am solely interested in the well-being of the State."

With Villa in control of the governorship, he could initiate reforms. In his first months in office, he issued a series of decrees aimed at the amelioration of problems faced by the general populace. First, he reduced the price of meat and thereby made it available to all. Second, duty-free goods — considered necessities — entered Chihuahua through Juárez. Third, Villa's love for children manifested itself through a decree creating schools where children congregated and where no such facility was available. Fourth, Villa made functional once again the electric power plant and also began operating the flour mill that had belonged to the Terrazas family. Fifth, using his soldiers as police, Villa ordered the summary execution of anyone involved in theft or in the sale of liquor. Sixth, under Villa's governance, the water system produced abundantly, and the telephones worked. Finally, Villa founded the Banco de Chihuahua, capitalized at ten million pesos that was secured by the large confiscated estates. Some of the lands belonging to the Creels and Terrazases were redistributed among the *campesinos*.

Through these reforms, Villa brought the countryside into closer communication with the capital of the state. This early reform activity on the part of Villa indicated that he was not just a bandit-turned-revolutionary. A very real spirit of reconstruction and reform infested his very being.

Supplying an army like the burgeoning División del Norte proved an almost full-time job. Villa established a most effective supply system through agents in the United States. As early as June 1913, Mexicans resident in El Paso sent supplies, money, and arms to Villa for his prosecution of the revolt against Huerta.

Felix Sommerfeldt, a German-Jewish immigrant, became one of the early *villista* agents. Sommerfeldt had, by 1913, become a Constitutionalist agent in the United States and worked closely with relatives of the murdered Madero and with Juan Sánchez Azcona. Through Sánchez Azcona, money was funneled to Villa. Sommerfeldt in turn used this same money to purchase supplies. There is some suspicion that Sommerfeldt through his connection with the revolution often played a tripartite game. He served as a German agent; he also served the Constitutionalists and later Villa; and there is the possibility that he acted as an informant for the United States Bureau of Investigation.

With the constant need for armaments and ammunition, the *villistas* remained uncritically supportive of Carranza between October 1913 and April 1914. Even when Carranza seemed penurious in terms of releasing ammunition, Villa continued to give his support. In late 1913, Shelton's, an outfit with which Carranza dealt for arms, had ammunition stored but would not release any to Villa. Already, Carranza was trying to control Villa through a miserly distribution of arms and ammunition.

As Villa piled victory upon victory through 1913 and into early 1914, a most expedient way of obtaining armaments came through picking up those weapons left by retreating *federales*. The field of battle received close attention by *villistas* to be sure that all arms and ammunition available came under their control. But as federal troops fled to Presidio, Texas, from Ojinaga, they took their rifles and ammunition with them. Villa decried the loss of about 2,000 rifles. Those that remained, however, were distributed among brigades that found themselves short of guns and ammunition. Villa cheerfully reported to Carranza that the División del Norte was getting enough guns and ammunition to be able to supply the entire army.

Soon it became obvious that the United States supported the Constitutionalists against Huerta. The arms embargo imposed by Taft and Congress almost two years before was lifted selectively: only Constitutionalists could buy arms from the United States. Rumors of such action abounded in northern Mexico. George C. Carothers, consular agent at Torreón and attached to Villa by Wilson, wanted verification of the lifted embargo. He claimed that if such rumors were untrue, "much hard feeling will result" with Villa. On February 3, 1913, the United States raised the embargo on munitions of war that entered Mexico.

The new availability of arms gave Villa the opportunity to purchase war matériel openly. He appointed Lázaro De la Garza as his commercial and fiscal agent and authorized him to appoint his own advisors as needed. Funds would be available through obtaining vouchers from federal and state offices in Chihuahua. Additionally, funds obtained through the sale of cattle, minerals, and other goods could finance the maintenance of Villa's war machinery. With De la Garza acting as the coordinator of fiscal activities, Villa's brother Hipólito traveled to New York to arrange for arms shipments to go to Villa through Juárez.

Villa's victories, his absolute control of Chihuahua, and his systematic organization of the revolution made him a darling of the press. His declarations about the protection of foreigners and their properties ingratiated him further with elements in the United States. While riding a wave of popularity, Villa's own sense of vengeance for the ills that beset Mexico occasionally took control. Two major incidents — one involving a foreigner and another a Mexican — would tarnish the Villa image.

Revolution unleashed primeval impulses among the revolutionaries. A strong, gut desire for vengeance characterized the revolutionary impulse for a forcible restoration of lands taken from the *campesinos* during the *porfiriato*. Pancho Villa's attitudes toward the Terrazases and the Creels clearly demonstrated the sense of vendetta released by the revolutionary whirlwind.

Tangible fear lay over Chihuahua City as the *villistas* prepared to take the city in late November 1913. No longer could the *orozquistas* serve as much protection for the privileged classes of Chihuahua. Rather, the *orozquista* defeat at Tierra Blanca forced the retreat of General Mercado and most of his garrison. Impending arrival of Villa and his legendary forces left the residents of Chihuahua City in fear for their lives and properties.

In most respects, the *chihuahuenses* were justified in their fears. Sophistry and hairsplitting did not enter into Villa's social thinking. To Villa, the Terrazas and Creel families had perpetrated unconscionable rapes of the state through their land manipulations, their banking interests, their mining, and their large, productive *haciendas*. Logically, at least from the *villista* perspective, large landholders should atone for past error by having their lands seized. The confiscation of Terrazas properties became one of Villa's first acts upon taking Chihuahua.

Declaration of confiscation did not, however, seem enough. Given the utterly negative attitudes that Villa held toward the Terrazas family, genuine fear existed that personal reprisals would occur. Enrique Creel, son-in-law of Luis Terrazas, Sr., asked that the United States intervene with Villa and attempt to gain some guarantees when he took Chihuahua City. There existed, in fact, a generalized fear over the fate of the Terrazas family.

Noncombatants left Chihuahua in the first week of December. Among them was the patriarch of the Terrazas clan, Luis, Sr. Yet some members of the family remained behind to close out the family's affairs. Among these was Luis Terrazas, Jr. On December 8, 1913, Villa captured young Terrazas by abducting him from the

British Vice-Consulate and demanded a ransom of $150,000 (dollars).

When the news reached the United States, various associates of the Terrazas family pressed the Department of State to assure that the younger Terrazas was not executed by Villa. Members of Congress, city officials from El Paso, and various members of stockmen's associations in Texas petitioned the Department of State for the protection of Luis Terrazas, Jr. Among these, Charles Goodnight stood out. A famous pioneer in the Texas livestock industry, Goodnight claimed that Terrazas "is not a politician but an unassuming gentleman. Get my friends behind it and save him." Senator Albert B. Fall of New Mexico also intervened. Fall claimed to have known the junior Terrazas for twenty years and had rented a house to Luis, Sr., when the old man fled to El Paso.

Importunities to the Department of State availed Luis Terrazas nothing. By early February 1914, Terrazas remained firmly in prison in Chihuahua City. Senator Fall pressed Constitutionalists in El Paso for the release of Terrazas. Although Villa in late December had given a "confidential guarantee that the life of this man would be spared," he kept Terrazas in prison.

In large measure, Villa hoped that keeping the son incarcerated would counteract any influence that Luis, Sr., might have. While meting out decent treatment to Terrazas, Villa viewed it as impossible to release the man. Citing a cattleman's aphorism, Villa declared that *"cuando se amara el becerro la vaca no anda muy lejos."* (When the calf is tied, the cow doesn't wander very far.) Villa felt his actions would keep Luis, Sr., from fomenting a counterrevolution against Constitutionalist control in Chihuahua.

The plight of Luis Terrazas, Jr., forced the women of the family to remain in Chihuahua City with little opportunity to leave and give aid to the ill Terrazas, Sr., who was in El Paso. Secretary of State William Jennings Bryan stated that "humanity demands that these ladies should be allowed to go to El Paso to give him such care and comforts as may be possible." Villa proved sensitive to suggestions by Special Agent George C. Carothers. By the end of January 1914, Villa was back in Ciudad Juárez because he had accompanied the remaining women of the Terrazas family to the border to see them safely into El Paso.

Reports began to circulate that Villa was torturing young Terrazas. Opinions to the Department of State carried with them the implication that the deparment should intervene actively on behalf of Terrazas. Carothers, however, noted that Terrazas had been moved from prison and was now "living with his family in Chihuahua apparently without molestation. I do not consider his life in danger at present."

A degree of desperation afflicted Terrazas's proponents and the diplomatic representatives of the United States. Because of his value to Villa, some talk circulated that Terrazas might be forced to march to Torreón with the División del Norte. Carothers received instruction to bring the matter up with Carranza. Carothers, however, felt that such a move would irritate Carranza because it dealt exclusively with Mexican citizens rather than foreigners. Moreover, Villa had convinced Carranza that the Terrazases in exile would successfully finance filibustering campaigns against the Constitutionalists should Luis, Jr., be released. By late March, Gen. Manuel Chao, civilian governor of Chihuahua, gave assurances that Terrazas would not be executed.

Villa released Terrazas in March, but he again incarcerated Terrazas in June for trying to get Terrazas cattle across the border. According to Villa, Terrazas hoped to provoke American intervention against the Constitutionalists. Again, the complaint went out about Villa's treatment of Terrazas. At the end of June, Villa telegraphed Carothers that he had ordered "full protection to Luis Terrazas, Jr., and hope that you will have no further reason to complain in his behalf. I have no intention of executing him."

The almost chronic persecution of the Terrazas clan characterized only one side of Villa's approach to so-called enemies of the revolution. Foreigners came under careful scrutiny, for foreign elements represented major concentrations of Mexico's wealth. The church, considered a foreign agency by the revolutionaries, also suffered abuse as a result of revolutionary antagonism toward all those elements that had ostensibly suppressed the populace of Mexico.

As Villa's forces continued to grow and *villista* influence gained a foothold in major towns of northern Mexico, retribution was exacted from wealthy foreigners in the area. In June 1913, for example, Tomás Urbina, Villa's *compadre*, held Durango. Summary arrests of foreigners occurred, many of whom were held for ransom. The Roman Catholic Bishop of Durango found himself incarcerated; his release would cost 500,000 pesos. The United States consul in Durango pleaded with the State Department: "Cannot help be sent?"

As Villa began to extend his hegemony over northern Mexico, his persecution of foreigners became increasingly selective. The seizure of Torreón on October 1, 1913, presaged a bad time for Spaniards and Chinese. Four days after the capture of Torreón, Villa had already executed seventeen Spaniards. Those who remained were assessed three million pesos. Americans and American interests, however, received exemptions. According to Carothers, Villa gave "assurance of exemptions for the future." The Chinese, another *villista* target, had heavy assessments laid on them. Yet the city, Carothers reported, seemed "well regulated and normal, with prices for necessities normal."

Villa's treatment of foreigners in Torreón signaled the *villista* tendency to cater to Americans. Because the División del Norte needed supplies from the United States, Villa could not risk alienating the United States through assessments and seizures against its citizens resident in Mexico. He allowed a train to haul Americans to the border if they wished to leave. Additionally, the rustic cavalier allowed the same train to take the women and children of prominent Mexican families to the border if they so desired.

Seizure of Torreón proved so rapid and complete that Spaniards who controlled the cotton industry there lacked time to heed the federal warning. The *federales,* even before October 1, had advised Spaniards that the rebels planned to kill them. While many left, a larger number remained behind and suffered the consequences of Villa's desire for revenge.

Pressures on Villa from the United States accelerated with regard to his treatment of foreigners. While exempting Americans, Villa's relations with other nationalities prompted the United States to petition him to ease up on foreigners. Writing to Lázaro De la Garza in late October, Villa claimed that he respected all nationalities except Spaniards, for this group was "bothersome" to Mexico. Also, if United States representatives spoke for the Spaniards, it would seem that the U.S. wanted to protect the enemies of the revolution.

Villa's antagonism toward Spaniards had its historical base. Spaniards controlled the church, much of the mercantile, banking, and wholesale establishments, and almost unanimously supported Victoriano Huerta. As *villistas* extended their control into Chihuahua and even before the Battle of Tierra Blanca, Villa ordered the confiscation of all Spanish goods. By November 19, all Spaniards would be expelled as "pernicious" to Mexico and their goods seized as spoils of war.

Once in Chihuahua City, Villa reiterated his decree, much to the horror of United States consul Marion Letcher. Villa also added that any Spaniards who remained would be shot. Letcher hoped to bring about the revocation of "this harsh, unjust and barbarous decree." Letcher continued and thus revealed his animosity toward Villa: "I submit that this decree marks Villa as violent and irresponsible. . . . The power he now wields is a menace for society." Not even his advisors, opined Letcher, could mitigate Villa's barbarity.

By mid-December, titular First Chief Venustiano Carranza continued to receive reports about *villista* excesses toward foreigners. Foreigners in Chihuahua hoped that Carranza might be able to curb Villa's predilection for summary treatment of selected foreigners and large landholders. Certainly, Letcher viewed any such optimism with disdain, for he stated that "although good will is professed for Americans I question whether conditions for them or any other foreigners will be sufficiently favorable to justify extension of business operations or even continuance of those now under way." Somewhat paranoically, Letcher sent his wife to El Paso, though Mrs. Letcher reported that Villa had been most accommodating toward her and had refused no request of the consul.

Systematic confiscation of Spanish property continued as Villa's hegemony over Chihuahua became more concrete. In late December 1913, Domingo Trueba, a Spaniard who owned warehouses in Juárez, complained to Carranza about Villa's seizure of his property. His employees, he recounted, were out in the streets without livelihood. Villa illegally sold the warehouses and goods to an American as a means of raising revenue. Trueba demanded restitution from Carranza.

Villa's anti-Spanish tendencies also manifested themselves in the individual treatment he meted out to Spaniards with a careless tongue. One American citizen complained that Villa had deported his wife, a Spaniard. The good lady had stated her gratification that Madero had been shot. Consequently, Villa deported her as an undesirable alien; he did not, however, take action against the husband or the property.

Villa's anti-Spanish policy, while not wholly condoned by the
U. S. consul in Juárez, was at least understood by that functionary.
He wrote:

> General Villa's policy, notwithstanding the seeming harshness
> and cruelty in some cases, is carrying out the only promising so-
> lution for restoring peace. The Spaniards are commercially in
> Mexico what the Jews are in Russia, with the addition of taking
> an interest in the political affairs of the country to the extent of
> being candidates for lucrative concessions . . . which [they] use to
> pauperize the natives.

At this juncture, appeals to Carranza about Villa's anti-Spanish policy failed to move the First Chief. Rather, he endorsed Villa's actions while cautioning prudence. Villa informed Carranza
that "I shall try to act in conformity with your ideas. . . . I was
grateful for . . . [your] prudent advice, and I shall proceed, in any
case, in a way that will best benefit our cause." Rather craftily,
Villa subtly informed Carranza that he still had the upper hand in
Chihuahua.

The seeming caprice with which Villa exercised his anti-for-
eignism left diplomatic observers somewhat nervous about how
rebel armies would act. While Villa prepared to retake Torreón,
foreign elements in that city and throughout Mexico feared that
Villa would again wreak vengeance on Spaniards. Throughout
January and February 1914, *villista* threats against foreigners in
general and Spaniards in particular prompted uncertainty on the
part of diplomats charged with the protection of outside interests.
Villa, however, rationalized his anti-Spanish pronouncements as
bombast issued in order to keep Spaniards in line. Villa claimed
that Spaniards would receive full protection as long as they did not
actually engage in combat against him.

Villista plans for the recapture of Torreón continued to devil
foreign observers. Although Villa guaranteed the safety of foreigners, he refused to guarantee their security during the actual heat of
battle. Some attempts were made to have Villa agree to a neutral
zone where noncombatants could take refuge.

By late January, increasing predictions emerged about a Constitutionalist triumph over Huerta. Revolutionary agents in Mexico
City proclaimed to the citizenry that if they afforded any protection
to the *huertistas,* summary executions would take place. Such a
statement horrified U.S. Secretary of State William Jennings

Bryan. He instructed George Carothers to impress upon Villa "the enormity of such a threat." Carothers also was to obtain promises that "foreign flags and the lives and property of foreigners and non-combatants will be respected." Moreover, all "summary and violent measures, whether proceeding from suspicion, from revenge or from other motives will be prohibited. All revolutionary forces should be so instructed." Apparently, Bryan genuinely believed that the revolution would be guided and controlled by the United States.

Despite guarantees, good intentions notwithstanding, Villa's ferocity often forced him to react viscerally to situations. The most celebrated incident involving an individual foreigner who suffered Villa's wrath occurred when William Benton, a Scotsman married to a Mexican, decided to take Villa to task for revolutionary seizure of Benton's cattle.

During mid-February, Villa was in Ciudad Juárez arranging for arms shipments in order to prosecute his campaign against Torreón. Benton, strong-willed and irascible, decided that Villa should be upbraided for his atrocities and personally went to Juárez to tangle with the commander of the División del Norte. At this point, the narrative becomes muddled. Various versions exist as to what happened. Some report that Benton went for his gun after exchanging harsh words with Villa. Villa's men, including Rodolfo Fierro, disarmed Benton, and Villa ordered that he be summarily executed. Thus, on February 17, 1914, William Benton was taken by Fierro and a squad of men to Samalayuca, where Benton was forced to dig his own grave. Sadistically, Fierro smashed Benton's skull with a shovel, dropping the body into the grave that was then quickly filled. Nowhere along the line did Benton's status as an Englishman receive any consideration. An attempt on Villa's life was sufficient cause for summary execution. Also, the English continued to support Huerta, reason enough to maltreat citizens of the United Kingdom.

Press reaction to Benton's death both in the United States and in Europe portrayed Villa as a heartless assassin. Villa, however, claimed that he had no choice, for more attempts by foreign *huertistas* to hide behind their nations' flags in order to subvert the revolution must be avoided. Benton, Villa claimed, was properly tried by a revolutionary tribunal and shot according to military custom.

British popular opinion with regard to the Benton killing

pressed for intervention in Mexico. In an attempt to flank interventionist tendencies in Mexico by the British, the United States offered to mediate the dispute. Benton's death highlighted the United States position vis-à-vis foreigners in Mexico. Because of the Roosevelt Corollary to the Monroe Doctrine, foreign complaints and grievances against Latin American countries had funneled through the United States.

Pressures for commissions of inquiry caused Villa some concern. He recognized the complex nature of the problem but did not know how to achieve a resolution. Benton had been struck on the head with a shovel. Villa ordered that the corpse be exhumed and then shot in order to give credence to his story about a proper military execution. His advisors, including the head of his medical department, informed Villa that a commission could determine rather quickly that the corpse had been executed after the fact.

Great Britain became increasingly bellicose. More pressure was brought to bear on the United States, and the British kept demanding action and threatening possible unilateral moves if the problem remained unsolved. George Carothers attempted to impress upon Villa the power that the British had. He pointed out the strength of the British navy. Villa rejoindered by wondering what the British navy could do to him in Chihuahua.

German officials, who also had interests in Mexico and also supported Huerta, viewed with some alarm the excesses of the *villistas*. Speaking through its ambassador to the Court of St. James, Germany recommended that the best solution for the United States would be total intervention in Mexico. Said the ambassador: "Make a desolation and call it peace." Strong hands were needed on the Mexican reins. Huerta demonstrated such strength.

Meanwhile, Carranza attempted to assert his authority over Villa. He claimed that representations needed to be made to him. When asked if the United States considered itself the protector of foreigners in Mexico, Carranza declined to comment. Instead, he viewed this as something with which the United States Congress would deal. Carranza did, however, order that the commission going to investigate the Benton affair should give open and aboveboard hearing to Benton's relatives in order to get all sides of the issue.

Villa's general treatment of foreigners and the fierceness of his relations with the enemy prompted the United States to attempt to modify and civilize the noted fighter. Gen. Hugh L. Scott, commander of the Southern Department of the Army, took on the task. Scott, an old Indian fighter who knew the Southwest intimately and spoke Spanish, met with Villa on the International Bridge between El Paso and Ciudad Juárez. Scott attempted to instruct Villa about civilized warfare. He even gave Villa a pamphlet about treatment of prisoners. The pamphlet so impressed Villa that he ordered it translated into Spanish and distributed to his army. Scott viewed his mission as successful because Villa did not order the summary execution of the next 4,000 prisoners that were seized at Torreón. Scott also noted that Villa continued to show no mercy to Orozco's *colorados*.

Scott and Villa developed a long friendship despite difficulties that would arise between the United States and Villa. The general described Villa as respecting truth and directness. "Like a child or a dog," Scott wrote in his memoirs, "these primitive people know well with whom they are dealing and are impressed accordingly." Villa, Scott argued, was quick on the trigger because of his long career as a bandit.

The Benton killing went unresolved. Foreigners continued to live under the threat of revolutionary dangers. Guarantees given one day might be withdrawn the next. Spaniards practically received direct assurance of persecution, as did the Chinese.

After the second battle of Torreón, some of Villa's men died from food poisoning. They had eaten in a Chinese restaurant, which was blamed for the deaths. In retribution, 300 Chinese allegedly died in Torreón. *Villistas* pillaged the Chinese sector of town, stole money from the Chinese, and drew and quartered some of them in vengeance. The latent violence and xenophobia of the revolution found expression in *villista* persecution of selected foreigners.

At no time did Villa ever consider himself as subordinate to Carranza or any other authority. When first approaches were made to Villa about his possible affiliation with the Constitutionalists and the Plan de Guadalupe, Villa insisted that he would be subordinate to no one. Originally, Carranza's emissaries had suggested that Villa would be militarily subordinate to Obregón and under the political jurisdiction of Manuel Chao. Villa refused. Carranza, at this time desperate for adherents to strengthen his ranks, accepted Villa's conditions and promoted him to a generalship.

As early as June 1913, it became apparent to the Constitutionalists that Villa would run his own show in Chihuahua. Consequently, the possibility of dissension always loomed as distinct. Gossip reached Carranza that adherents of Emilio Vázquez Gómez, one-time Madero supporter and later detractor, had made overtures to Villa. Hope was expressed that Villa might write to Carranza and reaffirm his adhesion to the Constitutionalist cause.

As the year progressed and as Villa continued to gain strength and renown, he remained steadfast in his support of Carranza. Villa, however, continued to note that he acted independently and without subordination to any other authority. Still, Constitutionalist agents found Villa to be "a chieftain worthy of your [Carranza's] trust." Villa also chose to give Carranza advice. Political intrigue within the Constitutionalist ranks irritated Villa. He told Carranza that anything he found bothersome "refer to me, and I'll straighten it out."

Carranza had some cause for concern. Villa already made independent contact with emissaries from Emiliano Zapata in the south. Gildardo Magaña met with Villa on November 16, 1913, in Juárez. Magaña, a contemporary of Villa's at Santiago Tlatelolco in 1912, had worked with Villa on his literacy. Villa felt a strong affinity for Magaña. Zapata wanted to be sure that Villa viewed social and economic ends as important. Upon his return to Morelos, Magaña reported that Villa was sincere in his dedication to social and economic reform.

Detractors of the Constitutionalist revolution — *huertistas, vazquistas*, or others — constantly attempted to separate Villa from Carranza. By the end of 1913, Villa continued to swear his allegiance to the Plan de Guadalupe. Carranza's own agents reported consistently that Villa remained loyal.

Villista conquest of Chihuahua and control of Ciudad Juárez also promised a fruitful ground for friction between Villa and Carranza. The appointment of local officials in Juárez, for example, had to be carefully balanced between Villa appointees and those made by Carranza, again demonstrating the regional and nearly independent nature of most of the revolutionaries.

Even the deployment of troops provided the possibility for friction. Villa, constantly anxious to get into battle, wanted troops sent from Sonora in order to extend his campaigns to Ojinaga and then to Torreón. When Carranza refused, Villa bit his tongue and merely sent his regrets.

Chores of administration began to wear on Villa. He had appointed Juan Medina, his one-time chief of staff, as interim governor of Chihuahua. Carranza, however, wanted Manuel Chao as governor. Villa demurred. He argued that while he loved Chao like a brother, he did not believe Manuel Chao sufficiently perspicacious to deal with intrigue and with attempts by enemy agents to operate in the state.

Villa, however, backed down. He viewed the military victory to be won at Ojinaga more important than a political dispute with Carranza. Villa took the appointment of Chao as a definite order. He told Carranza that he would follow all orders that fit his view of his obligations. Juan Medina was not worth a fight; he fled to the United States when it seemed that Villa and Carranza might be in conflict. A trimmer by nature, Medina wanted to see which way the battle would go before he committed himself.

Villa suffered provocation. After seizing Juárez and then Chihuahua, he entertained Francisco Escudero, an envoy from Carranza. Unfortunately, Escudero became intoxicated at a banquet and insulted Villa, calling him a savage and coward. Moreover, Escudero drunkenly claimed that Carranza had ordered such provocation to see if Villa possessed enough courage to defend himself. Villa, to the surprise of many at the banquet, did not kill Escudero — he merely got up and left. But the incident would add to the resentment that began to grow in Villa toward the First Chief.

By early 1914, Carranza kept receiving disturbing reports about Villa. Popular reaction to Villa in New York and Washington portrayed the northern warrior as a savage but still the only man for the times. Without Villa, popular opinion held, there would be no revolution. Carranza's own vanity was pricked over such news, for he saw it as detrimental to revolutionary unity and to his supremacy as First Chief.

Villa consistently invited Carranza to come to Chihuahua, but Carranza kept finding excuses not to go. The First Chief did not want to feel that he would lose control of the revolution. In Chihuahua, Villa's domain, Carranza would always be a guest. Problems were exacerbated even more when the governor of Texas asked if Texas should deal directly with Villa.

By February 1914, Carranza's advisors urged that he go to Chihuahua. They warned that the increased strength of the *villistas* might prove a threat if such a primeval force should be released. A meeting in Chihuahua might give Carranza an opportunity to straighten out the mess that Villa made of the Creel-Terrazas lands. Moreover, Carranza in Chihuahua would serve as a tangible demonstration of revolutionary solidarity.

In early March, Villa reiterated his invitation to Carranza. All facilities would be placed at Carranza's disposal. Also, such a move would join administratively the civilian and military arms of the revolution. By mid-March, plans were made for the arrival of Carranza in Chihuahua City. Gen. Felipe Angeles, undersecretary of war with Carranza, wanted assignment to Villa. Villa needed an artillery specialist. Carranza's visit on March 15, 1914, joined Villa and Angeles.

The meeting between Carranza and Villa did not go well. Villa warmly welcomed Carranza, but the latter received Villa's affectionate embrace somewhat coldly. While agreeing to most propositions, Villa felt that Carranza had surrounded himself with *chocolateros perfumados* — perfumed chocolate drinkers — who would misadvise the First Chief.

The arrival of Angeles, however, helped convert the División del Norte into a potent, disciplined force. For that, Villa was grateful. The career military man and the unlettered guerrilla joined forces. Their union would be a legend in Mexico.

Responsibilities of governance bogged Villa down. While he recognized the necessity of establishing political authority, his own personality constantly insisted on action. He knew that his own limitations would hinder his actions as a political leader. He did, however, want to exert influence over political choices.

Additionally, Villa represented an alien element to Carranza and his advisors. Villa came from the lower classes. Crude, rude, unlettered, and unsophisticated, Villa still remained intensely loyal to those who showed him respect. His loyalty was exemplified when he ordered the images of Madero and Abraham González to be imprinted on the currency of Chihuahua. On February 22, 1914, the anniversary of Madero's death, Villa returned González's body to Chihuahua for honorable burial and tearfully stood watch over the coffin.

Constantly fighting the image of bandit, Villa joined the Constitutionalists. But his name preceded his adhesion to that group. Elements anathema to the revolution quaked in terror at the thought of Villa and his hordes taking an area. No doubt existed in the minds of these counterrevolutionaries that, at the very least, lives would be shattered, if not lost, wives and daughters raped, and family fortunes devastated by the odious peasant who now called himself general.

Villa's alliance with Carranza and the Constitutionalists, however, did give him a modicum of respectability. During this early phase of the Constitutionalist Revolution, Villa demonstrated some political acumen and manifested some of the regional tendencies of his area. Fiercely individualistic, he constantly asserted his rights as head of the División del Norte. These assertions ultimately would bring about greater conflict and cause increased strife in Mexico.

CHAPTER VI

Coming Apart at the Seams

The relentless progress of Villa's march against Huerta was obvious. The seemingly indefatigable División del Norte represented the awesome military might of a people bent upon vengeance for centuries of perceived misfortunes. Manifest in Villa's action emerged a strong feeling about the role of foreigners in Mexico. Villa's attitude, however, proved discriminatory, for his principal target was Spaniards and others who might have supported the Huerta regime. At the same time, Villa continued to extend his hegemony over northern Mexico through the establishment and operation of governmental institutions in Chihuahua, and he sought to fulfill some of the barely articulated promises of the revolution about land reform and nationalist vengeance.

Villa's demons possessed two forms: Mexicans who supported Huerta and foreigners who supported Huerta. Acutely aware of the power of his name and the terror that it struck among the elite, Villa capitalized upon this in order to destabilize a social structure that attempted to cling tenuously to older forms.

Mexico's revolutionary *milieu* provided the ideal environment for terrorist activity as violent factions contended for power and as the society began to come unglued. Suppressed social groups found voices and avenues for expressing their discontent. Mexico's social traditions, especially those revolving around personal relations and family ties, combined with a pragmatic sense and vitiated the proto-terrorism of the Mexican Revolution. The social atmosphere also tempered the actions of Mexico's most notorious revolutionary leader, Pancho Villa.

Villa could well rest on some military laurels. His successful recapture of Torreón allowed him to give his troops a chance to recuperate for the final push southward and the ultimate defeat of Victoriano Huerta. While in Torreón, Villa made arrangements with an El Paso firm for large-scale outfitting of his swelling army. Villa wrote that "the manager of the firm, a Jew named Victor Carusoe, an intelligent businessman, gave me extensive credit and supplied me with everything. He knew our cause would triumph." Moreover, continued Villa, "he made money in dealing with me but he deserved it for his confidence in me and our cause when all the nations of the world were publicly branding our men as a gang of robbers and me, Pancho Villa, as the ringleader."

Villa used Torreón as a base to make his forays to secure the countryside for the Constitutionalist cause. Following the Battle of Paredón of May 17, 1914, Villa ordered that bodies of *huertista* commanders be found. The capture of a wounded but live lieutenant colonel netted a handsome bag for the *villistas*. Rodolfo Fierro, Villa's homicidal but loyal subordinate, of course wanted to do away with the lieutenant colonel immediately. Felipe Angeles, however, intervened by ordering that the prisoner not be turned over to Fierro despite the Carranza decree that all prisoners should be summarily executed. Villa, caught between his slavishly loyal friend and his brilliant artillery commander, finally made a Solomonic decision. With Jesuitical precision he stated that he certainly adhered to Carranza's decree, but humanity dictated that a wounded prisoner first had to be healed before he could face revolutionary justice. Such minor on-the-spot decisions would ultimately contribute to the growing fissure in the revolutionary ranks.

By the end of May 1914, Carranza and Villa were clearly at loggerheads. Carranza feared the military might of the División del Norte and hoped to keep Villa confined to the north and out of Mexico City. If Carranza could keep Villa corralled, then Obregón could sweep in from the northwest, take Mexico City, and leave Villa fulminating in the north. Thus, when the time came to move against the *huertista* positions in Zacatecas, Carranza ordered Villa to dispatch men to assist Pánfilo Natera in the siege of that provincial capital. This action nearly brought the two to an open rupture. Villa began moving against Zacatecas in mid-June. Despite Carranza's opposition, *villista* leaders declared that they merely wanted to free "the movements of troops and their leaders from the dictatorship of Carranza."

En route to Zacatecas, Villa told Special Agent George Carothers that when he reached Mexico City he would bow to the will of all the generals with regard to the selection of a provisional president, even if it was Carranza. Villa promised no direct hostilities toward Carranza but refused to carry out the First Chief's orders if they interfered with military operations. Carothers concluded that "Villa is not only a general but has keen political perceptions." Villa, he stated, showed an inclination toward considering advice from the United States.

On June 19, *villista* troops, numbering around 19,000, made contact with the 14,500 *federales* that garrisoned Zacatecas. Aided by 6,000 troops under Natera and the Arrieta brothers, Constitutionalist forces drove the *federales* toward the center of the city by June 21. Two days later, soldiers from the División del Norte engaged in heavy fighting that ultimately secured Zacatecas for the Constitutionalists.

Federal defenses proved inadequate. Trenches were badly laid out, supplies limited, and the troops demoralized as they faced the *villista* juggernaut. In the final body count, the *federales* suffered 5,015 dead and 2,500 wounded while the *villistas,* probably minimizing their figures, claimed to have lost only 900 men with 1,600 wounded. Practically, Zacatecas was reduced to near rubble. Heavy machine-gun damage and artillery fire pockmarked buildings and leveled whole streets.

The form of military action in which Villa engaged — heavy sieges accompanied by cavalry assaults — claimed high numbers of casualties. Zacatecas provided Villa's medical service an opportunity to prove itself. Of all the revolutionary armies, the División del Norte possessed the most sophisticated medical facilities. Headed by Dr. L. B. Rauschbaum, fifteen surgeons worked to treat all of the wounded without discrimination. Those immediately needing treatment received attention right on the field. More serious cases were moved behind the lines in cars, ambulances, wagons, litters, or on horseback to established field hospitals.

Good advice and his own perspicacity led Villa to set up his medical corps. Villa the bandit was also Villa the commander, and a good commander cared for the welfare of his men. According to Carothers, prisoners received good treatment. Many of them were later incorporated directly into the División del Norte. In addition to men acquired for the army, Villa also captured all federal artillery and weapons.

The stunning victory at Zacatecas further exacerbated Carranza's jealousy toward Villa. Villa recognized the necessity of consolidating his position. Rather than continuing south he headed north, distributing his army between Torreón and Juárez. Villa decided that he would leave Natera in charge of Zacatecas since the town had been secured.

Several reasons contributed to the change in Villa's plans. First of all, Pablo González failed to attack and subjugate San Luis Potosí and thus left the *villista* eastern flank exposed. Second, Carranza refused to send sufficient coal. Third, Carranza, who controlled the port of Tampico, would not send ammunition to Villa, who was nearly 1,000 miles from his point of supply at Ciudad Juárez. Finally, Carothers reported that Villa was utterly convinced that Carranza, "from a malicious sentiment of envy and jealousy," wanted Villa vulnerable to attack. Villa claimed that he would not attack Carranza unless he himself was attacked.

North again, Villa brooded about the injustice of his relationship with Carranza. By July, *carrancista* envoys attempted to heal the growing breach between the two headstrong leaders. *Villistas* and *carrancistas* met at Torreón and agreed that Villa would recognize Carranza as First Chief, while Carranza would recognize Villa's hegemony over the División del Norte. Carranza further agreed to furnish arms and coal to Villa so that he could proceed southward once again. He also agreed to call a convention of military chieftains to determine the fate of the country once Huerta had been driven from Mexico. Villa, for his part, confirmed the belief that Carranza was the chief civil administrative official of Mexico. In an act of generosity, Villa also agreed to release some *carrancista* officials imprisoned in Juárez and to relinquish a large sum of money to the *carrancistas*. But the agreement quickly proved a façade, for neither Villa nor Carranza truly believed that it stood a chance. As a result, their subsequent actions pointed to the resumption of strife and probable military conflict.

With such conflict just below the surface, the División del Norte sought to exorcise *carrancista* influence from northern Mexico. In Durango, Villa's native state, the Arrieta brothers, Mariano and Domingo, held sway with about 6,000 men. The Arrietas and their troops remained loyal to the Constitutionalists, and, as a result, Villa dispatched Tomás Urbina with 2,000 men to clean house in Durango. This and other *villista* activity clearly pointed to preparations for the upcoming battle with Carranza. Obregón had already marched into Mexico City, triumphant and flushed with victories in northwestern and western Mexico, and robbed Villa of his much-deserved glory.

Meanwhile, Villa continued to demonstrate limitless capacity supervising the civilian government of Chihuahua. In April 1914, Villa noted that Manuel Chao, the civil governor of Chihuahua appointed by Carranza over Villa's protests, was not administering Chihuahua with due respect for Villa's authority as military commander of the state. Rather quickly, Villa informed Chao as to who held the real power in Chihuahua and added a threat of summary execution if Chao did not conform. Chao, both out of intimidation and loyalty to Villa, subordinated himself to Villa's persuasive powers. Villa noted, however, that while Chao was bright and of good counsel, other Carranza appointees exaggerated their authority.

Once Chihuahua and its civil governor proved amenable, Villa extended his administrative hegemony to Torreón. The second capture of that cotton capital netted Villa an enormous amount of baled cotton in addition to that which still needed to grow and mature. The sale of cotton in the United States allowed Villa to liquidate a $75,000 debt that he had contracted with the Rio Grande Valley Bank and Trust Company of El Paso. Yet as Villa acquired more working capital in Torreón, budgetary demands in Chihuahua forced Villa to funnel more money into that state. Administrative machinery needed to be set up in order to distribute lands confiscated from so-called "enemies of the Revolution."

Silvestre Terrazas, shirttail relative of Luis Terrazas but no political coreligionist of the old patriarch, became the head of the agency charged with the administration of confiscated lands. In that position he constantly saw that some of Villa's subordinates took wheat and seed and sold them for dollars. While Terrazas recognized the need for money to acquire military ordnance, at the same time he decried the possibility of food and crop shortages as a result of these actions.

One result of this action came when Villa overtly accused Terrazas and the civil governor of the state with collusion and fraud. When he ascertained the enormity of the activity, Villa ordered the punishment of any individual who would violate the public welfare. Many of the military men engaged in such questionable activity claimed immunity because of the war and because of the intimacy with Villa. In one of his rages, Villa ordered punishment of all offenders, should the acts be repeated, and further declared that he would personally see to these executions.

In direct contrast to his fury over graft in his ranks, Villa's affection for children was well known. In the proposed budget for Chihuahua in 1914, schools received preferential attention. In spite of the perilous times the state and country were facing, Villa's government tried to keep all schools and institutes functioning as if the situation remained normal.

Educational reform on the part of Villa prompted curiosity in the U.S. Department of State. Secretary of State William Jennings Bryan inquired if Villa had in fact established new schools in the area. Marion Letcher, U.S. consul in Chihuahua and no friend of Villa, replied:

> Report is unqualifiedly false. Schools here and elsewhere . . . have continued with little interruption during all revolutionary disturbances but no new ones have been established. . . . I avail myself of this occasion to say that newspaper apologists for Villa have uniformly been shamelessly untruthful in their attempt to make a hero of Villa who is essentially a brutal illiterate and insolent, incapable of the fine aspirations and sentiments imputed to him and falsely reported as expressed by him.

Such an outburst from a senior diplomatic official in Mexico prompted Bryan to chastise Letcher. He thanked the consul for the information received but continued that

> the tone of your despatch suggests that you be cautioned against expressing to any one there an opinion about any of the Constitutionalists that might excite friction between them or alienate them from you. Villa's influence has been helpful to us in explaining the Tampico matter to the Constitutionalists.

Villa's popularity with newspapers in the United States received substantial assistance from the publication of *Vida Nueva*, an essentially *villista* organ published in Chihuahua. Villa ordered that 7,000 pesos be put at the disposal of the paper. Silvestre Terrazas, in communicating the order, said that such a sum was necessary with the end of "protecting the work of a good press, expressly dedicated to our Constitutionalist cause."

While Villa fought and bled for the revolution, he saw no reason not to indulge in some frivolity. Both as luxury and necessity, Villa built a home for his wife in Chihuahua City. The massive structure — Quinta Luz by name — contained fifty rooms and was half-home and half-fortress. These rooms, surrounding an interior patio, housed Villa's *dorados* whenever he was in town. In that way he could have some domesticity and at the same time be properly protected by his chosen bodyguards.

Villa's love for innovative things prompted Lázaro De la Garza, his chief fiscal agent in the United States, to indulge in a bit of pandering. A seven-passenger 1915 model Pierce Arrow was delivered to Ciudad Juárez and then sent to Villa in Chihuahua City. This ultramodern toy, reasoned De la Garza, would give a great deal of pleasure to Villa and would make De la Garza seem sensitive to the Centaur's whims.

More serious matters, however, occupied *villista* government in Chihuahua. Confiscation of large estates also needed their redistribution. The establishment of a state agrarian commission aimed at the reparceling of lands in Chihuahua. As a first step, members of the Villa-appointed commission obtained copies of land titles to determine which lands would be subdivided. In later months the state commission would effectuate some land redistribution.

Unstable political and financial conditions prompted Villa to try to set matters right in Chihuahua. His principal aim — the establishment of a bank of issue — sought the stabilization of currency in all areas under his control. In the process, Villa sought sufficient capitalization from New York banks for collateral for the new bank. De la Garza reported to Villa that one of his contacts, "of absolute solvency," had made arrangements to transfer credit to El Paso in order to facilitate the handling of bullion. Also, De la Garza ordered the printing of bills of emission by the American Bank Note Company of New York. These actions, predicated upon the idea that Villa would emerge as the supreme power of the revolution, later caused innumerable problems for all revolutionaries in Mexico.

An integral part of *villista* government in those areas directly under Villa's influence revolved around relations with foreigners, the church, and the large landholders. The general xenophobia of the revolution often branded foreigners indiscriminately. Felix Sommerfeldt, a *villista* agent in the United States, reported rumors that Villa intended to expel all Germans because it was a German boat — the *Ypiranga* — that attempted to deliver arms to Huerta at Veracruz. De la Garza, however, argued that the rumor should be squashed because "we too will bring ammunition on foreign ships."

The church and its clerics occupied a special place in Villa's attentions. In the spring of 1914, in Saltillo, Villa rounded up all clergy. Mexican priests, "for whom [Villa] bore no ill will," came to the defense of the hated Jesuits, most of them Spaniards. Villa contended that "Mexican priests . . . did not recognize their own interests and that the religious fraternity forced them to concede goodness to foreign priests who deprecated them," kept them from high church office, and generally treated Mexican clerics as second-class members of the church. In many ways, Villa articulated the almost chronic complaints of local clergy who had suffered discrimination during the colonial period and the first century of national existence. Villa informed Mexican priests not to waste energy on those who did not deserve it.

Villa's actions against foreign clergy in Saltillo, after he took that town in June, caused consternation among the pious leading ladies of Saltillo society. They decried Villa's contention that Spanish and foreign priests supported Huerta and ordered that Jesuits and foreign clerics would be watched carefully. The good ladies of Saltillo failed in their appeals to Villa, but he proved sufficiently charming that the ladies continued to be friendly to the revolution's most awesome warrior.

Villa saw the church as a foreign imposition that sought to cover evil through religious teachings, thus duping the people to whom clerics ministered. The obvious righteousness of the revolutionary cause forced Villa to conclude that if clerics refused assistance to that cause they were, *ipso facto*, evil in and of themselves. "In my opinion," Villa concluded, "our justice involves such holiness that the priests and the churches who deny us their help have forfeited their claim to be men of God."

Such a position found concrete articulation in Zacatecas on

the day after the *federales* fled the city. Villa learned that doctors and nursing nuns were hiding federal officers in the hospital. Villa, operating under the Juárez decree of 1865 and reaffirmed by Carranza as applicable to *huertistas,* wanted to find these officers so they could be summarily executed. The doctors and nuns refused to identify army officials in the hospital and even denied the presence of the individuals. Again Villa flew into one of his rages, and threatened to execute doctors and nurses if he did not get the accursed *federales.* Though running an exaggerated bluff, Villa ordered the immediate execution of the traitors and had them marched off with an execution squad. The doctors, Villa recalls, remained silent and the nuns prayed, convinced "on their Calvary" that they went to their deaths. The ruse worked. Apparently neither the doctors nor the nuns felt that federal officers were worth a test of faith, and Villa took some extra prisoners.

Consolidation of power required that dissident elements — foreigners, clerics, *huertistas* of whatever national stripe — be eliminated from Chihuahua and other areas under *villista* control. Among the first to feel the brunt of Villa's vengeful wrath were the Spaniards. As a matter of course the Chinese suffered mightily at the hands of all revolutionaries, for there existed an anti-Oriental prejudice in Mexico that dated to the colonial period but intensified during the *porfiriato.*

Because the Spanish expulsion was so elemental to Villa's actions, an analysis of the subject, previously mentioned, merits treatment.

As Villa approached Torreón in late September 1913, Spaniards, *huertistas* to a man, began to flee along with some of the federal officials. By the time Villa took the town on October 1, most of the Iberians had escaped, hauling themselves and their possessions in carriages, coaches, wagons, on horseback, on foot, and a few on burros. Those who fell into Villa's hands, however, suffered, for Villa demanded contributions of three million pesos for the support of the revolution. To buttress his demand, seventeen Spaniards were executed. While Villa exempted United States citizens in Torreón from any forced exactions, he showed no mercy to Spaniards. He needed the United States and was not about to jeopardize his relations with that powerful nation. He informed U.S. Consular

Agent George Carothers that the *gachupines* had better "watch their hides."

Once in Chihuahua City in early December, Villa intended to make his Spanish-expulsion decree a reality. On December 7, he called together all merchants of that city, especially the Spaniards, to meet with him at 3:00 in the afternoon. His guests had no idea why Villa wanted to see them. In short order, the Spaniards found out. Villa ordered them out of town in three days. Fortunately, Silvestre Terrazas arrived and tried to convince Villa that such a move was probably unjust since the Spaniards were a people who had "best assimilated with ours."

Villa remained adamant. These were the people who supported that loathsome, drunken Aztec and who, upon the advice of their diplomatic representative in Mexico City, had armed themselves against the revolution. These vile reactionaries deserved to suffer. Through the unending waves of Villa's *gasconades,* Terrazas finally made a point. The Sisters of Charity who ran hospitals and asylums were Spanish. In spite of his reputed ferocity, Villa still remained essentially tender-hearted and exempted the nuns as well as some other Spaniards, going so far as giving them "all sorts of guarantees for themselves personally and for their commercial and industrial enterprises."

Letcher, supercilious as always, failed to convince Villa to change his mind about the bulk of the Spaniards. Villa merely reminded the consul that it was Yankee intervention that brought down Madero. On December 12, Villa ordered the confiscation of properties belonging to enemies of the revolution. While aimed principally at Terrazas, Spaniards also came under that category as "accomplices."

Foreign governments began to worry about the treatment of their nationals by the Constitutionalists. William Jennings Bryan, secretary of state for Woodrow Wilson, ordered that Villa be informed of United States concern. He directed Carothers to tell Villa that Washington viewed with alarm the treatment of Spaniards and other foreigners. Villa, however, had more important things to worry about than the moralizing of a distant *gringo* politician.

Torreón remained to be recaptured at that time. The seizure of Chihuahua necessitated the transfer of troops from Torreón to the north. Federal forces moved in again. But this time Villa began to prepare the ground for his southward thrust. He launched propagandistic decrees aimed at frightening the Spaniards and other *huertistas* into submission. He declared that he had in his hands evidence of those Spaniards who had actively supported Huerta and the help they had given to the federal garrison in Torreón. Armed *gachupines* would be executed summarily. Those without arms would go into immediate exile. Offhandedly, Villa added that U.S. citizens had nothing to fear. Later, in February 1914, Villa knew full well the effect of his anti-Spanish decrees. He confided to Carothers that he made a lot of noise in order to keep the *gachupines* tame. A good threat kept them off-balance to the point that they would not actively oppose Villa and his program. In March, Villa reiterated his guarantees for Spaniards, though cynics scoffed about the sincerity of his declarations.

Meanwhile, Carranza began to get into the act. He ordered his field commanders to protect all foreigners and added that the seizure of property must be accompanied by written justification and could be carried out only in "extreme necessity." This ambiguity gave Villa a loophole to do as he pleased.

The second battle of Torreón proved bloody for both sides, but Villa again triumphed. He exiled all Spaniards for their own protection because anti-Iberian sentiments were so strong in the División del Norte. As a consequence, the benighted *gachupines* had twenty-four hours to get out of Torreón. Some Spaniards, however, felt that such rough treatment was unjust. They went to Villa, who remained adamant. *Vida Nueva* editorialized that those Spaniards who actively supported the usurper government would "have to receive the punishment merited by their conduct." So, on April 7, over 700 Spaniards went into exile, most of them going to border towns in the United States.

Exiled Spaniards left behind their goods and properties, all of which fell into the hands of the *villistas*. *Vida Nueva* supported its mentor and saw as just "the measures that General Villa has taken against the Spaniards who for many years had committed black deeds against the Mexican peasants who through bad fortune worked on 'THEIR' haciendas and properties." Any attempt to recoup damages by the Spaniards, editorialized another issue of the *villista* organ, "would have no result because it is public and notorious knowledge that [the Spaniards] have mixed in our internal affairs even to the point of picking up arms against the defenders of a just and legitimate cause."

Villa capitalized upon the absence of the Spaniards. He seized massive cotton crops valued at around twenty million pesos. With these, he hoped to provide money for his forces to buy arms and ordnance. Exiled Spaniards screamed extortion and claimed half of the price so that they could service debts incurred with the crop.

Villa quickly realized that he needed some of the Spaniards in Torreón. On June 20, 1914, he decreed that some could stay or return to Torreón because they were useful to society. "All Spanish subjects who have clean consciences," declared Villa, "— that is, not having meddled directly or indirectly in the political affairs of the nation — can return to our territory in which they can enjoy ample guarantees." He qualified this by stating that "those Spaniards whose consciences make them aware of having helped the Government of treason should refrain from returning to the revolutionary zone in order to avoid possible difficulties."

Villa's unconscious use of terrorist tactics against an entire social group was matched and surpassed by his singling out of individuals who might prove inimical to the revolution. Even more odious to Villa than Spaniards were Mexicans who had exploited the people through the *hacienda* and its concomitant peonage. In Chihuahua he zeroed in on the Terrazas clan.

"When the calf is tied," Villa had declared to George Carothers in February 1914, "the cow won't wander very far." Villa referred to his seizure of Luis Terrazas, Jr., scion of the wealthy family that had controlled the state of Chihuahua for nearly half a century. Villa readily recognized that control of the Terrazas fortune, especially the land and cattle, would provide him with necessary resources for the continuance of the struggle against Huerta. Control of a member of the clan would serve to keep other family members in check and thus staunch the flow of Terrazas money to Huerta and his supporters. Thus, another side of *villista* terrorism made itself manifest. Villa relied on the strong family ties that existed among the clan to protect Luis, Jr., from the announced vengeance that Villa had planned for him. Also, the older Terrazas would do anything to keep his son alive.

As Villa approached Chihuahua City in December 1913, Gen. Salvador Mercado and many of the city's leading citizens made their way to Ojinaga. Among those who sought refuge from Villa were Luis Terrazas, Sr. (a man in his eighties) and members of his family. Terrazas *pere* mounted a caravan of twenty wagons laden with personal effects, valuables, and about two million dollars in gold and currency. With the old man out of the way, ensconced in El Paso, Luis, Jr., was at great risk. He had remained in Chihuahua to care for some members of the family who had stayed and to guard the family interests. Hoping that diplomatic niceties would save him, he took refuge in the British Vice-Consulate. Villa, a stranger to the concept of asylum, grabbed Terrazas out of the Vice-Consulate and effectively held him for ransom.

Luis Terrazas, Sr., was now effectively neutralized. Villa pounded yet another nail into the Terrazas coffin with the December 12 decree of confiscation.

The kidnapping generated a great deal of sympathy in the United States. Southwestern and Texas cattlemen and politicians who knew the family pressured the State Department to come to the aid of the younger Don Luis. Alarmists along the border claimed that the Terrazas women were forced to remain in Chihuahua in order for the *villistas* to slake their vengeance upon them. Furthermore, Terrazas, Jr., would surely be killed when Villa had one of his attacks of uncontrollable fury.

Tentative representations by the United States notwithstanding, Villa allowed the implied threat of execution of Luis, Jr., to discomfit the family. He was not about to kill the golden gosling. Much of the Terrazas fortune had remained in the Banco Minero de Chihuahua, of which the Terrazases and the Creels had been founders. The junior Terrazas was on the board. Villa demanded a ransom of 250,000 pesos in order to offset the federal currency circulating in Chihuahua. Money from the Terrazas fortunes would allow the Constitutionalist government of Chihuahua to establish its own currency. Until that time, however, Terrazas money would suffice. Terrazas, Jr., was forced to sign Banco de Minero checks ranging in value from twenty centavos to five pesos, which then circulated as currency until such time as a revolutionary scrip could be printed.

Villa continued to avail himself of the Terrazas fortune. Terrazas cattle was sold in order to raise revenue. Eventually, old man Terrazas, under duress, of course, made Villa his agent for the sale of cattle in order for the *villistas* to sell livestock legitimately across the border. Without this arrangement, the cattle would be attached by the Texas Livestock Growers Association because Villa would not have a valid bill of sale and Terrazas was a member of that organization.

By this time Consul Letcher intervened. He expressed doubts about the safety of Terrazas, Jr. On December 18, Villa told Letcher that he was disposed to let the man go free, but the consul doubted that such would be the case. Three days later (December 21), Letcher reported that Villa had recanted on his assurance of release for the wealthy *chihuahuense*. Villa assured Letcher that Terrazas would receive good treatment and gave the consul a "confidential guarantee that the life of this man would be spared."

Villa went to Juárez to resupply his forces, but at the same time, reported the *El Paso Herald*, he planned to squeeze some more money out of the old man. Villa allegedly would be willing to release the entire clan for a lump sum payment of $1.5 million. But it became difficult for the senior Terrazas to lay his hands on that much money at once. Thus, he signed the duress contract for cattle with Villa. Cattle would no longer be attached by the Texas Livestock Growers Association. Still, by mid-January 1914, Villa continued to toy with the Terrazas clan.

Terrazas women remained in Chihuahua and stood little chance of fleeing the city. Bryan instructed Carothers to tell Villa that "humanity demands that these ladies should be allowed to go to El Paso to give him such care and comforts as may be possible. See General Villa and endeavor to make definite arrangements for the safe and immediate passage of these women to El Paso" in order to care for the old man in his infirmities. As in other matters, Villa simply ignored Bryan unless it suited his purposes. Once Ojinaga fell into Constitutionalist hands, Villa relented. On January 28, he allowed the ladies to leave Chihuahua and even accompanied them to Juárez.

To the horror of the Department of State, reports filtered to Washington that Terrazas, Jr., was being held, tortured, and forced to reveal where the family treasures were hidden. Carothers, however, deprecated the idea. He informed Bryan that Terrazas was "living with his family in Chihuahua [under house arrest] apparently without molestation. I do not consider his life in danger at present."

Carranza, however, decided to make his presence felt in the affair. He wanted to check Villa's excesses. He hoped to accomplish this by yielding to Villa's importunings about moving the Constitutionalist headquarters to Chihuahua. Carranza's own advisors urged this course in order to control the mercurial leader of the División del Norte. But little dissuaded Villa from his course *apropos* of Luis Terrazas, Jr. In February, Villa still held Terrazas, though Carothers reported that he received good treatment. Villa did shamefacedly acknowledge to Carothers that Terrazas had been "slightly tortured." He reportedly "scolded the perpetrators" and promised that no further mishap would befall the younger Luis.

Villa still found his prisoner a useful asset. In mid-March he demanded yet another 250,000 pesos. If such payment was not forthcoming, he warned, the consequences could be lethal for Terrazas, Jr. Money had to be delivered by March 10 or Villa would not be responsible for the consequences. March 10 came, and Villa took to the newspapers. He declared that Terrazas was well and walking the streets of Chihuahua. He further stated that Luis, Jr., was being held in order to stop the flow of reactionary support to Huerta.

The United States brought Carranza into the affair by making unofficial representations to the First Chief, who was then in Hermosillo. Carranza informed Villa that he was in a better position to deal with the international problem presented by Terrazas. The rarefied discussions in Washington and Hermosillo had little impact on Villa. One of Villa's agents in El Paso declared that Luis, Sr., certainly had sufficient money to pay for the release of his son. The cries of poverty beginning to emanate out of the old man sounded like an excess of protestation. The unnamed agent averred that "Villa is a man of his word . . . and, while the younger Terrazas is in no immediate danger, it is certain that Villa will expose him to the firing line [at Torreón] if his father lends aid and comfort to the enemy."

Villa extended the date for the old man to pay more ransom — he now had until March 25 to pay or his son would die. Luis, Sr., remained the loyal and supportive father. He offered to die in place of his son, for Luis, Jr., had thirteen children who desperately needed him. Civil Governor Manuel Chao reiterated assurances about the safety of young Terrazas.

The deadline for execution came and went. Terrazas lived, and Villa went on to recapture Torreón. Still, he threatened to use his prisoner as a common soldier as the División del Norte pushed southward to Mexico City. The family claimed that over $1 million had already been paid and that it would be extremely difficult to raise yet another 250,000 pesos.

Pressures from all sides caused Villa's mercurial temper to boil. In late June he informed Carothers that he had "ordered Governor of Chihuahua to afford full protection to Luis Terrazas, Jr. and hoped that you will have no further reason to complain on his behalf. I have no intention of executing him." Terrazas remained under heavy guard. His wife and daughters were evicted from their home in order to make room for Felipe Angeles and his staff. Consequently, the British Vice-Consulate offered shelter to the Terrazas women.

Issues of greater import than Luis Terrazas or a bunch of hapless Spaniards intruded upon Pancho Villa, especially in his relations with the United States. So far, Villa had proven conciliatory to the United States, recognizing in Mexico's immediate northern neighbor a bountiful source of supply for the División del Norte. Villa had minimized exactions from U.S. citizens. He purposely avoided the sort of blind pillage of American holdings that was being perpetrated against those of other nationalities. Yet the United States — in its own attempt to get rid of Huerta — almost achieved the unification of some revolutionary elements with the *huertistas*.

As a result of misunderstandings, arrogant trumpetings about national honor, and the pragmatic desire to keep Huerta from obtaining guns, the United States invaded Veracruz on April 20. Immediately, Carranza decried the intervention as an affront to Mexican nationality. Huerta called for reconciliation with the revolutionaries in order to fight the common Yankee enemy. By April 21, United States officials in Ciudad Juárez felt nervous about what Villa's attitude might be. *Villista* appointees grumbled about Yankee intervention and allowed their resentment to show openly. "It is impossible to predict," reported Carothers, "what attitude they will finally assume but I consider that there is no surety that they [villistas] will remain neutral."

Villa attempted to put timorous souls to rest both in Mexico and in Washington, D. C. He declared to Carothers that as long as the occupation of Veracruz did not constitute an act of war by the United States against Mexico, United States troops could hold Veracruz as long as necessary to rid Mexico of Huerta. Villa further apologized for Carranza's too rapid condemnation of the invasion. He added that "in his [Carranza's] well meaning patriotism he was ready to interrupt the Revolution in order to attack the United States and even to further Huerta's designs." Villa's conciliatory attitude received favorable response. Carothers informed the general that he could continue to buy armaments from the United States.

In a public statement Villa declared that "if Huerta wants war, neither we nor the United States will let ourselves be deceived. Sr. Carranza has given voice to the honor of our country, but he is not declaring war on the United States. . . . This is the true sentiment of all Revolutionaries."

Villa's colorful turn of phrase buttressed his opinion that there would be no war between Mexico and the United States over Veracruz. Mexico and the United States were too friendly to be suckered into such a conflict. It was Villa's opinion that "other nations would laugh and say, 'the little drunkard [Huerta] has succeeded in drawing them in . . .' " Villa hoped that the United States could hold Veracruz so tightly, "that not even water" could get to Huerta. Carothers privately hoped that Villa could force Carranza to accept conciliation.

Meanwhile, in Juárez, Villa's statements did not defuse the apprehension felt by United States officials on the border. Collector of Customs Zach Lamar Cobb saw Villa's recent arrival in Juárez as potentially explosive. "The grave danger of race conflict and bloody riots being started by irresponsible people," opined Cobb, "will be relieved by having adequate troops here." The subsequent announcement that Gen. John J. Pershing would bring in additional troops helped ease some of the tension.

Villa continued to take the sting from Carranza's hasty condemnation. In a telegram of April 25 to Carothers, Villa hoped that Wilson would not push Carranza too much, for Carranza's public bellicosity covered a more amenable nature. He urged Woodrow Wilson to tread cautiously, for all of the sister republics of the Americas hung on his words. "He has before him," wrote Villa, "the judgment of history which shall say with truthfulness whether he [Wilson] has only been moved by his high ideals of justice and democracy or if in the end he was influenced by the satanic machinations of one man [Huerta] and the pride of another [Carranza]."

By May 1914, Villa seemed the undisputed military hero of the revolution. From London, U.S. Ambassador Walter Hines Page reported that in the British view, Villa and Zapata would take Mexico City. Page passed along the British hope that the United States would be prepared to protect life and property belonging to foreigners. If not, continued the ambassador, European countries must be ready to act in concert against the barbarian horde. Should Villa succeed Huerta, this would constitute a "horrid anticlimax. . . . The British Government will demand satisfaction of Villa for Benton's death the moment they can get at him."

From Veracruz, Gen. Frederick Funston reported that a great exodus of people from Mexico City was coming to the port city. A general fear permeated the local ambience that if Villa and/or Zapata should take Mexico City there would be "a carnival of bloodshed and robbery." Consequently, Veracruz suffered from shortages and overcrowding.

The United States, however, proved reluctant to let Villa obtain already paid-for arms and ammunition. Villa continually argued that both he and Carranza demonstrated good faith about Veracruz. He further noted that federal generals Maass and Caraveo were recruiting men throughout the country to fight ostensibly against the United States. In actuality, the misguided recruits were aimed against the División del Norte. Carothers passed on the opinion that Villa had surely demonstrated his good faith and that the United States should honor its commitments to the man. Finally, arms began to trickle in to Villa, and he successfully withstood a renewed *huertista* effort to defeat him.

By July, the United States itself became concerned about the conflict between Villa and Carranza. Carranza neutralized Villa in the north, and Obregón began to push toward Mexico City from the west. On July 14, the revolution had achieved its objective: Huerta resigned and took a train for Veracruz. Huerta's arrival at the port city of Veracruz on July 17 and his departure a day later should have signaled an end to hostilities. Secretary of State Bryan wanted to impress upon Villa that personal quarrels should be avoided and that Mexico, with Huerta gone as of July 18, now possessed a bright and prosperous outlook. "Villa has played an important part in winning the victory," wrote Bryan, "and the President feels sure that he will use his influence on the side of harmony and cooperation among the Constitutionalists."

With the end of summer 1914, general war began to engulf Europe. Germany sought to keep the United States out of the European war and enticed the Japanese to make overtures to Villa about a possible alliance. A delegation headed by a Japanese vice admiral visited Villa and expressed Japanese sympathy for the cause of the revolution. While Villa certainly liked the flattery, he remained cautious. To a man of Villa's background, attention from high officials assuaged his self-image and gave him a sense of importance. He still needed United States support and matériel for the impending conflict with Carranza.

Villa continued to praise the United States. While Wilson and Bryan continually urged feuding revolutionary factions to reconcile their differences, Villa remained a steadfast public admirer of the northern colossus. In his *Memorias,* Villa recalled that "our neighbors were giving us proof of their friendship and their interest in our cause. If they had wanted to harm us, and not to help us, they would have tried to add to our discord instead of relieving it as they were doing."

While Villa may have felt somewhat tenderly toward the United States, his actions gave pause to the administration of Woodrow Wilson. For all purposes, Villa exercised an instinctual terrorism without consideration of the niceties involved in dealing with a people over whom he exercised control. His treatment of the Spaniards initially and the protracted capture of the younger Terrazas demonstrated that Villa, whether he realized it or not, had capitalized upon an unstable situation in which he kept opposition forces off-balance through a variety of terrorist techniques. There was no need for him to have read Bakunin or other advocates of political violence. Political violence already existed. Villa used the ferocity of his name to keep his enemies under control.

Yet, with an element of terrorism as a part of the Villa approach to revolutionary success, his administration of Chihuahua demonstrated a marked interest in affairs of state. He especially showed concern over some type of land reform. Villa's sincerity about redistribution of land was coupled with his hatred of the large landholders such as the Terrazas family. He had never forgotten López Negrete and refused ever to be in a position where privileged people would intimidate him. Practicality, however, intervened, for Villa used confiscated lands as a means of rewarding his followers. Sale of confiscated lands also helped to finance the División del Norte and provided Villa with needed matériél for the prosecution of his campaigns.

Villista pacification of Sonora also elicited high praise from the United States. Villa, in turn, thanked the United States for sending Zach Cobb as an intermediary for the sincerity of its motives. He called the United States Mexico's "best friend" and declared that the U.S. provided an example of tolerance to all Mexicans. Moreover, Villa congratulated Wilson on the removal of a large contingent of soldiers from Veracruz, for this provided a faithful interpretation of the aspirations of the Mexican people. But in spite of good intentions on the part of Villa and the United States, the revolution would find itself rendered by personalities and factionalism.

CHAPTER VII

"Sir, you are a son-of-a-bitch!"

Contact between Carranza and Villa in Chihuahua in the early spring of 1914 probably did more to undermine the unity of the revolution than any other factor. While egos and personalities constantly intruded into the decision-making process that occurred in far-flung revolutionary armies, the meeting between Carranza — titular leader of the Constitutionalist Army — and the Centaur of the North — the major military might of Carranza's movement — threw the two men into conflict. For Villa, Carranza and his advisors constituted an effete group of "perfumed chocolate drinkers" who did not know how to sweat and die for the people of Mexico. Nor were these pretentious snobs particularly sympathetic to the populist aspirations of many *villistas*. Carranza saw in Villa an untamed animal, feral in his instincts, nearly impossible to control, to be used but not given positions of influence in the decisions that in the long term would affect Mexican development.

Clear social differences separated Villa and Carranza. The barely literate Villa saw a powerful threat to popular aspirations in Carranza, a man who had served as a senator under Porfirio Díaz and still represented a landholding elite in northern Mexico. Carranza, on the other hand, viewed Villa as an unbridled peasant who sought to rise above the station in which God and the natural order had placed him.

Additionally, the direction of the revolution provided a source of conflict between the different factions. Carranza continually attempted to assert his authority as First Chief of the Constitutionalist Army, a title that bore no military rank nor military perquisites. Villa at the same time took the position that the División del Norte was in fact an independent entity allied to the Constitutionalist cause but not controlled rigorously by it. Consequently, policy decisions often suffered from the insertion of personal differences in their effectuation. In foreign affairs, in reform programs, in the prosecution of the war against Huerta, the personalities of the leaders of the revolution intruded into the smooth execution of revolutionary objectives.

Before March 1914, Villa and Carranza had met briefly. It did not take long for a mutual suspicion to grow as Villa attempted to take his own course in the revolution. Carranza, almost constantly on the move, ultimately decided to go to Chihuahua and to take part of his staff with him. He finally acceded to Villa's importuning and made an official visit of the Centaur's lair.

The meeting between Carranza and Villa underscored their differences. Villa, who hated such ceremonies and felt most uncomfortable dancing attendance on political functionaries, was not told of Carranza's arrival until the last minute. He appeared, unshaven, dressed in a bedraggled-looking field uniform and an old sweater. Carranza and his retinue, conversely, appeared immaculate. Always effusive, Villa attempted to embrace Carranza. But the latter coldly accepted Villa's mumbled words of welcome and affection. Put off, Villa saw the beginnings of problems for himself and the revolution, for Carranza the aristocrat refused to mingle with those who were not afraid to sweat.

The United States remained apprised of the developments in the revolutionary camp. George Carothers kept a constant stream of telegrams flooding the Department of State as he reported the progress of talks between Carranza and Villa. Many of the issues that beset the two men remained unresolved. Carranza wanted Villa to stop printing paper money. Villa wanted Carranza to supply him with money for the purchase of arms, ammunition, and military supplies. Carranza expressly ordered Villa to direct all foreign relations to the first chieftaincy. On this Villa acquiesced, for his memory of the Benton affair remained too vivid for him to want another foreign entanglement if he could avoid it. Carranza demanded accountability while Villa pursued his own course in the purchase of goods and disposition of confiscated properties. On April 9, Carothers hoped that unless Carranza intervened, there existed the chance that Villa would continue "his somewhat reckless course and violate property."

Villa was quick to take umbrage when Carranza countermanded orders. Villa saw Chihuahua as his personal sphere of influence. If Carranza wanted to operate in Chihuahua, then it behooved him to recognize who in fact ran the revolutionary operation there. Again, the kernel of conflict had been sown, for Carranza would insist on obedience and loyalty from those he considered his subordinates. Carothers noted rather quickly, however, that the breach between Carranza and Villa did not as yet seem serious.

For his part, Villa attempted to maintain at least a façade of conciliation toward Carranza. When the First Chief moved his Constitutionalist government to Torreón, Carranza at a banquet in early May proclaimed his intention to continue resistance to the United States in Veracruz. Wild applause greeted an essentially nationalistic crowd. Villa, at the same time, publicly but implicitly agreed with Carranza. The Centaur of the North grabbed some headlines when he proclaimed himself subordinate to Carranza.

By the end of the month, Villa continued his public attempts to give cohesion to what was becoming a many-headed movement. In a proclamation he called for togetherness in the Constitutionalist ranks. He threw down a gauntlet to

> whoever contradicts these ends and means, sowing lack of confidence, awakening suspicions, and blowing vicious ambitions in the ears of the *caudillos,* should be considered a traitor to the cause of the fatherland and of peace. I also declare emphatically that I will not tolerate that my humble but unstained name be used as a rallying point of discord. Whoever does this I shall consider him both as a personal enemy and one of the fatherland.

But United States officials reacted with some sensitivity to reports of an open breach between Villa and his titular chief. Secretary of State William Jennings Bryan constantly asked Carothers to keep him abreast of developments. Carothers, increasingly a Villa partisan, pointed out that El Paso newspapers tended to be a bit sensationalist and could not foresee any difficulties between Villa and the First Chief.

From another quarter, Villa's subordinates faced harassment from some of Carranza's underlings. Felix Sommerfeldt, a trusted *villista* agent in the United States, reported that some of Carranza's minions like Luis Cabrera and Rafael Zubarán Campany impeded the progress of *villista* labors in the United States. This, in turn, caused Villa to complain that Sommerfeldt was failing him. Lázaro De la Garza, Villa's chief fiscal agent in the United States, intervened on Sommerfeldt's behalf and cooled Villa's temper. Sommerfeldt, however, was quick to note that Carranza's people were "doing everything possible to keep Villa from receiving war materiel. They fear that Villa will be first into Mexico City, snatch up the glory, and possibly the presidency."

In spite of his unlettered beginnings, Villa, when he wanted to, demonstrated a ready political perception. In early June, he confided to Carothers that Carranza was obviously trying to undercut his authority. Villa predicted that should trouble between the two erupt, the blame could be laid at the feet of "politicians advising Carranza." Villa complained that he could get no coal because Carranza had placed his own people in charge of the railroad's coal supply. Carranza also attempted to control access to rolling stock. Additionally, Villa could not proceed southward in his march to Mexico City but was forced to operate only in the north because of limited railroad fuel. More critically, Villa ordered and paid for ammunition that was due to arrive in Tampico. Carranza's officials constantly kept placing obstacles in Villa's way as he attempted to get much-needed supplies. This, more than anything else, would force Villa to declare against Carranza. Political wrangling, it seemed to Carothers, forced Villa to lose much of his old energy, for he was being diverted from his principal objective: the ouster of Huerta.

In his reports to the secretary of state, Carothers remained Pollyannaish about the growing schism between Villa and Carranza. Visiting Carranza in Saltillo, Carothers reported on June 13 that relations between the two antagonists seemed better and that initial alarm over their split could be laid to rest. Carothers, however, only saw what he wanted to see, for on June 13, 1914, the split between Carranza and Villa became a giant fissure.

Carranza had hoped to keep a lid on Villa. His imposition of control over railroads and ammunition seemed to restrain Villa. Villa, however, would not be abused. His statements against Carranza became increasingly inflammatory, with questions regarding Carranza's military judgment. The major break came over the seizure of Zacatecas.

On the southward path of the revolution lay Zacatecas, a provincial capital in north central Mexico. A mining and cattle district, Zacatecas lay on the rail line that led directly toward Mexico City. The town was a prize military objective that would move the Constitutionalists farther south. Carranza, however, feared that if Villa took control of Zacatecas, the División del Norte would then sweep into Mexico City, a situation that for Carranza seemed highly unpalatable.

To relieve himself of some concern, Carranza took two major steps that affected Villa directly. First, he ordered that Villa move on Saltillo instead of Zacatecas. Second, Carranza ordered that Pánfilo Natera and the Arrieta brothers take command of the siege of Zacatecas. Indirectly, Carranza chose to hedge his bets and moved Alvaro Obregón toward central Mexico in order to have the capital under his control before Villa could arrive there.

Natera and the Arrietas proved to have more bluster than ability. On June 11 they began their attack on federal positions around Zacatecas. By June 13, Carranza realized that the bravado of Natera and the Arrietas would not carry the day. Yet he did not want to dispatch Villa to direct the attack personally. He saw such action as an undermining of Natera's authority and as presenting to Villa too great an opportunity to enhance his own ends. Instead, Carranza chose to command Villa to place 6,000 of his *muchachitos* under Natera's command.

Villa demurred. For one thing, he had advised Carranza against placing Natera in command of the Zacatecas campaign. Villa had declared that while he had respect for Pánfilo Natera, he recognized the limited abilities of the man, for it was Natera whom Villa bailed out at Ojinaga in January. Carranza, however, thought differently. He used Natera and the Arrietas as a counterploy to Villa. Carranza repeated his order. Again, Villa refused.

With Caranza in Saltillo and Villa in Torreón, a telegraphic argument between the two began on June 13. Villa had become more than a little irritated with Carranza. He asked that if he should send troops, who would be the commander, Natera or the

Arrietas? Additionally, and this aimed to injure Carranza's pride, Villa asked who ordered the seizure of Zacatecas without being reasonably sure of success. Finally, Villa declared to Carranza that "if you want to replace me, let me know with whom and I will judge if he is capable of directing my men."

Carranza, chronically testy, chastised Villa for his criticism of Natera and the Arrietas. Moreover, he told Villa that "I don't think you should resign, but for the good of the Constitutionalist cause I would accept your resignation." In a huff Villa quit and asked who would be his successor. Carranza, himself a reasonably shrewd *político*, did not name a successor to Villa. Instead he ordered that Generals Angeles, Robles, Urbina, Herrera, Fierro, and others select a replacement for Villa. Readily they acceded to the request and named Francisco Villa as his own successor. Carranza declared the selection unsatisfactory. In a fit of temper, Maclovio Herrera, a loyal but impetuous *villista*, pulled his pistol, held it to the head of the telegraph operator, and began to dictate a telegram to be sent over the names of all of those present. He began: "Sr. Venustiano Carranza, Saltillo, Coahuila. Sir: You are a son-of-a-bitch. . . ."

Quaking, the telegraph operator wrote down the message. By this time Felipe Angeles calmed Herrera down and convinced him that a more judicious tone would accomplish more with Carranza than a direct confrontation and name calling. Instead, Angeles informed Carranza that serious internal and diplomatic overtones could develop if Villa was not reinstated. It was further pointed out to Carranza that all of the commanders that comprised the División del Norte could resign as did Villa and thus dissolve the most powerful arm of the revolution. Angeles respectfully suggested that Villa be reinstated and that the whole matter be dropped. Angeles, however, was not all honeyed words, for he informed Carranza that

> We hope you understand our reasons and accept them with good faith, but if you capriciously offend our leader more and thus risk the cause of the people, then we shall withdraw our recognition of your First Chieftaincy and gather around our beloved leader . . . who, with or without your permission, shall follow the path of victories until the triumph of the people is consummated.

The breach between Carranza and Villa did not heal itself; it only remained quiescent. While preparing to move south to Zacatecas, Villa also began to prepare for the eventual conflict with

Carranza. Villa rapidly deployed men to Ciudad Juárez and again seized control of that city. As a means of assuring *villista* hegemony in Juárez, he jailed all Carranza appointees. Even then, one of Villa's legal advisors, Alfonso Madero, saw that the breach could be healed unless "Carranza is a fool."

As the schism became increasingly public, many of those committed to both sides hoped to see the conflict mediated. Eliséo Arredondo, a close Carranza confidant, approached De la Garza with an offer of mediation. Villa, however, rejected the offer because "there are no differences with Mr. Carranza." Therefore, he could not accept Arredondo's "bounteous services."

As Villa's forces subdued trapped *federales* in Zacatecas, the leader of the División del Norte attempted to isolate Carranza from his support. On June 25, for example, he telegraphed Obregón and complained about the obstacles that Carranza constantly placed in his path. Now Carranza wanted Villa to divert some troops to Pablo González for the capture of San Luis Potosí. Villa refused. He asked Obregón to join him in a mutual march to Mexico City and thus ignore Carranza. Obregón, however, had no love for Villa. A week later he finally responded and stated that Villa could not be the sole arbiter of revolutionary problems. "It is not one man who is in jeopardy," he continued, "but the nation." Finally, he refused Villa's offer to join forces. Obregón remained cognizant of the potential problems. He acknowledged the proposed meeting between Villa, Pablo González, and Carranza in Torreón and urged that such a meeting should result in a renewed harmony between the different factions.

Obregón covered his bets quite well. He did not like Angeles and did not trust him, for he saw in the slick, educated artilleryman a manipulator of the first order. On June 18, Obregón assured Carranza of his support.

Meanwhile, the Department of State continued to wring its hands over the incomprehensible mess in Mexico. Bryan kept pressing Carothers to mediate between Villa and Carranza. With the imminent defeat of Huerta, the Constitutionalists would need to meet with the *huertistas* in order to assure a smooth transition from one government to the other. To achieve this, however, it was necessary for harmony to prevail among the revolutionaries.

Finally, Carranza decided not to meet with Villa personally. Instead he dispatched some advisors to Torreón with the expressed hope that if problems could be resolved Villa's lack of discipline could be overlooked. Carranza, however, could not resist a dig at Villa when he stated that in the future he hoped that Villa could "preserve order, restrain his passions, and recognize constituted authority." Nobly, Carranza continued that he would not place any impediment for the resolution of differences. He would not, for example, force an apology from Villa nor demand some public submission. Villa, warned Carranza, needed to restrain his passions in order to avoid further international embarrassment. Without this, Villa could easily become a menace to the revolution. Leon J. Canova, yet another state department denizen, summed up Carranza's attitude by reporting that if Villa's excesses "are tolerated and condoned today he will be a peril tomorrow. . . . Villa was not indispensable."

Zach Cobb, however, took a different view. Cobb used his position as a special representative to the Department of State and collector of customs at El Paso as a listening post into Mexico. The conferences, he hoped, would succeed in maintaining revolutionary unity. Should they fail, he noted, the fault would lay with Carranza because he was so "obdurate."

All of the grievances that Carranza and Villa held against each other were aired at the conference in Torreón. Villa continued to complain about Carranza's failure to supply the División del Norte with coal for its trains. By the same token, Villa promised that he would provide locomotives for Pablo González's forces. Carranza proved as sensitive to innuendo and rumor as Villa, for he demanded that *villista* agents in the United States should cease maligning him. Villa, however, responded that he knew nothing about this and asked for a list of these so-called slanderers in order to effect their punishment.

By July 8, a tentative agreement had been reached at Torreón. On Villa's part he would release all *carrancista* prisoners and monies in Chihuahua and apologize for the action. Villa also would recognize Carranza as First Chief, whose authority would be limited to civil and diplomatic matters. Carranza, on the surface, seemed to be giving up more, for he agreed to elevate Villa to division general and thus put him on a par with Obregón and González. Additionally, Angeles would take over as supreme military commander. A caveat to this, however, was that such action must be kept quiet in order to avoid injury to Carranza's pride. Carranza also agreed to leave Villa unmolested in his territory and to grant him command of the División del Norte in its push toward Mexico City. Villa also received control of railroads and coalfields. Both sides agreed to make a final push for Mexico City within one month and to make personnel changes mutually acceptable to both sides in order to maintain some harmony.

Villa proved willing to accept the arrangement. Carothers, skeptical of Carranza's sincerity, noted that Carranza would have to accept the agreement, for lack of ratification might lead to the separation of Pablo González from the *carrancista* ranks. Carothers, however, failed to recognize the venality of González.

Rather quickly, Carranza temporized and made snide innuendos about where the fault lay for the breach in the revolutionary cause. Leon Canova argued for Carranza to respect foreign property. Carranza pointed out that most of these difficulties really started with Villa. He reiterated the Benton case, Villa's treatment of Spaniards, and his confiscation of cotton stores in Torreón.

Another problem — and one that would constantly plague Villa — lay in Sonora. José María Maytorena became governor of Sonora and opportunistically though cautiously threw his support to Villa. Carranza's agents reported that Maytorena was in fact the cause of much of the corruption and disruption in Sonora. Roberto Pesqueira, another Carranza agent, informed his chief that Villa was obviously surrounded by scoundrels such as Maytorena, Urbina, and Fierro. This cadre hoped to make Angeles the head of the state and thus displace Carranza as the legitimate authority.

Meanwhile, on the day Huerta left Mexico (June 18), the Mexican consul in El Paso attempted to bring about a united front between Villa and Maytorena. He felt that they would be willing to treat with an interim government after Huerta's removal, while Carranza would remain headstrong throughout the attempt at orderly transition. Villa, reported Carothers, seemed willing to accept a civilian president. As an afterthought, Villa relented and allowed Spaniards to return to Mexico under certain limitations.

Carranza, too, played the conciliation game. He let it be known that a train was destined for Torreón loaded with guns and ammunition for Villa. To some observers, this was Carranza's "first display [of] generosity towards Villa and may terminate that difficulty." Carothers also echoed that fond hope. He viewed Villa as tolerating "everything except actual isolation." Hopefully, the wound in the revolutionary *corpus* had now healed.

But events did not allow Villa to demonstrate goodwill. Huerta's resignation brought an immediate reaction from an exiled Pascual Orozco, who declared himself in rebellion against the interim government of Francisco Carbajal. Orozco saw that he had no choice, for Villa had vowed to get Orozco and deal with him most unpleasantly. While hoping for peace, Villa continued to prepare himself for conflict with Carranza. In Chihuahua, Consul Letcher, a Villa antagonist, reported that Villa was recruiting men and horses as quickly as possible and was provisioning his army "as fast as arms can be smuggled from the United States. Nobody here doubts the purpose of his activity."

On July 25, Villa took additional steps that pointed toward preparation for a showdown. He removed 10,000 men from his garrison at Torreón and sent them to Chihuahua, thus raising the number of troops in Chihuahua to 30,000. Leon Canova, no friend of Villa's, accused the Madero brothers and other venal politicians of attempting to gain political *entrée* on Villa's coattails. "So," he wrote, "we have General Villa surrounded by a number of elements, all with axes to grind for their own benefit and every one of them is getting to turn the stone."

By the end of July, Carranza's strategy against Villa became clear. On July 31, Obregón occupied Irapuato and effectively cut off Villa's southward advance, for Irapuato provided for western Mexico the same railroad nexus that Torreón supplied in the north. Villa continued to collect supplies, arms, and men though cut off by Obregón. He was preparing for war, not against the already deposed Huerta but against Carranza and his men.

The split became increasingly public. The Madero family stood firmly with Villa as he accelerated his recruiting efforts. *Villista* smugglers also worked overtime avoiding border patrol and customs personnel. Zach Cobb noted that Villa's agents purchased large quantities of coal and hospital supplies. Villa, additionally, shipped twelve trains loaded with matériél to Chihuahua. Villa had prepared for action. Cobb, ever the Wilson Democrat, could not help moralizing about the *villista* preparations. He noted that "through concessions to associates Villa is surrounded by corruption . . . and is in imminent danger of being drawn into alliances with big special interests."

Villa, too, could put on a good public face. In early August he declared his willingness to continue the alliance with Carranza for the good of Mexico. He even offered to help Carranza begin the long process of calling and supervising elections. In this way Villa hoped to push Carranza to a declaration of his political intentions.

Accusations aimed at the Maderos forced one of them, Emilio, to resign as counsel to the Comandancia Militar of the División del Norte. He said that he wanted to avoid accusations about personal or family ambitions and declared himself free of political connections.

The United States continued to look with alarm at the apparent schism between Villa and Carranza. Well-intentioned but deluded Bryan reflected Wilson's own fond hope of helping the Mexicans mold their destinies. He instructed Carothers to bring about a meeting between Carranza and Villa. Naively he wrote "that if these two gentlemen could meet under favorable circumstances, free from partisan influences, and discuss in a spirit of patriotism, which, we believe, inspire both of them, an amicable understanding and a practical working basis would be reached."

Maytorena and Sonora, meanwhile, continued to provide sufficient irritation to keep wounds suppurating. Plutarco Elías Calles moved to Nogales and abandoned Cananea in mid-August. The State Department transmitted a request to Villa that he use his influence over Maytorena to reduce the lawlessness and banditry rampant in the area. At this juncture, however, Villa needed unsettled conditions in Sonora, for such near-chaos made his recruitment efforts more effective among the *sonorenses* who would look to him for salvation. Yaqui Indians, a particularly fearsome tribe in Sonora, carried on a reign of terror that Maytorena did not seem able to quell. The Yaquis also supported Obregón. Upon Villa's orders, troops were dispatched to the Yaqui valley to stop the Indian depredations.

Maytorena, an officious politician, hoped to ingratiate himself with Villa through flattery. He ordered 2,000 buttons bearing Villa's portrait. Maytorena's agent, however, reported that he could not get these made on time. Meanwhile, Obregón and Villa attempted to reach some understanding about Sonora and the roles of Maytorena and Calles.

Carranza prepared to enter Mexico City on August 20. Troops from everywhere in Mexico except Morelos and the División del

Norte marched in the victorious parade. Disgruntlement and a sense of hurt pervaded the *villistas*. Carranza refused to name a single *villista* to the new government and thus increased the possibility of a permanent rupture between himself and Villa.

Villa still hoped to bring at least temporary peace to Mexico. He contacted Carranza and requested that Obregón come to Chihuahua in order to work toward a peaceful resolution of mutual problems. On August 24, Obregón arrived in Chihuahua. Villa proposed almost immediately that he and Obregón join forces against Carranza and even offered to support Obregón for the presidency. Obregón, according to his own account, told Villa that "the battle is over. We should no longer think of war. In the next election the man with the most votes shall win."

On August 28, Villa and Obregón headed for Nogales. The next day they met in Nogales and agreed to recognize Maytorena as military head of Sonora. Under him would be Calles's forces in Naco, Agua Prieta, and Cananea. Villa crossed into Arizona in an attempt to calm Maytorena, who accused Obregón of undermining his position in Sonora. Secretly, however, Villa informed Obregón that he would dump Maytorena if this could assure peace, for Villa obviously wanted some conciliation. He told Obregón: "If you had not come, little buddy, the División del Norte would already be 'kicking ass' [*echando trancazos*]."

Obregón's presence in Chihuahua did much to ease some of the tension both in Mexico and in Washington, D.C. Carothers reported that conditions looked favorable for an amicable settlement between the two hostile factions. Villa and Obregón seemed close to an agreement that would then be delivered to Carranza for his concurrence.

By the first days of September, the two outstanding generals of the revolution had in fact hammered out a workable compromise. In it they agreed that Carranza should become provisional president complete with a cabinet of ministers. Carranza would then name interim supreme court justices, and the governors of the states would serve only on a provisional basis. These would then call local elections in the *ayuntamientos* (roughly county governments) for offices running from local officials to representatives in the federal legislature. Finally, as one of the stickier items of the agreement, the provisional president would proceed with a detailed program of constitutional reform, once the full governmental struc-

ture was in place. This reform would have as its purpose an attempt to remake the Mexican constitutional structure and remove
from it some of the more odious aspects of the *porfiriato*. Heading
the reform list came the removal of the vice-presidential office. The
restoration of the vice-presidency under Díaz gave to that office a
particularly onerous taint. In an attempt to exorcise *porfirista* influence, the vice-presidency would have to go.

Constitutional reform also meant calculating how much time
the interim president should serve in office. Here, clearly, Villa
hoped to undercut Carranza's long-term influence. Obviously, too,
Obregón, while nominally supporting Carranza, appeared willing
to dump the bearded aristocrat if some modicum of stability could
be restored to Mexico and thus remove an obstacle to Obregón's
own advancement. Additionally, both men hoped to minimize the
power that Carranza might wield in Mexico when they agreed that
none of the provisional officers — president, governor, or other
elected officials — could succeed themselves immediately after the
end of their provisional terms. Political opportunity would be more
readily available to those who chose to exercise their talents in the
electoral lists.

Both Villa and Obregón — outstanding military leaders —
agreed that no officer of the Constitutionalist Army could run for
any elected office unless he resigned his commission six months
prior to an election. While this might seem onerous to professional
military men, Villa and Obregón came to military life as a result of
the revolution and, unlike Angeles, were not reared in a military
tradition. At the same time, both men seemed to want to minimize
the influence of the army in Mexico's political life. Much of this, it
seems, came from Obregón, who subsequently as president in the
1920s would in fact begin a process of removing the military from
active political participation.

News of the agreement between Obregón and Villa reached
Washington quite rapidly. Secretary of State Bryan praised Villa's
patriotism and unselfish sacrifice of personal ambitions for the
good of the common cause. On September 3, Villa personally contacted Bryan through Carothers that he would be willing to "sacrifice all," including his health and well-being, "for the health and
welfare of [the] country and people."

Meanwhile, as Obregón and Villa's secretary, Luis Aguirre
Benavides, headed toward Mexico City to deliver the agreement to

Carranza, an ominous note injected itself into what seemed an amicable resolution to potential anarchy. Aguirre Benavides had observed Villa closely for over a year. In that time he apparently became increasingly disillusioned with Villa's political acumen and his susceptibility to influence. Aguirre Benavides said to Obregón: "Now you see Villa so tame! Well, in two hours his advisors will have changed him completely."

When Obregón and Aguirre Benavides arrived in Mexico City on September 6, they faced a Carranza who remained absolutely adamant about Villa. Villa as a force would have to be eliminated before there could be any agreement between the *carrancistas* and other factions. Somewhat taken aback after his initial optimism, Obregón hoped that a meeting with Carranza and Villa's representatives might still alleviate the situation.

For too long Villa had faced deceit and duplicity from Carranza and his cohorts. As Carranza temporized, so too did Villa begin to act independent of any agreements reached with regard to problems in Sonora. Between September 7 and 9, Villa sat in Chihuahua and dispatched a flurry of telegrams to Obregón. He demanded that a replacement for Maytorena be sent at once in order to wrap up that piece of business. When there appeared to be some reluctance, Villa then ordered Maytorena to seize towns that had formerly been under the command of Gen. Benjamin Hill. Obregón, patient but no Job, finally accused Villa of violating the agreements that they had both worked so hard to effect.

A major sore point between Villa and Carranza remained Veracruz and United States occupation of that major port city. Carranza still felt that Villa had failed to act in good faith when he refused to support Carranza's jingoistic declaration about the troops that occupied Veracruz in April. Obregón, attempting to bring the agreement between Carranza and Villa to completion, informed Villa that many revolutionary chieftains in Mexico City generally agreed with the declaration signed by the two leaders. However, the sour note remained the Yankees in Veracruz. "With the disappearance of the so called government of Huerta and with the dissolution of the federal army . . .," wrote Obregón "there should no longer exist in our land another flag other than the beloved tricolor." Villa, again quixotically, readily agreed on September 10. Within a matter of hours, Obregón received another telegram from

Villa asking that any joint declaration about *gringos* in Veracruz be delayed for yet awhile.

In large measure, Villa reacted to news from Mexico City sent to him by his delegation. On September 9, Carranza met with Obregón and the *villistas* and received the agreement signed by Obregón and Villa. He skimmed it cursorily and then dismissed Villa's emissaries, telling them that he would take the document under consideration. Again Villa felt a sense of betrayal by Carranza, and he, too, began to hedge his bets.

Carranza also trimmed a bit. On September 13 he informed both Obregón and Villa that the profound questions raised in the agreement required study by the entire nation. While he agreed immediately with the idea of the provisional president, some modification was required about *ayuntamiento* elections. Such elections, opined Carranza, should only be held in those areas where such officials were customarily elected. Carranza then took his cue from Woodrow Wilson.

In an attempt to get a broad consensus about the restoration of stability, Carranza called for a meeting of revolutionary leaders on October 1. Wilson and Bryan had urged this course on Villa and Carranza as a means of hammering out differences. Carranza added that from this meeting there should come a definitive statement about the future political and economic progress of the country.

Events began to sour. Obregón found himself on the road to Chihuahua once again amid rumors that Villa intended to have him killed. Heading north from Mexico City, Obregón passed three days observing the bleak and war-torn countryside. He arrived in Chihuahua on September 16 and talked to Villa that afternoon. Before going to see Villa, Obregón observed Villa's military preparations. It seemed that Villa wanted Obregón to see the strength of the División del Norte. At a military parade held in his honor, Obregón saw 15,000 men pass by, as well as sixty artillery pieces under the command of Felipe Angeles. Villa hoped that the display of power might convince Obregón to change sides with regard to Carranza.

Obregón's presence in Chihuahua did not stop problems from developing in Sonora. Forces commanded by Calles and Hill clashed with those under Maytorena while Obregón visited Villa. On September 17, Villa demanded that Hill go to Casas Grandes and Obregón acquiesced. Still not mollified, Villa ordered that twenty of his *dorados* seize Obregón and "shoot this traitor!"

Luis Aguirre Benavides genuinely feared for Obregón's life. He called Raúl Madero to intervene in Obregón's behalf. At the same time, U.S. agent Leon Canova arrived to see Villa. But the Centaur was in such a rage, fulminating against Obregón and his treasonous activity, that he refused to see Canova.

Once his rage was spent, Villa calmed down and dismissed the firing squad. He did a complete about-face, for he genially invited Obregón to join him for supper. "Come eat, little buddy," he said to Obregón, "everything is over." Though skeptical, Obregón joined Villa for supper and then was treated to a big party in his honor.

The temporary goodwill of meal and party dissipated the next day. Benjamín Hill proved just as obdurate as Carranza. He refused to move any troops and argued that as long as Obregón was in Chihuahua any telegram signed by him would obviously be exacted under duress. Villa's rage rekindled while he ordered 2,000 men to pursue Hill and eliminate him from the Mexican scene. At the same time, Canova worked out an arrangement whereby Obregón would be freed and sent to Ciudad Juárez. Obregón refused and stated that he needed to return to Mexico City.

Three days later, Villa decided to send Luis Aguirre Benavides and José Isabel Robles as well as a full contingent of generals with Obregón to Mexico City. After another change of plans, only Obregón, Aguirre Benavides, and Robles boarded the train in Chihuahua headed for Mexico City.

Villa's anger again manifested itself the next day. At Ceballos a telegram intercepted the train and ordered that it be returned to Chihuahua. Robles and Aguirre Benavides said that if they returned, Obregón would surely be executed. Obregón, however, demonstrated some of his daring when he said that if that were the case, then it would be better to get it over with and avoid a lot of humiliation. Early on September 23, the train arrived in Chihuahua. Villa stormed and thundered and cast imprecations at Carranza. The day before, he had wired Carranza. Showing the telegram to Obregón, Villa disavowed Carranza as head of anything and refused to attend the convention of revolutionary leaders scheduled for Mexico City on October 1.

Obregón was again placed on a train and ordered to go to Torreón. He knew that in Torreón Villa would have him killed. Met by Aguirre Benavides and Robles, they urged Obregón to go to Saltillo instead. Neither of these two *villista* aides seemed ready to turn on Carranza yet. Obregón finally arrived in Mexico City on September 26, having lived through some harrowing days in Villa's lair.

Villa's changeable actions caused more than one man to question his ability to play a major role in national affairs. Luis Aguirre Benavides finally decided to leave Villa. To Aguirre Benavides, men like Angeles played too large a role in the political thinking of Pancho Villa and would retard national progress should power come to them.

At the same time, Villa cast about for alliances with different revolutionary leaders. Pánfilo Natera in Zacatecas remained loyal to Carranza. Still smarting from Villa's criticism of his handling of the Zacatecas campaign, Natera chose to stay holed up in Zacatecas and give his allegiance to Carranza. Villa's approach to the Arrieta brothers in Durango brought a more cautious response. On September 23, he telegraphed them and asked that they join him against Carranza, for the First Chief had "offended . . . the honor and dignity of this Northern Army." Villa told the Arrietas that Maytorena had already joined against Carranza and asked for their support as well. The Arrietas, however, urged Villa to wait and see what happened at the convention before any definitive action occurred. They pointed out that such a rupture would leave the country even more bloodied and "more at the mercy of the United States which has still not withdrawn its forces from Veracruz."

Maclovio Herrera, the man who had held a pistol at the head of a telegraph operator while he called Carranza a son-of-a-bitch, seemed to have changed his tune. He urged Villa to desist from his resistance to Carranza and admonished Villa to "be a good Mexican. Be a good patriot as you have been until now and sacrifice your humiliation and slights received from the First Chief for the good of the nation." He urged Villa not to become another Pascual Orozco. If Villa could not abide Carranza, then honorable retirement should be in order.

Villa hoped to assuage the fears of some of Carranza's generals be denying any political ambition. On September 26, he informed Gen. Lucio Blanco, Ignacio Pesqueira, Rafael Buelna, Eduardo Hay, and J. C. Medina of his disavowal of political ambition. He renounced the idea of either the presidency or vice-presidency for himself, explaining that his split with Carranza grew out of the latter's "incapacity to reestablish . . . democratic government and to avoid armed conflict" among the revolutionaries.

Villa accelerated his approaches to new allies. As early as March 1914, Emiliano Zapata and his contingent in Morelos grew increasingly receptive to overtures from Villa. By mid-August, Villa pushed Zapata to show himself as opposed to Carranza. The *carrancistas* feared that Zapata, never a staunch supporter of Carranza, would be lost to the *villistas*. Villa's appeal to Zapata carried notes of patriotism when he wrote that they "must save our country from the consequences of the caprice of the so-called First Chief of the Constitutionalist Army. On this date [September 22]," he continued, "we have withdrawn recognition of him as head of the nation and will make every effort to force him to deliver power to the true representatives of the people."

Villa's appeals for support began to have an effect on Carranza. Various generals began to press Carranza with their doubts, and some of Villa's commanders demanded that Carranza retire. In response, Carranza declared that he had no other desire than to return authority to the Constitutionalists who gave him power in the first place. While he offered to retire, Carranza demanded that Villa also leave center stage and retire. Carranza offered to resign at the upcoming convention, but, he pointed out, should his resignation not be accepted he would "fight the reaction which is showing itself led by General Villa, the perhaps unconscious instrument of *porfirismo* and *cientificismo*." Carranza had begun to plant the label of reactionary on Villa in an attempt to wean away those *villistas* who feared a return to the *porfiriato*.

Villa made his break definitive. Carranza accused him of financial mismanagement and of perpetuating the struggle that had for so long left the country bleeding and weary. Villa also had the Benton incident thrown in his face again. Carranza's accusations of irresponsibility stung Villa, for he perceived his actions as growing out of a commitment to revolutionary goals and devoid of personal ambition. While a bit farfetched, Villa nonetheless held to his declarations.

In large measure, the turmoil between Villa and Carranza grew from the nature of the revolutionary situation. Instability, lack of political expertise on the part of many military commanders, and marked social differences too quickly divided the Constitutionalists. "Along with obedience to revolutionary chieftains there also grew jealousies and frictions between different captains," writes one Mexican observer, "who became repeatedly disobedient and [caused] open conflict which ultimately led to the ferment that separated Villa from Carranza."

The perpetually aristocratic Carranza refused to grant validity to Villa, bandit chieftain-turned-revolutionary hero. Villa suffered the fate of those who rose quickly in the turmoil engendered by the revolution. He was not allowed to do anything other than put his head on the block for the nation while Carranza and his advisors thought great thoughts and formulated plans without ever consulting the man who made the ouster of Huerta a reality.

CHAPTER VIII

Shattered Egos, Shattered Nation

Vainglorious megalomania plunged Mexico into another year of continued strife as Villa and Carranza hurled insults at each other and prepared to join in Herculean battle for dominance of the Mexican Revolution. For Carranza, the upstart Villa refused to submit to constituted authority and thus give a semblance of hegemony to the Constitutionalist movement. Villa felt slighted. Carranza failed to acknowledge openly his massive military contribution to the ouster of Huerta and consequently felt that he, a man emerging from the lower classes, was deemed not fit to mingle with upper-class reformers represented by Carranza. Additionally, the United States, long suffering in its patience with Mexico, played the role of fickle harlot as it toyed with the different factions represented by Villa and Carranza. Ultimately, Woodrow Wilson was forced to choose between the two men. His choice finally reflected a yielding to his own prejudices rather than what genuinely represented the barely articulated aspirations of the Mexican people.

The formal break between Villa and Carranza came in September 1914. As different revolutionary leaders prepared to meet in convention in Mexico City to determine the political destiny of Mexico, Carranza set about to systematically eliminate possible Villa supporters in the capital. *Villista* agents in Mexico City found

106

themselves sitting in the federal penitentiary because Carranza hoped to undercut their chief.

Both sides, however, indulged in fairly shady tactics, for a *villista* agent in Mexico City constantly attempted to suborn those generals who were loyal to Carranza and openly referred to Carranza as a "stupid goat." To the north, in Baja California, Villa's artillery genius Felipe Angeles began recruitment of ex-*federales*, including Baja California Governor Esteban Cantú.

Generals began to convene in Mexico City. All of them were, at least initially, Carranza supporters. Obregón still attempted to effect a reconciliation between Villa and Carranza. In one of its first official acts, the convention voted to reject Carranza's grandstand resignation on October 3. Two days later it decided that only military men could be participants. On October 5, the delegates voted to move the assembly to Aguascalientes on October 10. The move to Aguascalientes aimed at placing the convention on neutral ground, for it bordered on territories controlled by Villa and Carranza.

Villa, however, blustered and sputtered about the gutlessness of the convention in not accepting Carranza's resignation. Obregón, still perilously straddling the fence, viewed such a move as inopportune and hoped to postpone such a decision until the convention was more suitably ensconced in the Morelos Theater of Aguascalientes. Villa persisted in his view that the continuation of Carranza in office threatened the long-term success of the revolution. Villa quickly noted that he had offered to remove himself from the field and even to commit suicide if Carranza would join him. How much of this was bluster and bravado is hard to judge, but Carranza hastily rejected the offer.

Delegates to the convention provided a fine circus for the nation. They still clutched rifles and revolvers, punctuated speeches with volleys of small-arms fire, and hooted and howled in a most raucous manner. Yet a sufficient number of them saw that without either Villa or Zapata as adherents to the convention it would be nothing more than a rump congress of *carrancista* generals. As a result, on October 16, Felipe Angeles was designated by the convention to go to Cuernavaca and secure *zapatista* attendance in Aguascalientes. Ten days later the *zapatistas* arrived, but instead of going directly to Aguascalientes they traveled a hundred miles north to Villa's headquarters.

Villa's attitude toward the convention began to soften once he had his *zapatista* delegates to help offset the overwhelming numbers of *carrancistas* in Aguascalientes. The alliance between Villa and Zapata turned the tables on Carranza and placed his delegates in the minority. Villa continually informed the convention that he would accept anyone as president, provided it was not Carranza. Carranza did not prove as magnanimous, for he refused to recognize the sovereignty of the convention. Smugly, Villa declared that "at last the country and world at large should be convinced that Carranza is not a patriot."

Throughout, Villa's actions and public statements in the formative days of the convention pointed to a determined effort to be accommodating. On October 17 he addressed the convention, broke down and blubbered about his beloved country, embraced Obregón in front of the Morelos Theater, and tried to act like a properly contrite supporter of highly touted political ideals. Carranza, by refusing to attend or send a representative, did not even grant tacit legitimacy to the convention. Such a move caused strong animosity toward Carranza even among those military men who wavered between him and Villa.

The arrival of the *zapatistas* in union with their *villista* comrades galvanized the convention. Ringing speeches and outraged responses — even to the drawing of guns — underscored the strong emotions that were present in Mexico. This alliance would ultimately alienate some of the more moderate elements who preferred to stick by Carranza rather than hand the country over to *zapatista* radicals or to the unpredictable *villistas*.

On October 29 the convention again received word from Carranza that he would consider retirement if both Villa and Zapata would leave active participation as well. Confusion broke out on the convention floor. While no action was taken with regard to Zapata, the convention did vote to ask both Carranza and Villa to set aside their personal animosities and retire. Angeles hoped to convince Villa. Prepared to take any measure to rid Mexico of Don Venus, Villa not only offered to join Carranza in retirement but also suggested that the convention should have them both shot to assure peace and tranquility in Mexico.

Again, however, Villa dealt from strength. He controlled the railroads in and out of Aguascalientes and the supply lines that ran from the north. The convention, while claiming sovereignty, still remained tied to the magnanimity of Francisco Villa.

Off and on the convention had met throughout October, and as it moved into its second month, most delegates recognized the necessity of selecting a president who would function as head of the convention and also as the duly constituted executive in Mexico. On November 2, after wrangling between the candidacies of José Isabel Robles (*villista*) and Antonio I. Villarreal (radical *carrancista*), a third candidate emerged. Eulalio Gutiérrez, a moderately successful general, became the compromise choice of the convention.

Carranza proved obdurate. While citing his disposition to retire, he quickly backtracked and said that conditions had not been met. Neither he nor Villa seemed disposed to quit. Carranza steadfastly refused to recognize the sovereignty of the convention and refused to deliver the executive authority to Gutiérrez. Villa refused to make any moves that hinted at retirement until he was assured that Carranza would no longer pollute the political environment of Mexico. The strong commitment of both of these men to their personal ambitions as well as their mutual personal animosities slowly led Mexico back toward war.

The convention declared Carranza in rebellion on November 10. Carranza issued a call to his loyal followers to join him against the illegal convention. *Carrancista* delegates began leaving Aguascalientes to join their leader and take their soldiers back to prepare for battle. Villa further provoked men like Pablo González by offering his troops to the convention should Carranza fail to retire and turn over the executive authority to Gutiérrez. At the same time, Villa made preparations to move on Mexico City. *Carrancista* officials saw his advance as difficult to contain.

Villa gauged Carranza's reaction quite correctly. While optimistic that he could control Mexico, Villa still worried about Carranza and Veracruz. Villa considered Carranza of such low moral character that he strongly believed the First Chief would provoke an incident with United States forces in Veracruz in order to garner support from the Mexican people. Continued presence of United States troops in Veracruz concerned Villa. He felt that since Carranza no longer bore the official imprimatur from the convention that Veracruz should be turned over to convention forces. "Otherwise," he noted, "the Convention could not be held responsible for the enforcement of guarantees."

Carranza's act of rebellion still left the convention wondering which way Obregón would jump. His organizational genius was critical to Carranza. Eulalio Gutiérrez, however, helped Obregón decide when Villa was appointed commander of all convention forces. Obregón, joined by other *carrancista* generals, declared for Carranza. Obregón had tried one last-minute mediation as Villa prepared to move to Mexico City. On November 11, Villa received an eleventh-hour appeal from Obregón asking that Villa get out of the country for a while in order for Carranza to transfer power without duress. He wrote: "It would not be a sacrifice for you to save the nation of yet another battle."

Gutiérrez, the compromise candidate, also attempted to be a compromiser. Through Pablo González he kept trying to get Carranza to retire for the good of the nation and extended the deadline twenty-four hours at a time. Gutiérrez, however, saw that if Mexico should again be torn by civil strife "it would be chargeable to his [Carranza's] obstinacy and [the] country would hold him alone responsible."

By this time, Villa hoped to cement a firm military alliance with Zapata and to convert his new political ally into a strong military supporter as well. Villa informed Zapata that hostilities were inevitable and that both of them should join forces to hound Carranza into the sea. Zapata, by sending delegates, tacitly recognized the sovereignty of the convention and found himself with little maneuverability. Villa pushed Zapata to strike at Carranza from the south since Don Venus had gained the status of *un rebelde* (a rebel).

Carranza felt dual pressure from both Villa and Zapata. On November 20 he began preparations to evacuate Mexico City, though he made no provisions for the protection of the city other than the regular and ineffectual police force. Carranza began to move toward Veracruz. Both Carranza and the convention had pressed Washington to leave Mexico now that Huerta had been defeated. United States forces began marching out of Veracruz on November 23, secure in the assurances of Carranza regarding treatment of civilians who cooperated with the occupying forces. Carranza now had a base of operations and assured income from the customshouse in Veracruz. From there he could launch a relentless campaign against Villa and the convention.

Mexico City prepared for the onslaught of the northern and southern barbarians. For over a year, tales of the brutalities of the *villistas* and the *zapatistas* had titillated the denizens of Mexico City. Zapata's forces were the first to arrive. Instead of launching a campaign of rapine and looting, they stared, bewildered, at the incredible sights of the big city. Their attention concentrated on the splendid horses throughout the city, and these they confiscated with impunity. On November 26, Zapata arrived from Morelos, while Villa was making his way southward from Aguascalientes.

Agents from each man arranged a meeting for the two leaders at Xochimilco. On December 4, Villa and Zapata met for the first time. The meeting was coldly formal until Villa blurted out Carranza's name. Zapata called the First Chief a "son-of-a-bitch" and began to list his grievances about Carranza. With that outburst the session became less formal. Zapata, always the dandy, wore an elaborate *charro* suit, while Villa arrived at their meeting in a pith helmet, his favorite baggy sweater, and khaki trousers. The conversations ranged over every conceivable topic. Publicly, they drank a toast to their mutual alliance. Villa, not much of a drinker, nearly choked on the fiery *aguardiente* that he threw back in one swallow.

While full of camaraderie, the meeting between Villa and Zapata had a serious purpose. These two men, preeminent in Mexico, needed to divide jurisdictions for fear that they might inadvertently step on each other's toes. Villa had been urged by Angeles to pursue Carranza to Veracruz and there destroy him before he had an opportunity to organize his forces. Villa, however, refrained because he had agreed with Zapata that Veracruz was within the *zapatista* jurisdiction. Such an action would lead to Villa's final defeat, for Zapata never felt comfortable outside of Morelos and its immediate environs and did not pursue his side of the military alliance vigorously.

On December 6, Villa and Zapata rode at the head of their forces into Mexico City. They went to Madero's tomb, where Villa unashamedly wept, then entered the National Palace, where Villa, more outgoing and fun-loving than Zapata, sat in the presidential chair "just to see how it felt." They met with Eulalio Gutiérrez and informed him about their plans to crush Carranza. Gutiérrez felt somewhat out of the picture, for his two principal military leaders did not consult him but rather presented him with a *fait accompli*.

The *entrée* of Villa and Zapata into Mexico City was accomplished with little violence. But neither Villa nor Zapata could control men who just sat around and found themselves into mischief. Throughout December the chaos in Mexico City accelerated. Killings and lootings replaced the peaceful entry of the two leaders and the awed stare of their soldiers. Vengeful, Villa hoped to find some *huertista* and *carrancista* targets still in Mexico City. Rodolfo Fierro, Villa's somewhat homicidal henchman, killed two leading members of the convention merely because they spoke critically of Villa. Villa hoped to arrest and execute Eduardo Iturbide, the man who handed Mexico City over to Obregón in August. Luckily, Iturbide received a safe-conduct from Gutiérrez and escaped to the United States with the help of presidential agent Leon Canova.

The occupation of Mexico City by the forces of Villa and Zapata demonstrated the limitations of both men in dealing with a national problem named Carranza. Both Zapata and Villa ultimately remained tied to their regional origins. Rather than strike boldly and pursue Carranza all the way to Veracruz, Zapata's forces stopped at Puebla. Villa constantly worried about his northern supply lines and did not move vigorously to the southeast. All the while, Gutiérrez urged them to make good their plans to crush Caranza's opposition to the convention. He was ignored, and by the end of the year felt that a conspiracy was aimed at him by Villa and Zapata.

The pillage committed by the *villistas* and *zapatistas* finally forced Gutiérrez to prepare to leave Mexico City. He knew that he was at Villa's mercy, but he continued to correspond with Obregón and other moderate *carrancistas* in an attempt to resolve the strife in Mexico. Unfortunately, captured documents brought to Villa by Angeles forced Villa to order Gutiérrez's execution. Gutiérrez then fled Mexico City and headed, eventually, for San Luis Potosí. Much to Gutiérrez's discomfiture, Tomás Urbina held that town, and Gutiérrez finally took refuge in a little town that no one wanted. There he remained until June 1915, when he returned to civilian life.

Gutiérrez's removal forced the convention to select a successor. Dominated militarily by Villa and his forces, the delegates selected Roque González Garza, a *villista,* to fill the precarious presidential chair vacated by Eulalio Gutiérrez. As a major official act, González Garza confirmed Villa's appointment as head of the convention armies and commander of all military operations. In a note to Villa, the new president declared his certainty that "the nation puts its faith in your support of the Revolutionary principles and that you will succeed in realizing these, as well as all the dispositions and decrees of the Convention."

While politicians wrangled in Mexico City, *villista* forces continued to consolidate their northern positions. In mid-January 1915, Villa's men seized Saltillo, Coahuila, in a bloody battle that was complicated by fog and carried on in hand-to-hand combat. Continually, the *villistas* poured the pressure on the *carrancistas*. Railroad men defected from Carranza's forces and made the escape of the *carrancistas* nearly impossible, thus forcing them to stand and fight.

Success in the north, however, did not stop the *carrancistas*, headed by Obregón, from pushing the *convencionistas* out of Mexico City. By January 27, the pressure became so intense that Villa, watching from the north, offered to send a train to move the convention to either Chihuahua or Torreón. But it was too late. Most of the delegates, *zapatista* and *villista* alike, headed to Cuernavaca, where they hoped to reestablish convention headquarters.

The ability of the *carrancistas* to regroup and begin an offensive against the convention forces caused some of Villa's former supporters to reconsider their original allegiance to the Centaur of the North. Eugenio Aguirre Benavides soon followed Eulalio Gutiérrez in denouncing Villa. His denunciation, growing in part from Villa's treatment of Obregón in September and from the growing chaos in Mexico City, was repudiated quickly by Felipe Angeles. Angeles remembered the way in which the Aguirre Benavides brothers became cozy with Obregón. When approached to defect, Angeles rejoindered:

> I remember . . . our oath at Aguascalientes and its consecration of the flag of the Convention. . . . We were struggling in defense of his [Carranza's] government, and he [Obregón] in the meantime was negotiating a plan for the enemy to advance on us from Saltillo and Monterrey. . . . General Villa is a great man and a patriot, and if he were not, your acts would be enough to make him so.

Defections, a revitalized Constitutionalist Army, and general chaos contributed significantly to the nervousness of the convention delegates. The decision to move the convention south to Cuernavaca still made most of the delegates feel uncomfortable, for they feared the inability of the *zapatistas* to protect them from Obregón. As a result, Villa, at the urging of his advisors, began to move beyond his military role and to assume civil duties. Reluctantly, Villa decreed on January 31, 1915, that he would begin to take charge of political and civil functions as well as military ones. In his decree he accused Carranza of wanting to establish a dictatorship and rehashed his side of the problems with Carranza. He reiterated his grievances against Gutiérrez, and concluded that

> it occurs, however, that by force of circumstances the armies are now separated and even without communication, a part of them concentrating in the north under my orders, with headquarters in Aguascalientes, another part in the south under Zapata, and the President of the Convention with general headquarters in Cuernavaca — all of which now obliges me to take over the civil authority, which I will not exercise personally but through three offices situated in the City of Chihuahua.

In his rationale, Villa decreed the creation of an office for Justice and International Affairs. Secondly, he created an office for Communications and Internal Governance of Mexico. Finally, Villa established the office of Treasury and Development. Pure rhetoric rolled from Villa in the final words of his decree:

> But I, Pancho Villa, declare that the new authority circumstances force me to assume will be no authority of dictatorial form but only that of the man who, in his devotion to the people, has already expressed his ideals of redemption, the authority of the man who swore to be faithful to the Convention, to respect and obey its orders, and to recognize whatever government it might establish.

While on the defensive, Villa still pushed his forces to retake key urban targets. Obregón had forced him out of Guadalajara in January. By mid-February, Villa's forces recaptured Mexico's second largest city. Crowds of citizens lined the streets to welcome the *villistas* back to the city. The United States vice-consul reported that the great popular demonstration represented all classes of people. He added that "the largest concourse of people that I have ever seen gathered in the plaza and streets" treated the *villista* forces like deliverers from the *carrancistas*.

However successful some of the convention and *villista* military efforts appeared, the convention itself struggled against the factionalism of the *villistas* and *zapatistas*. Regional differences and attitudes underscored the growing schism between *zapatista* and *villista*. To Villa's supporters, the peasants from the south arrogantly flung about their singular commitment to a narrowly perceived social reform. *Zapatista* adherence to a social philosophy made them arrogant and hungry for power. What rankled the *villistas* most, however, was the failure of the *zapatistas* to live up to their military promises. Their refusal to expand beyond the confines of Morelos seriously weakened convention efforts to crush Obregón and Carranza.

Zapata's followers also had their grievances. They complained about the paucity of arms and ammunition promised by Villa. Without these, they declared, General Zapata and his men could not effectively prosecute a campaign against Carranza. Moreover, the *zapatistas* felt like ugly stepchildren, for they viewed themselves as excluded from the inner circles of power that made policy and decisions that bound all convention delegates. Finally, the *zapatista* ideologues saw in the *villistas* a weak to nonexistent commitment to social reform, agrarian or any other kind.

Such serious differences in mid-March again forced the convention to consider another move, this time to Chihuahua. In almost three months, Obregón had forced the convention to Cuernavaca, stripped Mexico City of anything of value, and declared worthless all currency of *villista* issue. Carranza remained fortified in Veracruz while Obregón led the renewed offensive against the convention forces. Consequently, a move north removed the convention from serious entanglements with the vengeful soldiers under Obregón's command.

Obregón's abandonment of Mexico City in March brought almost immediate reoccupation by the *zapatistas*. They came to dominate the convention more and more as their ideological harangues increasingly irritated and drove away *villista* delegates. Thus, while Zapata's men played and talked in Mexico City and while Villa began to concentrate his forces in the north, Obregón moved northward toward Querétaro and Celaya. Again the convention felt threatened and cut off from Villa's protection. Too late, the *convencionistas* accepted Villa's hospitality in Chihuahua. Obregón had cut off rail communications between Mexico City and the north.

Villa himself had become disgruntled with Zapata. He argued rightly that the *zapatistas* could at least protect Mexico City from Obregón. But other areas also plagued Villa. Rodolfo Fierro had lost Guadalajara, and Angeles faced troubles in Monterrey. Villa's presence there finally turned the tide, and he began to head south. The battle to be joined would, in the long run, decide the course of the revolution.

As Villa and his army headed south they knew that they would run into Obregón somewhere along the line. They did. Obregón, aware of the weaknesses of his enemies, had dug trenches and placed machine guns around Celaya. He was waiting for Villa.

As Villa approached Celaya, he easily subdued Obregón's outposts. But on April 6, the situation began to change. Confident of victory, Villa crowed to Carothers that he would happily agree to a neutralization of Mexico City if Carranza would also agree, but since he was about to give Obregón a thorough thrashing, such an agreement would be moot. Villa bragged a little early.

Too impatient to sustain a long siege of Celaya, Villa ordered mass assaults on the enemy's positions. Obregón's barbed wire did its work. The battle raged throughout the day of April 6. Hospital cars overflowed with wounded, and more than a thousand dead lay on the plains of Celaya. On April 7, Villa again tried his human wave against the trench warfare of Obregón. At one point the *villistas* broke through to Celaya but were driven out by the defenders. His infantry in disarray, 2,000 men dead, and his *dorados* literally wiped out, Villa conceded defeat. While he lost no artillery, the División del Norte was dispirited.

For a week Villa collected forces from all over Mexico. Angeles cautioned him to wait until he should arrive to direct the artillery barrages that would reduce Celaya to rubble. Obregón remained hunkered down in his trenches, secure that the barbed wire would protect him from Villa. Villa, however, grew increasingly restive, and on April 13, he ordered another frontal assault on Obregón's positions. Obregón had rebuffed an attempt to lure him into the open. Villa had appealed to Obregón to fight out in the open and thus avoid civilian bloodshed, but to no avail. Obregón stayed behind his barricade.

For two days the battle raged. Time and again Villa hoped to render Obregón, and Obregón held. Bodies littered the battlefield. Some estimates placed Villa's losses as high as 4,000 dead and 5,000 taken prisoner. The most relentless war machine of the Mexican Revolution had suffered ignominious defeat. Obregón proved that Villa could be defeated. Unfortunately for Villa, he never recovered fully from the blow to his military vanity and to his armed strength.

Carranza's supporters were jubilant at the defeat of Villa. Dr. Rafael Cantú, the head of the Constitutionalist medical services, wrote to Carranza that "*villismo* is now dead, never to rise again, because it is eternal law that evil shall be suppressed by the sinister weight of its crimes."

Though demoralized, Villa and his army began to reorganize in Aguascalientes toward the end of April. Angeles finally arrived and began to take stock of the situation. Rifles, especially Mausers, were in short supply. Ammunition was not adaptable to the Marlin .30-.30 sporting rifles that about half of the División del Norte carried. Frustrations at every turn drove Villa into one of his rages.

Indiscriminately, Villa began to shoot some of his own subordinates. Gen. Dionisio Triana, an unfortunate nephew of one of Obregón's own commanders, was ordered executed by reason of blood relation. Villa saw in this relationship an intolerable treason that could only be extirpated through the firing squad. In Aguascalientes almost daily executions occurred. The United States viceconsul feared that his ability to protect foreigners and others had come to an end. Villa "evidently resents my active intercession and his resentment is so gross that it is impossible for me to treat him with any dignity or satisfactory result."

Personal tragedy also complicated Villa's life. In mid-May his brother, Antonio, fell in battle to the Constitutionalists. Silvestre Terrazas sent condolences to Villa and added his assurance that God would give him the strength and resignation to "see [your] fortitude as an exceptional man, conserving [your] energy for the good of the Fatherland." Bent on vengeance, Villa headed toward Chihuahua and postponed yet another engagement with Obregón.

Obregón meanwhile pushed north again and established a defensive perimeter around León, Guanajuato. Obregón well knew what Villa would do. Against Angeles's advice, Villa pressed to the attack. Rather than withdraw to Aguascalientes and force Obregón to pursue him, Villa attacked. For two days again, wave after wave of *villistas* fell to Obregón's machine guns and became entangled in vicious barbed wire coils. By June 5, the *villistas* were decimated. While Obregón lost an arm in the engagement and nearly committed suicide, his well-disciplined forces delivered a decisive blow to Villa's ambitions and hopes.

Blood flowed freely on the Mexican *altiplano* as Villa and Obregón locked in combat. Politicians in Mexico City, however, continued to harangue each other throughout the spring of 1915. *Zapatista* delegates showed more interest in the passage of land reform bills than in opening a second front against Carranza. *Villista* and *zapatista* delegates blamed each other for the food shortages that daily occurred in Mexico City. Again the convention changed presidents, this time naming Francisco Lagos Cházaro, an ardent *villista* from Chihuahua, as its titular head. But all of the political wrangling did nothing to help Villa.

Villa's decisive defeat at Celaya and León boded ill for his future as a dominant figure in Mexico. His temperament forced him into illogical military situations that cost him men, equipment, and morale. Also, his political allies refused to make a wholesale commitment to the defeat of Carranza. Bruised egos on all sides of the political questions in Mexico prolonged the national exercise in fratricide that had become the Mexican Revolution.

CHAPTER IX

"I shall teach those Latins to elect good men"

He cut an imposing figure as he stepped before the assembled delegates. Thomas Woodrow Wilson, president of the United States, prepared to address the Pan American Union in June 1913. His principal topic was Mexico. Huerta's rise to power offended Wilson's moral sensibilities, and the president was determined to oversee the downfall of Mexico's usurper and Madero's murderer. In his address Wilson promised a policy of patience with the struggle that strove to unseat Huerta and with the movement that would bring needed changes and reform to Mexico. Yet Woodrow Wilson could not forget his own training and background. College professor, college president, son of a Presbyterian minister, governor of New Jersey — all of these plus a steadfast conviction in his own righteousness ingrained in the new president a sense of mission and a pedagogic bent that made most of his pronouncements professorial and slightly didactic.

To Wilson, Mexico could not keep her house in order. His Central American neighbors threatened to erupt into chaos. The Caribbean festered at the doorstep of the United States. Professor Wilson concluded by stating that he would "teach those Latins to elect good men." In that short statement, Wilson set the tone for his Latin American policy and for the specific relations that his government would have with the different factions that contended for power in Mexico.

For two years, Wilson watched as the Constitutionalist revolution drove out Huerta and then turned on itself. Throughout the first year of the struggle against Huerta, Wilson's policy tended toward the División del Norte. Of all the Constitutionalist leaders, the flamboyant Villa seemed the most outwardly amenable to Wilson's teachings. Carranza, on the other hand, testily rejected all of Wilson's attempts to mold and guide the revolution in his preconceived image of what a Latin American revolution should be like and what should constitute its goals. Carranza bristled at United States invasion of Veracruz and came close to making common cause with Huerta. Villa welcomed the presence of United States marines in Veracruz, for they provided a diversion of *huertista* troops from the capital.

Villa had excellent press coverage. A Mexican Robin Hood, always with good words about the United States, emerged from the pages of United States newspapers. Additionally, Villa avoided the pillage of United States-owned holdings in the parts of Mexico where he held sway.

In large measure Villa calculated his friendship toward the United States. He readily recognized that the United States was the primary provider of arms, ammunition, and other military supplies for his growing and powerful División del Norte. As a consequence he exercised caution in his dealings with President Wilson. As matters worsened in Mexico and a struggle between himself and Carranza loomed as a distinct probability, Villa wanted an uninterrupted supply of equipment available through El Paso and Ciudad Juárez.

Wilson, however, mired himself in a quandary. Certainly, of the two major leaders in Mexico, Villa seemed the most malleable and easily influenced. Yet he was a peasant, a sweating cattle rustler devoid of civilized sensibilities. Carranza, while a testy old curmudgeon, shared many of Wilson's faintly aristocratic views about social reform and the function of the upper classes to make genuine efforts to uplift their less fortunate brethren. This longstanding distinction, plus immediate political developments, ultimately forced Wilson to make a choice.

But the choice that Wilson made failed to take into account some of the solid achievements of *villista* government, especially in

Chihuahua. Wilson could see only the chaos and anarchy that revolution engendered in Mexico; he saw economic collapse precipitated in part by irresponsible fiscal policies. These factors combined to force Wilson to reject Villa as his anointed for leadership
in Mexico.

The Conventionist routing of Carranza and his flight to Veracruz in November 1914 gave early indication of Wilson's leanings
in his choice between Villa and the Constitutionalist First Chief.
United States occupation of Veracruz, beginning in April of that
same year, did in fact provide some diversion of *huertista* forces and
contributed to a reduced number of supplies entering Mexico destined for Huerta's army. Carranza, however, viewed the entire operation jaundicedly and promised revenge on any *veracruzanos* who
cooperated with the illicit forces of foreign occupation. Villa's position proved much more benign since he felt that United States presence helped rid Mexico of Huerta that much more quickly. Consequently, when Carranza fled to Veracruz at the end of November,
the United States moved its forces out, handed the port over to
Carranza, and also gave him the customshouse receipts that had
been kept in trust for Mexico's government. Thus, tacitly Wilson
stamped approval on Carranza long before he finally granted *de
facto* recognition to the First Chief.

Carranza held an immediate advantage over Villa once Veracruz came into Constitutionalist hands. The First Chief could now
with impunity move goods in and out of Mexico. His lines of supply
were protected by a safe harbor on the Gulf of Mexico. Villa, however, received most of his material through Ciudad Juárez. Time
and difficulty often made the procurement of supplies and equipment more difficult on land routes than the sea routes available to
Carranza.

Villa did not read the signs very well. He continued to court
United States favor throughout 1914 and 1915 (at least until October). Japanese overtures to Villa provoked virulently pro-United
States sentiments, for Villa declared that in any foreign entanglement he would back the United States against it adversary.

Villa continued to be optimistic about his chances. In spite of
military reverses in the winter of 1915, Villa still saw the convention as the legitimate government of Mexico. In a conversation
with Special Presidential Agent Duval West, Villa contended that
his faction should receive recognition from the United States. He

thanked Wilson for preventing war in Mexico and for exercising restraint in order to avoid war between Mexico and the United States. But because Wilson had demonstrated "his ability to enforce law and order throughout Mexico, and was actuated solely by a desire to promote the welfare of his country, disclaiming any personal ambition whatsoever," Villa thought the president should recognize the convention government. Wilson, however, pursued his policy of waiting patiently for conditions in Mexico to right themselves.

By early April 1915, Villa noted a slight change in attitude on the part of the United States. Immediately prior to the Battle of Celaya, Villa complained about the paucity of ammunition. He wired his brother Hipólito in the United States, who replied that a change in United States attitude made the delivery of ammunition to the División del Norte difficult though not impossible.

Major military reverses for Villa threw him on the defensive. Two defeats at Celaya in April threatened to force Wilson to look toward Carranza. Wilson, however, harbored little love for Don Venustiano. Instead, Wilson issued an Olympian proclamation just prior to the last great battle between Obregón and Villa at León, Guanajuato. In his statement, Wilson noted the patience which for two years the United States had displayed toward Mexico. Protection of foreign nationals, noted Wilson, continued tenuous, and in the two years of "watchful waiting" Mexico had not resolved its monumental internal problems. "It is time," declared Woodrow Wilson,

> that the Government of the United States should frankly state the policy which in these extraordinary circumstances it becomes its duty to adopt. It must presently do what it has not hitherto done or felt at liberty to do: lend its active moral support to some man or group of men, if such may be found, who can rally the suffering people of Mexico to their support in an effort to ignore, if not unite the warring factions of the country. . . . I feel it to be my duty to tell them that, if they cannot accommodate their differences and unite for this great purpose within a very short time, this Government will be constrained to decide what means should be employed by the United States in order to help Mexico save herself and serve her people.

Villista defeat at León, shortly after Wilson's dicta, led to a variety of speculations about the disruption of the *villista* forces. Principal among these was the rumor that Angeles had left Villa. Angeles, however, traveled to the United States in order to prevail on Gen. Hugh L. Scott to arrange an interview for him with Wilson. Villa rightly saw in Angeles the perfect emissary. His urbanity and sophistication would readily appeal to Wilson. The president of the United States would treat with a civilized, traveled, educated military man, not a cattle rustler or a bandit. Angeles's mission, however, aborted, for Wilson was not receiving direct appeals from Mexican revolutionaries no matter what patina they presented to the world.

Meanwhile, various Mexican groups exiled in the United States hoped to bring together some reconciliation in Mexico. While divided by differing political views, these exiles met in San Antonio, Texas, and formed the Mexican Peace Assembly in mid-January 1915. As an initial step they communicated with leading Mexican revolutionary leaders including, of course, Villa, Obregón, Angeles, Zapata, and others and implored them to lay down their arms. Only Villa, Obregón, and Angeles replied and rejected the Peace Assembly's plea out of hand. In the wings, however, stood Victoriano Huerta. His return to the United States coincided with the formation of the Mexican Peace Assembly, which began to look toward Huerta as the possible unifier for the restoration of peace in Mexico.

Soon the Mexican Peace Assembly took on a reactionary mantle as it continued to flirt with Huerta. *Carrancista* agents and informers in the United States drew parallels between Villa and the different reactionaries operating in Washington, D.C. One anonymous correspondent told Carranza that Villa hoped to enmesh the Constitutionalists in the same reactionary net as the one in which the convention found itself.

In league with Pascual Orozco, Huerta's abortive comeback in August 1915 resulted in the death of Orozco and the capture and incarceration of Huerta in the United States. Villa granted a posthumous lifting of animosity between himself and Orozco, also from Chihuahua, and informed the family that they could return his body to Mexico for burial. The family, however, chose to bury Orozco in El Paso.

Exile activity did not deter Wilson from trying to bring about a reconciliation between Villa and Carranza. In August, joined by the ambassadors from Brazil, Chile, Argentina, Bolivia, Uruguay, and Guatemala, Secretary of State Robert Lansing issued a call for a conference on neutral territory between the different factions in Mexico to resolve their differences and thus save the country further bloodshed. Many of the diplomats who joined Lansing offered to act as intermediaries between the warring groups in Mexico. The plea also called for the formation of a provisional government that would ultimately lead to constitutional reconstruction of the country and a call for general elections.

Villa realized that his military posture was now tentative. His enthusiastic and positive response to Lansing's requests came as a means of gaining support both inside and outside of Mexico. The failure of Carranza to acknowledge such an overture would undoubtedly place Don Venus in a rather bad light. Villa, in his reply, claimed that he could continue the struggle against Carranza, but the good of the nation dictated that peace must come to Mexico. Villa concluded that "all military chiefs and civilian officials affiliated with the Convention Government desire only to witness the reestablishment of a government in Mexico that will bind itself to hold popular elections."

Villa continued to stall, hoping to neutralize Carranza. He asked that Hugh Scott treat in his name for an armistice between all factions for three months. In addition, all railroads would be opened to commercial and passenger travel while all troops would remain in place. Villa, however, wanted to include Zapata in the conferences, for Zapata defended the same ideals as did the División del Norte. Any faction that refused such magnanimity would automatically be refused supplies of any kind from the United States. George Carothers, hopelessly taken with Villa, urged the immediate adoption of such a policy and volunteered to accompany Scott on such a mission.

Hugh Scott was no stranger to Villa. When he commanded the Southern Department of the United States Army he had had frequent contact with the commander of the División del Norte. In early 1915, fighting between the forces of Maytorena on the one side and Hill and Calles on the other forced Scott, now commander-in-chief of the army, back to the border to talk with Villa. Scott remained adamant. The border had caused enough problems, and fighting around it must cease, he declared. Civilians continued to catch errant bullets fired by the different revolutionary factions. Villa wanted a day to finish off Hill and Calles; Scott replied that he would not even have eight minutes. Still, good relations between the two men continued, and, in some ways, Scott was the most vocal advocate of the *villista* position in the United States government.

Thus, when Villa and Scott met again in August 1915, some problems that rankled the United States were resolved. Villa remained desperate for funds. He had called a meeting of mine owners in Chihuahua with the intention of extorting funds from them in order to purchase much-needed equipment and ammunition. Scott, however, convinced Villa that such action could only weaken his cause in the eyes of President Wilson, and Villa subsequently canceled the meeting. Villa, moreover, agreed to return inventory to foreign merchants in Chihuahua and to allow the Santa Rosalía Light and Power Company to devolve back into the hands of its original owners. Obviously, Villa still tried to curry favor with the United States and continued to make concession after concession when his own position remained untenable.

The superficially cordial relations between Villa and Scott became almost an embarrassment to the American general. Villa's irascibility, his desperate moves to stay in favor, and the obviously defensive nature of his posture in Mexico made his public advocacy by Scott almost impossible. Heriberto Barrón, a Carranza supporter, talked with Scott, explained even further the justness of the Constitutionalist cause, and tried to make any support of Villa by Scott a degrading thing for the general to do.

With Barrón working on one side and Manuel Chao working on the other, Hugh Scott found himself barraged with conflicting views and pleas from the contending parties in Mexico. Chao went to Washington to meet with Scott and informed the old Indian fighter that the Pan American Peace Plan of the month before had obviously failed, because Carranza refused to submit to any kind of arbitration. Chao also told Scott that Obregón would be an acceptable provisional president.

On another front, Villa's military reverses forced him to search every available avenue for funding the *villista* hordes. Since he still controlled Chihuahua and Juárez, he had to look there for more sources of revenue. A major step came in the acquisition of the public slaughterhouse in Ciudad Juárez. Villa could begin processing cattle that he rounded up. Reasoning that he could eliminate the middleman if he sold freshly killed meat, Villa began to

make the *abbatoir* functional once again. By mid-August he was
ready to begin selling meat both in Mexico and in neighboring El
Paso. A serious snag developed. Without a veterinary inspector
present at the border post, the meat could not enter the United
States. American government reluctance to send a veterinary inspector back to Juárez should have tipped Villa off to his loss of
favor with Wilson.

In response, Villa offered to pay the salary of the meat inspector.
He placed monies on deposit in El Paso so that the monthly salary of
the inspector could be guaranteed. Frustrated, Secretary of State Lansing tried to obtain the cooperation of the Agriculture Department in
keeping Villa's fresh beef out of the United States. Lansing reasoned
that most of the beef had been obtained illegally by Villa. The Department of Agriculture, however, found nothing in its regulations to
prohibit passage of the meat. Also, added the secretary of agriculture,
there was no way to ascertain whether the beef coming across the border had the correct political beliefs or not.

Throughout most of the fall of 1915, the Juárez slaughterhouse
became a minor *cause célèbre* between Villa and the United States.
Minor bureaucratic details temporarily closed down the export of
beef by Villa, but overall the business provided at least some source
of revenue that was reasonably dependable.

The slaughterhouse in part indicated more tellingly a change
of policy toward Villa by the United States. By the end of September, more signs pointed toward an eventual *rapprochment* between
Wilson and Carranza. Villa asked for and was refused permission
to move his hospital trains through El Paso and across New Mexico
and southern Arizona to Nogales. Since no wounded were aboard
the trains, no humanitarian reason existed to allow medical supplies to be shipped through the United States, argued the secretary
of war. *Villista* forces supporting Maytorena needed the supplies
and were denied them by the executors of a yet unarticulated policy.

By this time, even Zach Cobb had become less of a friend to
Villa. In early October, Cobb viewed Villa's movement as near collapse and argued that *villista* delegates in the United States were in
fact refugees. Furthermore, the Madero family used *villismo* as a
means of dividing the *carrancistas* and of fomenting constant revolution until the Maderos could once again dominate the Mexican

scene. Cobb concluded that "except as bandits Villa's Coxey's Army is not entitled to consideration as a direct element."

Refusal piled upon refusal as Villa tried to move equipment, men, and supplies through the United States to reinforce his troops in Sonora. A customs broker employed by Villa again asked permission of the Department of State to ship medical supplies in bond to Sonora. Again he was refused. Gen. John J. Pershing claimed that such a request had been denied earlier by the War Department, and Cobb enthusiastically urged that no change in policy should occur.

Villa's defensive posture and the roll call of successes that Obregón had gained, coupled with increasing Constitutionalist hegemony in Central Mexico, left little choice to the United States when it decided with whom it would cast its lot. The final fillip, of course, was the attitude of Woodrow Wilson. In spite of personal differences between himself and Carranza, Wilson found that he had to go with the man who most closely represented his own views about reform and about the role of an educated elite. The sense of *noblesse oblige* lay heavy on both Wilson and Carranza. Villa was an outsider. His blunt, often crude, and unpredictable populism frightened both Wilson and Carranza.

Carranza still remained immovable about any outside mediation. Such "meddling" did not deserve the dignity of a response. The Latin American countries that had made the original approach to the major factions in Mexico finally concluded that since Carranza already controlled Mexico City, he probably was the most viable candidate for recognition. Carranza had not, however, offered any guarantees about foreign properties or about the treatment of members of opposing factions in Mexico. Still, when the time came, Woodrow Wilson extended *de facto* recognition to Venustiano Carranza on October 19, 1915. In so doing, he laid the groundwork for augmented and vengeful *villista* activity, devoid of consideration for American sensibilities and interests.

Throughout the months prior to the recognition of Carranza, a major component in United States consideration revolved around the protection of United States and other foreign interests in Mexico. While Wilson had publicly declared that Mexican policy would not be dictated by special interests, threats to foreigners chronically rankled Wilson's sense of propriety. Carranza, of the two contenders for Wilson's fickle favors, at least appeared predictable. He made no concrete statements about guarantees. Villa, however, often changed his positions depending upon the need to project a more favorable image in the United States.

Mines, stores, warehouses, livestock, and land all became fair game for Villa in his quest for dominance over the *carrancistas*. Cattle provided a steady and reasonably reliable source of income for all the revolutionaries, but Villa, an experienced cattle thief and cattle dealer, controlled Juárez and from there found ready markets for stock taken from ranches throughout Chihuahua. Availability of such stock provided a constant temptation to Villa. Ranches within his domain often found themselves making contributions of cattle for Villa to sell to American dealers looking for inexpensive feeder stock.

One such company, the International Land and Cattle Company of Jimenez, Chihuahua, wanted to get the rest of its cattle out of Mexico before rebel forces exhausted their herds. The company hoped Consul Letcher could intercede with the *villista* authorities of Chihuahua. Letcher met with some success, for Villa's officials in Chihuahua granted permission to the company to export old bulls, old cows, and old steers. They would, however, still be subject to a ten-dollar-per-head export tax. Young and still productive stock would remain in Chihuahua, for Villa and his people saw the need to replenish herds if they were to use cattle as a source of income.

When Villa took over civil as well as military control of the convention government in Chihuahua on January 31, 1915, he made his position clear — for the time being — about guarantees to foreigners. To begin with, all foreigners who had remained scrupulously neutral would have their rights "religiously respected." He noted, however, that foreigners who became involved in Mexico's internal affairs would be detained until a full investigation of their involvement had been completed. Finally, Villa concluded, "contrary to the policy of Venustiano Carranza, . . . I believe that . . . the legal organization and functions of the tribunals of justice are essential elements in the restoration of order and consolidation of the government." Villa in part hoped to impress on fence straddlers both in Mexico and the United States that he at least had some of the outward trappings of legitimacy, as opposed to the arbitrary and high-handed attitudes of Don Venus.

Expediency most often dictated policy in Villa's part of Mexico. While foreign rights might be theoretically guaranteed, by early spring of 1915 Villa still had not ceased his confiscations of foreign lands, goods, and properties in Chihuahua. Cobb argued that it was the right of foreigners to have their investments guaranteed by the contending factions. Still, Villa needed his supplies. If the only way to get them was through the seizure of goods and property, he believed, foreigners would have to make some kind of contribution to the process of revolutionary justice.

Villista appropriation of foreign properties continued throughout 1915. Influential Americans with interests in Mexico wanted United States intervention for the protection of their investments. For example, owners of the *Los Angeles Times* — Harrison Gray Otis and Harry Chandler — opposed Wilson's policy of patience and forbearance with regard to Mexican policies. They owned two million acres in the form of the C-M Land and Cattle Company originally granted by Díaz. To their discomfiture, Villa and Carranza were agreed on one point: to annul all Díaz grants. Consequently, Otis and Chandler hoped to bring about United States intervention in Mexico as a means of protecting their interests.

No doubt desperation drove Villa to extremes. His actions, however, would ultimately boomerang on him in his relations with the United States. By September 1915 rumors of kidnapping and ransom demands by *villistas* increasingly filled reports reaching Washington, D. C. from border points such as El Paso. By mid-September, Cobb had turned against Villa. He urged State Department officials to encourage the disintegration of *villista* activity without further endangering United States lives and property in Chihuahua. Stridently, Cobb declared that "cold water [should] be thrown upon Villa publicity agencies and their desperadoes' propaganda deception."

Villa had once been the darling of the American press. His reverses caused the United States press and border *políticos* to look with a more jaundiced eye at *villista* activities. In August 1915, Villa's desperate measures provoked a reaction from Mayor Tom Lea of El Paso. In a rather direct and unequivocal declaration, Lea lambasted Villa and all of his activities:

> I hear that they had that bandit [Villa] from Juárez over here posing for moving pictures this morning [August 10, 1915]. . . . If this thing happens again, I will stop it if it takes the whole police force of El Paso. . . . If that bandit comes to El Paso again, the police force has orders to throw him into jail. . . . Certain people

raised sand around here because a few people gathered on the streets and shouted Viva Huerta. That bandit over in Juárez is not one bit better and he is going to jail if he comes back to El Paso.

During the initial phases of the struggle against Carranza, Villa seemed to possess abundant press support in the United States. Lázaro De la Garza reported in October 1914 that the United States press viewed Villa as moderate and prudent, energetic but tactful. The press, according to De la Garza, noted that relative stability existed in areas where Villa's forces dominated. Those areas over which Carranza and his minions held sway fell to "complete anarchy where the lives and properties of the citizens are at the capricious mercy of a bunch of military chieftains uncontrolled by their leader."

The press effort for Villa in the United States continued through the first two-thirds of 1915. Propaganda bulletins in Mexico were translated into English for circulation in the United States. One such pamphlet entitled ¿Quién es Francisco Villa? [Who is Francisco Villa?] made the rounds in New York and Washington and aimed at placing Villa in the most favorable light as compared to Carranza.

Other Villa actions sought to engender support both in Mexico and the United States. In early January 1915 he offered amnesty to all ex-*federales* except those who had been implicated in the overthrow of Madero. He invited the ex-*federales* to join the convention government in order to establish peace and order in the country. In part, Villa recognized that continual fractionalization of the body politic would leave Mexico in a state of constant turmoil. He sought to reduce that condition by making overtures to former but defeated enemies of the revolution.

While Villa hoped to improve his image in the United States and in Mexico, Carranza and Obregón worked equally hard to destroy the Villa mystique from their headquarters in Veracruz. Obregón publicly denounced Villa for stealing millions of pesos from the treasury of Ciudad Juárez. Additionally, continued Obregón, Villa exploited gambling in territories under his control in order to squander public monies on a debauched life.

Such propaganda, especially when directed at a moralistic president in the United States, was effective but contained little basis in fact. Villa, when he occupied Ciudad Juárez originally in

1913, sought to regulate gambling and saloons and saw to it that those establishments paid their fair share of taxes to the revolution. Like most revolutionaries, Villa actually opposed gambling because of its negative impact on the society in general. But for pragmatic fiscal reasons, he allowed it to operate in areas that he controlled.

Obregón's propaganda barrage continued from Veracruz. In December 1914 he accused Villa of making common cause with Orozco in April 1911 in opposition to Madero. Obregón even went so far as to claim that Villa had joined in a conspiracy to assassinate Madero. Obregón further noted that Villa irresponsibly and capriciously ordered the executions of wide numbers of people, including William Benton. Villa was also a thief, for he had lifted five million pesos from the national treasury. Finally, reactionaries now backed Villa in his attempt to consolidate power in Mexico.

Turning to Angeles, Obregón loosed a volley of propaganda at him as well. To Obregón, Angeles was both a *porfirista* and a *huertista*. He and Villa both aided and abetted José María Maytorena in his Sonora power grab. Paradoxically, Obregón also claimed that Angeles had also suborned Villa. Finally, Angeles, Villa's grey eminence, proved instrumental in the recruitment of former *huertistas* into the División del Norte.

With a firm groundwork laid upon which to base propaganda for export, the *carrancistas* began the publication of a bulletin called the *Mexican Letter* in the United States. Aimed solely at the vilification of Francisco Villa, the *Mexican Letter* served as a constant source of misinformation aimed at swaying Woodrow Wilson in the direction of Venustiano Carranza. In the issue of January 5, 1915, for example, the sheet claimed that Villa was the most unpopular man in Mexico and alleged that "the Mexicans have no intention of exchanging a Huerta for a Villa."

Mudslinging became indiscriminate. Even the more righteous Zapata came in for his share of libel and Villa's enemies attempted to undercut all support that Villa and his allies might find in the United States. Propagandists declared that Villa had joined the assassins of Madero, and he and Zapata fought "Constitutionalism not for the good of the people but to resuscitate the accursed old regime."

Just prior to Wilson's recognition of Carranza, it became apparent that the propaganda had done its work against Villa quite effectively. The *carrancistas* came to believe their own propaganda when Enrique Lascurain, a former *huertista*, thanked Carranza for remaining atop of the situation. He asked rhetorically "what would the nation have done had we stayed in the hands of that degenerate being, that vicious assassin Arango [Villa]."

At no time did either Carranza or Villa have total unanimity in their ranks. Villa's adherents, more blunt and direct than the *carrancistas*, often expressed their dissatisfaction with their leader in a more violent manner. As assassination attempt on Villa by one of his own officers was met with gunshots and executions.

Defections from the *villista* ranks began to filter to Carranza's faction. Carranza willingly accepted all help, as did Villa. They were locked in a brutal struggle for survival that could only be met with numerical superiority as well as the best available information.

The seeds of Villa's ignoble descent became obvious in June 1915. His major defeat at León and the increased insensitivity of *villista* officials along the border prompted Zach Cobb to note that the possibility of a Huerta comeback loomed as a major threat. He reported that Huerta showed greater force than many of the Mexican leaders. "He impressed me," wrote Cobb, "as being dangerously sober and resourceful rather than the drunkard he has been pictured. I . . . urge the importance of speedily bringing the better elements with Carranza and Villa together, fearing a collapse soon that would benefit Huerta."

Meanwhile, Carranza's forces closed in on Mexico City and finally reoccupied it in July. The convention had died, and Mexico for a while had no government. Carranza's forces in Mexico City headed by Pablo González presided over chaos until government could be reestablished.

Villa at the same time frantically tried to reorganize his forces from Torreón. With his fiat money now worthless, Villa found himself hard-put to find the fuel to move supplies from one point to another. Graft among military commanders was on the rise, for the anarchy of revolution began to have its effect on those who had risen on the coattails of chaos.

Carothers, however, remained optimistic. He reported that Villa was abundantly aware of conditions and planned sweeping reforms to eliminate the worst problems, including the reorganization of his commercial agency headed by brother Hipólito. "I do not see immediate signs of complete collapse," wrote Carothers. "I cannot see how existing conditions can last much longer without it. If any agreement can be brought about between the revolutionary factions it will have to be done soon or the country will be confronted with anarchy which only military intervention could stop." Even Carothers, probably the most attuned of the U.S. agents in Mexico, began to make interventionist noises.

By August, Villa ran the government from his shirt pocket. His ministers served in name only and only at his caprice. Confiscations and rough treatment of foreigners intensified. Villa's ministers prevailed on Carothers to try to get Villa to modify his actions. But Villa was desperate and broke. His campaign for money to fuel his fight against Carranza pushed him to extreme measures that ultimately backfired on him in his desire to obtain recognition from the United States.

Carothers's reports continued in an increasingly pessimistic tone. He saw conspiracies against Villa headed by some of Villa's closest advisors, including Angeles. Carothers feared that Villa would take bloody reprisals against putative traitors and added that "I myself have been advised . . . to stay out for the present."

The disintegration of Villa's movement in the middle of 1915 contributed to increased pillage by Villa's supporters and subordinates. More devastating for Villa than almost anything that had happened to him was the necessity of executing his *compadre*, Tomás Urbina. Urbina had absconded with millions of pesos from the *villista* treasury. Taking refuge in Las Nieves, Urbina declared that if Villa came after him he would give him a warm welcome with bullets. On September 9, Rodolfo Fierro captured Urbina. No action was taken, however, until Villa arrived. Enraged, Villa ordered the execution of Urbina and fourteen members of his staff on September 10. Gleefully, Fierro carried out the grisly work.

Vida Nueva reported the death of Urbina in Chihuahua City. Consul Letcher chortled that "the death of Urbina removes one of the most ferocious and uncontrollably terrible figures [of the revolution]." Villa's Mexican detractors used Urbina's death as evidence of the bestiality of Francisco Villa, a man who would arbitrarily order the death of his own *compadre*.

Recouping the money taken by Urbina and his cronies served to allay Villa's problems only temporarily. Troops began to defect from Villa as he passed from Chihuahua to Juárez. Villa sought re-

venge through execution and reportedly left a mound of bodies in
Chihuahua City as evidence of his displeasure. Yet Villa did not
take his vengeance on Luis Terrazas, Jr. Terrazas escaped from his
incarceration, was joined by his son Guillermo, and made his way
to the United States. Yet the Terrazas extortion, editorialized
Cobb, typified Villa's actions and was a "black record representative of his [Villa's] highest ideals."

No doubt existed in Cobb's mind about the deterioration of
Villa's army. Yet Villa's real strength lay in the commercial net-
work he had established in the United States, by which he could
obtain arms, ammunition, supplies, and other articles of war and
sell goods such as cattle and sheep — often stolen from Mexico.
"Villa can continue to operate after losing any number of officers,"
opined Cobb, "so long as he is permitted in conjunction with
American and Mexican grafters to market his loot here."

In large measure, the diplomacy that the United States con-
ducted with Villa, especially throughout 1914 and until his defeat
at Celaya, was tempered by some of the proto-terrorist activities in
which Villa engaged. The Benton case was one example. The
United States, operating under the Roosevelt Corollary to the
Monroe Doctrine, became the principal representative of European
powers who had complaints against the revolutionaries. Since the
U.S. had no relations with Huerta, only unofficial representations
could be made. But, as in the case of Benton, the British appealed
to the United States to use its good offices in resolving the problems
surrounding Benton's death.

Spain also used the paternalism of the United States in attempting to protect its citizens. With so many Spaniards seeking
refuge in Texas after the second battle of Torreón, the government
of King Alfonso asked that the United States intervene in order to
protect the interests of Spaniards who had been exiled from Torreón. The United States, however, could only offer to care for Spanish refugees resident on American soil. It could not jeopardize the
interests of its own citizens and the tenuous protections afforded to
Americans living in Mexico by the *villistas*. While representations
were made to Villa, Bryan and Wilson were careful that they did
not offend his own particular sensibilities. Villa's loathing of the
Spanish was more than apparent; too much pressure might provoke more attacks on Spaniards and their properties.

Interestingly enough, the Spanish minister to Mexico, Juan Riaños y Gayangos, had been the principal cause of the Spaniards' misfortunes. He had suggested that they arm themselves against the revolutionaries, and he constantly reported to his government that the *villistas* carried out brutal reprisals against Spaniards. Thus, when King Alfonso's government changed representatives in Mexico, the new agent, Don Manuel Walls y Merino, viewed his assignment with some apprehension.

With Huerta gone and the split between Carranza and Villa now definitive, Walls y Merino attempted to make contact with the fractured elements of what had been Constitutionalism. When Walls y Merino finally talked to Carranza, he described the experience as one that caused his blood to turn cold. This, in turn, increased his apprehension about going to Chihuahua to visit Villa. But as a good servant of his monarch, he embarked on his journey. When Walls y Merino arrived, his fears were laid to rest. Villa saw the need to pacify the Spanish government. He effectively held them in check in those areas under *villista* control. Thus, Villa greeted Walls y Merino in Chihuahua City with assurances of comforts and guarantees. The agent emerged suitably impressed with Villa and so informed his government.

Villa's image notwithstanding, Walls y Merino found a Centaur of the North who was the exact opposite of the rabid hispanophobe who had plagued and terrorized Spaniards in Chihuahua and Torreón. Carranza's offensive treatment of the new Spanish agent gave Villa the opportunity to display a new image to the world. In this he was successful, at least in the short term. According to *Vida Nueva,* Walls y Merino declared that foreign interests would receive all possible protections from Villa and not from Carranza. "From what had been seen," wrote José Fuentes Mares, "Pancho had become the consummate diplomat. . . . Now our Pancho had even become an *'hispanista'.*"

Villa also kept foreign powers, especially the United States, off-balance about Luis Terrazas, Jr. Excessive importunings by U.S. representatives merely angered Villa, and appeals to Carranza only frustrated the United States. Villa effectively carried on his own diplomacy with regard to his major golden hostage.

Unlike modern-day terrorists, Villa approached the capture and retention of Luis Terrazas, Jr., and his persecution of the Spaniards from a strictly nonideological perspective. These were pragmatic situations that required capitalization and not theoretical blandishments. Yet, in both of these instances, Villa demonstrated the quirkiness of his personality. Threats to kill young Terrazas never materialized, and Villa finally allowed some Spaniards to return to Torreón. Even when his fortunes were reversed, Villa did not commit the ultimate atrocity against Terrazas or the Spaniards. An odd sort of compassion characterized Villa in these actions and, if possible, lent a bizarre humanity to this Mexican brand of terrorism.

Villa's failure to obtain recognition from the United States also stemmed from his inability to bring instant stability to areas under his control. Wilson wanted orderly revolution, an odd contradiction in terms. No Mexican revolutionary — Villa, Carranza, Zapata, or Obregón — saw the establishment of order without exacting a modicum of vengeance whenever feasible. When Villa and Zapata occupied Mexico City, the city found itself in precarious condition. Prices were high; stocks of foods and drugs remained in short supply. Charcoal had to be rationed through the police stations, and beggars roamed the streets, many of them merely children. Villa, always compassionate when it came to children, took sixty young beggars and sent them to Chihuahua to be reared and educated at his expense.

Such magnanimity, however, did not forestall the executions of political enemies in Mexico. In part, Villa mixed personal vendetta with political expediency and was prompted along this course by Fierro and other, less squeamish, advisors.

Villa further tarnished his image through the peremptory way in which he treated the *gente decente,* the respectable folk. When he first took Guadalajara in December 1914, he addressed a meeting of the better folk on December 18. The assembled citizens of that town were not happy when they came out of the meeting. According to the U.S. consul in Guadalajara, Villa claimed not to seek higher office for himself but only wanted the restoration of order and justice. He warned them, wrote Consul W. B. Davis, "that a government exclusively for the rich classes . . . was forever at an end — that this was as sure as God reigned in Heaven." He promised strong reprisals if those assembled did not come up with one million pesos to pay for revolutionary expenses. One man who left the meeting cried out that Villa *"no es más que otro chingado intentado para encharnos a la calle* [Villa is just another son-of-a-bitch who wants to throw us into the streets]."

Lack of military and political stability in those parts of Mexico under *villista* control further undermined Villa's argument about his actual influence over the country. Currency devaluation and the conflicting claims of the different currencies for validity indicated a fragile fiscal policy. Fiat money from one side was not accepted by another.

Not all reports to reach Woodrow Wilson were negative. In March 1915, Duval West sent positive impressions of Villa's governance of Chihuahua. West saw that Villa maintained order fairly in his territories, though the military courts used for this purpose often handed out summary justice. West hedged a bit and said that, should the United States grant recognition to Villa, the real problem lay in Villa's total disregard for laws, property, and women.

The Centaur's real decline, however, came with Celaya. His money dropped in value, prices for staple goods spiraled, and Villa had to bring pressure to bear on foreign companies for forced loans or use outright extortion. Villa's fiat money was easily counterfeited. He launched a campaign of reprisal against those passing counterfeit currency and argued that the United States needed to exercise some control over the banknote companies who manufactured bogus currency. In all fairness, however, it was extremely difficult to distinguish real fiat money from phony fiat money.

The consequences of this difficulty came with the need to revalidate currency at different intervals. In Sonora, for example, one Chinese merchant took his money for revalidation and it was done promptly. Yet when Villa arrived in Hermosillo he called for all money to be brought back for another revalidation. The Chinaman soon had his cash declared counterfeit.

Loss of value of Villa's money was reflected in prices. In Chihuahua City in June 1915, for example, Villa ordered that state currency be accepted at a value of sixty centavos silver per peso paper. Villa also fixed prices. Coffee could be no higher than four pesos per kilogram, while sugar was limited to two pesos per kilo. Fixed prices also applied to flour, rice, wheat, and beans. Villa tried to assure the availability of foodstuffs to all classes in Chihuahua. He also decreed that those merchants who hoarded merchandise would be jailed. Without these decrees, Villa feared that runaway inflation would leave his people devastated. However, he was not wholly successful in keeping his currency problems from getting out of hand.

By September 1915, Villa poured products onto the El Paso market. Cattle, bullion, ores, and cotton came into the United States. Carothers feared that the El Paso courts might attach these properties in order to restore them to former owners. Given Villa's frame of mind, the possibility existed that Villa might even raid El Paso.

Villa failed to gain recognition from the United States. While he tried to institute decent government in those parts of Mexico under his control, the factional rivalries even among his allies undercut all efforts to achieve some unanimity. Some of his commanders loathed the idea of land reform on the scale envisioned by the *zapatistas*. They bristled when the convention formed a National Agrarian Commission. Villa saw land reform as something to be done on a regional and state basis. Carranza hoped to wean away some *zapatistas* by issuing land reform decrees in early 1915, and Villa himself lobbied a moribund convention in June for reasonable land reform laws.

All of Villa's good intentions did not help him with Woodrow Wilson. The chaos of revolution was attributed to Villa's essentially bestial character. Yet Wilson implicitly seemed to favor the northern chieftain over Carranza. The fickleness of Wilson's behavior would have profound consequences for Mexico and the United States.

CHAPTER X

"The common enemy of Mexicans"

Venustiano Carranza received recognition from the United States, and Pancho Villa again turned to the hills. He intended to recoup and continue the struggle against the people who had betrayed him and those who now dominated Mexico. The radical change in status suffered by Villa unquestionably altered the condition under which he would wage war against his enemies. Villa became a man possessed to drive Carranza out of power, despite the numbers of nations that were aligned with the bearded aristocrat.

Villa's altered state vis-á-vis the United States appreciably modified the means by which he would acquire ammunition and the other necessities of war. Smuggling, extortion, theft — any means would be acceptable, provided the protracted battle against Carranza could continue, for Villa's honor had suffered a severe blow. His previously benign attitude toward the United States became malignant as he nurtured a sense of betrayal and personal hurt.

On October 19, when the United States granted Carranza recognition, Villa was already heading toward Sonora to deal with Calles and other *carrancista* supporters there. The journey was arduous; the División del Norte suffered from a reduced number of men and pack animals. Yet shortages only made the remaining *villistas* work all the harder. With success they took two batteries of artillery across high peaks and prepared to do battle in Sonora against the hated Calles.

The United States, however, began to take steps rather quickly to stop Villa from defeating Carranza. With the recognition announcement, Zach Cobb recommended the complete closure of the port of El Paso-Juárez "to his loot and cancelling his privilege of entering the Juárez packinghouse." The *carrancista* consul in El Paso predicted that, with the increased tempo of Constitutionalist military activity, Villa would not last long. Recognition of Carranza would give Mexico peace at last. Mexico's El Paso consul joyfully reported the prohibition on contraband destined for El Paso through Juárez, though the stipulation that goods had to be released if their duty was paid within three days slightly marred the initial reaction to the news. Thus, within three days after recognition, the United States took its first decisive steps against Villa.

Villa, however, did not suffer from universal opprobrium along the border. In Brownsville, Villa had some supporters who complained bitterly to the Department of State about the Carranza recognition. Wrote one county official: "It is Carrancistas who have murdered and robbed along the Rio Grande. If embargo is beneficial along Villista territory, we feel that it would prove equally so here against Carrancistas whose outrages have been much greater and appeal to you to include this border." Like so much of the United States, the lower Río Grande Valley and most of the Southwest found itself divided as to who should receive official sanction from Washington.

Bureaucratic regulation made the prohibition against the sale of livestock in the United States difficult to enforce. One week following recognition, *villistas* continued to sell sheep and cattle in El Paso. Cobb surmised that threats to livestock owners about the fate of their remaining herds obtained owner cooperation. The secretary of agriculture noted that the acts of Congress that regulated the importation of cattle aimed primarily at the curtailment of livestock disease. "These acts," he wrote, "refer rather to the animal than to the owner or shipper." Consequently, the Department of Agriculture had no authority to "establish, by regulation or otherwise, a distinction between shippers, favorable to Americans and others in Mexico not engaged in the continuance of the Revolution and unfavorable to those who are so engaged." Thus, as long as Villa could keep the cattle clean that came into the U.S. through his aegis, there existed no means to stop him from obtaining money in this fashion.

Villa's long and arduous drive into Sonora had as its objective the defeat of Calles at Agua Prieta. If he could drive Calles out, he could effectively break the *carrancistas* back in northwestern Mexico. Villa prepared to lay siege to Agua Prieta, situated directly across the border from Douglas, Arizona.

Calles — no military genius in the mold of Obregón, Villa, or Angeles — still possessed sufficient perspicacity to recognize that the only way to defeat Villa was to make him come to the attack. Barbed wire and deep trenches surrounded Agua Prieta on three sides. Additionally, Carranza became a legatee of United States recognition rather quickly. He was allowed to pass troops (unarmed), matériel, and medical supplies from El Paso through United States territory to Douglas and thus provide Calles with much-needed men and supplies. Woodrow Wilson had made the decision for Carranza. Rightly or wrongly, he would now support Carranza. If it meant an open, overt action like permitting passage through United States territory, it would happen.

When Villa began his raid on Agua Prieta, a strong sense of *déjà vu* pervaded the engagement. While stolid Calles learned from Celaya, mercurial Villa did not. Again he poured men and equipment directly at the barbed wire and machine guns. Proximity to United States territory, however, hampered Villa. He could only direct his artillery in an east-west direction, fearing that northbound shells might land in the United States and cause retaliation.

Again Villa suffered a massacre. The utter mangling of his forces by Calles's concealed machine guns forced the *villistas* to retreat. After dark on November 1 and into the early hours of November 2, the *villistas* tried again to crush Calles. Unfortunately, Calles also prepared for this contingency. Bright, blinding floodlights powered by United States generators illuminated the *villistas* and made them more ready targets for the Constitutionalist machine guns.

Devastated, mortally wounded, and spiritually flattened, the *villistas* were forced to retreat. Villa and about 3,000 men made their way toward Naco, hoping to gain control there of a border town that could be used as a base of operations. At the same time, the manager of the Cananea Copper Company dispatched two doctors to care for wounded *villistas*. Villa at first was delighted with the unplanned-for medical assistance. His joy, however, soon turned to anger, for at this juncture he learned that the United States had allowed *carrancista* troops to cross to Agua Prieta through El Paso. Consequently, Villa imprisoned the two doctors and accused them of being spies. For several days he ritually took them out of incarceration and ordered their execution. At the last minute, he would grant them a reprieve. Managers at Cananea offered to pay Villa $25,000 in "taxes" if he would release the doctors. When he finally let them go to make their own way to the border, the two doctors suffered from exhaustion and exposure. One of them died as a result of the harsh treatment.

Villa still needed a base of operations safe from the reaches of Carranza. He looked toward Hermosillo as such a base and sent money to Maytorena to purchase arms. Maytorena, however, proved to be the slippery opportunist that his detractors said he was. He fled the country with the money and made his way to the United States. When Villa arrived in Hermosillo, Angel Flores and Manuel Diéguez had occupied the town for Carranza. On November 15, Villa made an unsuccessful attempt to take the capitol of Sonora.

Villa tried to soften up lukewarm *carrancistas* with some blustering accusations of his own. Before attempting to take Hermosillo, Villa declared that Carranza had sold the country to the *gringos* for a loan. He further accused Carranza of giving to the Yankees the right to regulate the Mexican economy and body politic through the appointment of officials amenable to United States direction. Villa further questioned the naiveté of the *gringos* if they really believed that Carranza could give them any guarantees whatever about the protection of foreign interests in Mexico. Villa genuinely believed that Carranza and Wilson had made such an agreement. While no evidence exists about such a pact, Villa's assumption remained reasonable. Pushed by his own sense of betrayal and his personal loathing of Carranza, Villa saw in these two men the utter loss of the ideals of the Mexican revolution.

Villistas throughout northern Mexico saw that their cause had been devastated. Many operated independently of Villa's peripatetic command and continued to traffic in stolen goods. They still ran cattle into the United States, making handsome profits as they decimated what were once vast herds in northern Mexico. El Paso remained the center of *villista* activity even after October 19. Active and former *villistas* continued to congregate in El Paso and hatch plots for the overthrow of Carranza. George Carothers, former *villista* sympathizer and special agent from Woodrow Wilson, had now changed his view. He saw the elimination of Villa and his supporters as an absolute imperative of American policy. Carothers's new tune chorused that Villa "should be eliminated as quickly as possible, as he is a menace and could never rehabilitate himself in Mexico." Additionally, Villa adherents wanted to start up a new party in conjunction with the old Catholic Party and with the Madero family as a means of regaining power. Villa would become a member of the party and would have a military command, but he would be politically subordinate to others more appropriately trained.

The United States remained cagey throughout the rest of 1915. While it supported Carranza, Wilson feared that any shipment of arms to the Constitutionalists might be intercepted by the *villistas* and thus give Villa even more power. Carranza's need for matériél continued to nag, and in mid-December, Wilson relented when he permitted the shipment of two million rounds of ammunition to Carranza through El Paso and Nogales. His final criterion became that "these munitions of war will reach their destinations in safety, and that they are not used to promote conditions of domestic disorder, but are intended for the protection of life and property in Mexico." Probably because he had to, Wilson chose to believe that Carranza actually intended to continue guarantees to foreigners in a country seized by nationalist revolt.

By the end of the year, Villa again became nothing more than a regional bandit leader. His thousands of men became but a few hundred. Many of his best commanders had died or defected; friends were dead. Urbina had betrayed Villa and suffered the ultimate penalty. Fierro also died, but unlike Urbina, Fierro's death resulted from the arrogance of the man and not from his venality.

Fierro drowned in Lake Guzmán as he led troops from Juárez to Sonora. His troops were afraid to cross the lake; Fierro called them all cowards and commanded that they see how a man handled water. Weighted down by a money belt, Fierro sank out of sight. Not one of the men moved to succor him. Fierro, the most frightening of Villa's subordinates, died unloved except by Villa.

Villa demanded the recovery of the body. When the body arrived the money belt was still in place, and Villa used the money to reward those who had brought Fierro to shore.

Frustrated, reduced to little influence, ignobly treated, Villa still dreamed of a comeback. He began to plan for a means by which he could make a daring and flashy attack and humiliate both Carranza and the United States. His followers also shared his sense of frustration and betrayal. *Villistas* crossed the international boundary in December and threatened Americans. On December 21, just before abandoning Juárez to Obregón, *villista* troops willfully fired into El Paso and killed a railway inspector. United States troops massed at the border, but Obregón's forces soon took over before the U.S. could actually intervene.

The flight of *villistas* from Juárez came about as a result of negotiations between Silvestre Terrazas and other Villa adherents and the Constitutionalist consul, Andrés García, in El Paso. The terms read that all *villista* troops who surrendered would receive amnesty, provided they pledged allegiance to the Constitutionalists. Villa, however, would be exempt from any amnesty agreement. Those troops that fired into El Paso were hard-core *villistas* who refused any such agreement. When Obregón arrived in Juárez, Villa left Chihuahua with 800 men. His destination was unknown. At this point Villa began to plan his grand coup against both Carranza and the United States.

Villa had hoped to reestablish himself in Chihuahua. Again he had harped on the sellout theme of earlier declarations. He continued to accuse Carranza of turning the country over to the United States and accused Leon Canova of plotting with *huertistas* for the conversion of Mexico into a United States protectorate. Such bloody-shirt tactics failed even in Chihuahua, Villa's principal stronghold. Mexico had tired of political histrionics and of the flamboyant accusations of one *caudillo* against another. Pancho had been the darling of the north, but the general population was not quick to forgive the failures at Celaya, León, and Agua Prieta. The surrender of *villistas* at Juárez merely reflected the exhaustion of a people after seven years of fratricide, pillage, and social and economic devastation. Now, perhaps, Mexico could have some peace.

Such a hope, however, was couched in guarded terms. As on other occasions when Villa prepared to wage all-out war against his enemies, he sent his women into safety. On December 20 many of his family, including Luz Corral de Villa, the widow of his brother Antonio, his sister Martina, and children from these different families including some of Villa's from another wife, set sail for Cuba. Villa hoped to join them. Cobb, sitting in El Paso, misread the signs, for Villa now prepared for a last desperate gamble that might catapult him back into prominence.

Inability of United States officials to keep track of Villa's movements caused increasing tension along the border at the end of 1915. In El Paso and Ciudad Juárez, Cobb saw conditions as extremely tense. Some rioting in the few days before Christmas and the arrest of Hipólito Arango over a conflict with Victor Carusoe forced Cobb to conclude that "it is wiser while General Villa remains in Mexico for the Government not to arrest H. Villa here." The possible arrest and incarceration of Hipólito convinced Cobb that Villa would mercilessly sack El Paso and Juárez.

The advent of 1916 did not decrease the preoccupation along the border with what Villa intended to do. Officials in the United States continued to worry over the use of El Paso as a means of supplying Villa with money, arms, ammunition, and other war matériél. The United States Senate, in a resolution, asked the president and his cabinet for all information that would illuminate the possibility of closing El Paso to *villista* commerce. Since meat continued to be a principal source of income, Lansing duly informed the Senate that no *villista* meat was prohibited entry to the United States except when specific USDA standards were not met.

While U.S. officials worried and fretted over Villa's intentions, the wily Centaur continued to regroup his forces in Mexico. In Chihuahua, he moved on to the Babícora holdings that belonged to William Randolph Hearst. In so doing, he underscored to his *gringo* antagonists that Carranza was in no position to protect them from *villista* wrath.

Villa's newfound antagonism to *gringos* in Chihuahua specifically and to the United States in general infected his followers. No longer did United States citizens in Villa-held territory enjoy any of the former immunities extended to them by a now angered *guerrillero*. Blindly, *villistas* struck out at all Americans who represented the odious *gringo* presence in Mexico. Carranza meanwhile had issued assurances that all foreign investors residing in Mexico would receive ample protection. Unfortunately for some members of the Cusi Mining Company, they believed Carranza.

In early January, Charles Watson, the general manager of Cusi, arrived in El Paso with substantial quantities of gold for the express purpose of reopening the mining operation near Cusihuiriáchic. From El Paso he traveled to Chihuahua City, where he was joined by American members of his staff and their Mexican assistants. There they boarded a train and headed westward. Near Santa Ysabel, the train was stopped on January 17. Mexican rebels led by Col. Pablo López boarded the train and herded the American mining personnel systematically out of the railroad cars. Maliciously, López selected two men as executioners and proceeded to kill seventeen American mining engineers. Shouts of *¡Viva Villa!* and *Death to the Gringos!* were punctuated with rifle shots. Only one American escaped.

Villa denied any involvement in the Santa Ysabel massacre. He personally swore to execute the perpetrators of the massacre. The Centaur, however, could not duck the ultimate responsibility, for the murders at Santa Ysabel were carried out in his name.

The effect of the killings along the border exacerbated an already tense situation. With the return of the bodies of the murdered men, a huge demonstration in El Paso almost caused the destruction of South El Paso, the Mexican district (called Little Chihuahua), that was stopped at gunpoint and federal troops. Martial law was proclaimed and a curfew imposed. Armed intervention became the cry along the border and among those members of Congress who represented border districts. United States citizens residing in Mexico actually welcomed the massacre as a means of provoking armed intervention by the United States. But the United States did not intervene; its dreams of a romantic bandit-hero named Villa were quickly terminated, but there was no intervention.

Increasingly, however, throughout February 1916, Mexicans living in the United States became subjected to harassment and actual physical violence by supposed law enforcement officers along the border. Hunting Mexicans almost became an acceptable pastime for Rangers and deputies with time on their hands. Such action undoubtedly increased the tension along the border and provoked anti-*gringo* actions on the part of Villa and other rebels.

Santa Ysabel, in a sense, marked the formal termination of Villa's attempt at cordiality with the United States. From this point forward, he remained the implacable enemy of the *gringo* who had betrayed him and had attempted to manipulate him for vague philosophical ends. Carefully, Villa planned reprisals. On January 8 he dispatched a letter to Zapata asking him to join in an alliance against all Americans in Mexico. He also sent couriers to all sections of Mexico asking for vengeance against the hated *gringo*. Villa's pitch became that the *gringo* was the "common enemy of Mexicans."

Without the friendship of the United States, Villa cast about for a new source of funding for his continued campaign against Carranza and now Americans. War in Europe left United States officials in Mexico uneasy about what the Germans were doing with regard to Villa. The death of Huerta in early January 1916 took away the German hope for a pro-German Mexico. Villa, who seemed now strongly anti-U.S., encouraged the Germans in their belief that Mexico would be in the German corner, should he be triumphant. Marion Letcher, Villa's antagonist in the U.S. Consulate in Chihuahua, reported that German interests in northern Mexico increasingly looked to Villa to protect them from "such hardships as might be visited upon Americans in the course of [his] campaign of destruction and massacre."

Independent action by different groups loyal to Villa extended to the oilfields in and around Tampico. In early February 1916, *villista* forces routed the *carrancistas* in the oilfields. Extortion and the demand for payment of taxes by the oil producers provided yet another source of income for the *villistas*. Oil producers were forced to pay taxes backdated to January 1, 1916, if they wanted to avoid unpleasantness with the now victorious *villistas*.

A month after Santa Ysabel, Villa controlled the area of Chihuahua that bordered on Columbus, New Mexico. The somnolent border town of Palomas lay directly south of Columbus, and Villa used this out-of-the-way port as a staging area for his men. Villa kept the *gringos* guessing. His emissaries were reported in Japan and then back again, helping Villa prepare for a continuation of his dual campaigns against Carranza and the United States.

Villa now controlled the border area west of Juárez. No longer did he attempt to mask his movements. Instead, Villa openly led his troops for all to see, assured that Carranza's forces were too few to give any kind of pursuit. Cobb reported on March 8 that troop shortages and lack of enthusiasm by the *carrancista* garrisons in Chihuahua gave Villa *carte blanche* in the north.

On March 7, Villa stopped south of Columbus and rounded up cattle belonging to the Palomas Land and Cattle Company.

These cattle, however, were not sold but became a source of provisions for his mobile force of 400 men. No one knew what Villa would do next.

Mexicans and Americans did not have long to wait, for Villa graphically illustrated what he would do. At about 4:30 A.M. on March 9, 1916, Francisco Villa crossed the United States border and led a lightning strike against Columbus, New Mexico. Shouts of *¡Viva Villa!* and *Death to the Gringos!* again provided counterpoint for the sounds of small-arms fire as Villa's men charged through the town, setting fire to the principal buildings of the area. Three American soldiers from the small garrison outside of town were killed, as well as four civilians. Several soldiers, rousted from their sacks, were injured and so were a handful of civilians. The soldiers, caught unprepared, still gave pursuit to the fleeing *villistas* and actually crossed the border into Mexico. The attack by Villa provoked the soldiers. In their pursuit of the *villistas*, they took no prisoners.

George Carothers now saw Villa as an unleashed animal. "Villa and his men are half crazed," reported Carothers, "and constantly make absurd statements that they intend conquering the United States." Villa's next moves defied anticipation, though it could be assumed that he still planned to continue his campaign of depredation and reprisal against Americans in Chihuahua. Cobb seconded Carothers's views. "This massacre," wired Carothers to Lansing, "like that at Santa Ysabel, is a murder of commission by Villistas and omission by Carranzistas who have lacked both strength and sufficient effort to adequately go after Villa." No doubt remained in Cobb's mind that "it is the duty of our government to now require respect for our people. National honor can make no stronger appeal than is now made that our people shall not be foresaken." Intervention, though reluctantly recommended, became the only answer to assure American safety in Mexico.

Gen. John J. Pershing prepared his forces in the event of an all-out effort against Villa. Pershing wanted to know if the Mexican government would accept the help of the United States in the pursuit and capture of Villa and his men. By March 10, 5,000 men began to concentrate around Columbus. While making no claim about intervention, military leaders in the United States clearly wanted to get Villa.

Carranza actually feared the possibility of United States intervention, for such an action could unseat the First Chief from his precarious perch. He quickly apologized to the United States for the attack and pledged renewed efforts to control the *villistas* and ultimately destroy them. Wilson, however, could no longer listen to empty apologies from Carranza. No pledge of renascent effort by the Constitutionalists could keep Wilson from venting his moral outrage at the attack on Columbus. By March 10, Wilson ordered that a punitive expedition be sent to capture or disperse the *villista* forces. Wilson quickly noted that such an action did not impugn Mexican sovereignty; the expedition merely aimed to assist Mexico in controlling its undesirable elements. Quick action by Wilson in ordering up troops outraged Carranza.

Carranza had earlier replied that any similar acts by Villa along the border would constitute reason enough for the United States to send in troops. When he heard of American forces gathering at Columbus, he changed his attitude. Carranza ordered northern forces to do everything possible to impede American entry into Mexico, though nothing should be done that would rupture relations with the United States.

Pershing faced a monumental task of pulling together a fighting force from an ill-prepared standing army. National Guard units complemented the contingents sent to the border. Yet, within a week, United States troops moved in two columns into Mexico to pursue Villa.

Such action by the United States did not sit well with Carranza. He saw the Pershing expedition as an invasion of Mexico and sent 2,500 men under Gen. Luis Gutiérrez north to establish order. Carranza argued that under the terms of the treaty of reciprocity, worked out in the 1870s between the United States and Mexico, Mexico also had the right of hot pursuit of *villistas* into the United States. Carranza further averred that only in the event of another *villista* invasion of the United States could American troops enter Mexico. His arguments were of no avail. Pershing ordered the columns into Mexico.

Carranza fumed impotently. He accused the United States of intervention, noting that "the Mexican Government cannot but wonder at the fact that the said troops should have crossed the boundary line and entered our territory without previous agreement, official communication, or notice of any kind and reached [Casas Grandes] which is much more distant from the boundary line than any other point. . . ." Again he demanded the removal of American troops from Mexico.

Villa now faced twin enemies: the Punitive Expedition and augmented *carrancistas*. Villa tried to keep out of sight. Though not ducking a fight, Villa knew that he could not dissipate his forces. When the opportunity presented itself, he would join battle. On March 31, after eluding Pershing for two weeks, Villa laid waste a troop of *carrancistas* at Guerrero, Chihuahua. While militarily successful, Villa received a severe leg wound that forced him into hiding for most of the spring.

Pershing's troops operated in hostile territory. While the citizens of Chihuahua no longer supported Villa overtly, sentimentally they remained with the Centaur. They continued to give emotional backing to the man who had risen to virtual stardom in the revolution and now needed their support. No help was forthcoming to either Pershing or the *carrancistas* that attempted to stop Villa.

With Villa wounded and his troops dispersed after Guerrero, *villista* sentiment became diffuse. On April 12, Americans and *carrancistas* tangled at Parral, Chihuahua. Several Mexicans and one American lost their lives. Restraint did prevail as *carrancista* authorities attempted to calm the indignant citizens of Parral over the United States presence. Popular indignation over Yankee presence spread to the *carrancista* troops that garrisoned Parral. Shouts of *¡Viva Villa!* came from Mexican soldiers. Obregón, now secretary of war, raged that such action was tantamount to treason. He ordered the military commander of Chihuahua that "if such soldiers are thus shouting *vivas* for Villa, they should be summarily shot. To hope victory for such a bandit is a high criminal act."

The *villista* raid on Columbus also prolonged the disturbed conditions in Chihuahua City. Fear of a *villista* conspiracy in Chihuahua itself resulted in the imprisonment of a number of *villista* civilians by the *carrancista* authorities. In large measure, the unsettled social and economic conditions prevalent in Chihuahua contributed to the tense ambience. Severe fiscal problems plagued the city. Prices for goods had doubled, provided they were paid for in silver, and paper currency stood in value at about twenty to one. Clearly unsettled times still remained very much a part of Villa country.

Though Carranza sulked and tried everything short of an open break, he did agree to allow Obregón to meet with Generals Frederick Funston and Hugh Scott at El Paso at the end of April. Their meetings attempted to cement relations between Washington and Carranza in order to subdue Villa. At El Paso, both sides agreed that the Pershing expedition would begin leaving Mexico at an unspecified date. Carranza, however, still wanting to pin down the United States, remained an obstacle to settlement.

Pershing's forces desperately searched for Villa and his men. *Carrancistas* captured the notorious Pablo López and wounded him. He faced a firing squad while standing on crutches. Then Lt. George Patton captured and killed three Mexicans, among them the commander of Villa's *dorados,* Julio Cárdenas. On May 25, Candelario Cervantes, probably the most able of Villa's remaining men, fell to American guns.

But these successes proved too few and too isolated. The capture of Villa himself eluded Pershing. Beset by political agreements, Pershing found himself increasingly restricted in his actions. By early June, he could no longer progress southward. Carranza had ordered that any southward progress would result in attack by Mexican forces. In mid-June the Punitive Expedition suffered a devastating defeat by *carrancista* forces at Carrizal. From this point forward, it became a matter of extricating Pershing from Mexico with some degree of honor. The Punitive Expedition had been neutralized.

Along the border, meanwhile, the fear remained that Villa would make yet another strike into United States territory. Citizens of Langtry, Texas, petitioned Funston for additional protection. Hugh Scott, however, noted the grievous condition of most American forces and replied that no relief could be given. Apologetically he told the secretary of war,

> General Funston . . . is sick with apprehension over safety of border in which I consider he is justified. . . . We also believe that all munitions of war now held up in border customshouses should be removed away . . . to points in [the] interior not subject to attack and preparation be made now to keep munitions from entering Mexico through any port or across any frontier.

Villa's wound, while severe, did not keep him in perpetual isolation or at least Villa allowed rumors to circulate that he was again on the move. He was reported around Canutillo and Parral in July 1916, and the news of his recuperation sent shivers through United States and Mexican officialdom. In mid-July, Villa had a reunion with some of his old commanders, and they began to regroup. Estimates of as high as 7,000 men coming together under Villa and his subordinates gave a degree of pause to those who wanted to extend Constitutionalist hegemony over Mexico. Carothers, no longer in intimate contact with Villa but still receiving information about him, reported that great numbers were defecting from Carranza. "This is increased by the fact that Villa," wrote Carothers, "clips off one-half of the right ear of prisoners taken in battle as punishment but pardons those who voluntarily join him." Revivified, cocky again, Villa promised his followers that they would celebrate September 16 (Mexican Independence Day) in Chihuahua City.

Throughout the summer, Pershing found himself and his men hounded by restrictions. His men could not prosecute the campaign effectively, Villa remained at large and was apparently recuperating from his wound at Guerrero, and Carranza remained adamantly opposed to the presence of the United States in Mexico.

No question remained in Villa's mind about his intentions. Publicly he proclaimed his plans to retake Chihuahua City. By September 13, three days before the projected attack, *villista* infiltrators worked their way into the city in order to make the conquest by Villa more effective. Villa lived up to his pledge. On September 16, accompanied by approximately 1,000 men, Villa began his attack on Chihuahua City. Eight hours of bloody fighting saw many *villistas* killed, but also saw Villa emerge triumphant in his recapture of the city. From horseback, the *villistas* fought in the patios of government buildings. Bloody hand-to-hand combat inflicted heavy damages on both sides. By the end of the day, Villa capped off one of the bloodiest encounters of the revolution with a harangue of the populace.

Villa admitted that he could not hold the city with the forces he had immediately available. Also, he confessed to being unable to ameliorate the poor conditions in the city and thus would not retain control of the state capital. He did, however, announce that he planned to return after seizing Juárez. In short, he assured his followers that Pancho Villa still remained a force with which Carranza and his goons would have to reckon.

Government reaction to Villa's pronouncements came instantaneously. Gen. Jacinto Treviño declared that all citizens found with arms in their possession would be summarily shot. Moreover, no passenger train had gone north to Juárez since September 20. A curfew was imposed, but the government showed little inclination to go after Villa with any kind of gusto. From Juárez, the United States consul offered the view that Carranza officials in Chihuahua showed great reluctance to pursue Villa with any vigor. "They are making too much money out of the situation," he opined. Consul Edwards declared that much of the money was going into officers' pockets, which resulted in missed payrolls and greater and greater numbers of defections to Villa.

Villa augmented his forces when he captured Chihuahua on September 16. He proceeded to unlock the doors to the state penitentiary and release political prisoners, most of whom were *villista* sympathizers. Thus augmented with former prisoners and with *carrancista* defectors, Villa again attacked Chihuahua on November 23, holding it until December 7, when a large relief column threatened the *villista* position.

Villa, however, was not through with his bravado. If he could take Chihuahua, why not Torreón? On Christmas Eve, he fell on the unsuspecting town and effectively rendered it. Gen. Severiano Talamantes, the *carrancista* commander at Torreón, could not face Carranza and preferred suicide to the First Chief's wrath. Villa carried with him fond memories of the richness of Torreón. He repeated his action of two years past, extracting a forced loan from the leading citizens of the town, and disappeared to the north.

Villa remained at large. By January 1917, the Punitive Expedition was removed from Mexico. Earlier, in December, National Guard units were released from border duty. Pershing and his men, while failing in their attempt to capture Villa, still kept him sufficiently off balance to give some respite to the *carrancistas*.

But the ultimate aim of the expedition — the capture of Villa — rankled American pride. Villa's flirtation with Germany and the possibility of a Japanese alliance made United States citizens aware of Mexico as a major problem in United States world relations. Rumors about Villa's movements — whether true or merely fabricated by fear and lack of information — forced one United States citizen in Ovando, Montana, to write the attorney general's office complaining that "as Villa is said to be on his way to Japan and as the U.S. Extradition Treaty with that country, why can't you cable Japan to arrest the murderer and hold him for the United States? Villa, being the leader of a lot of murderers, does not exempt him from arrest . . . and give him the right to kill Americans or Europeans."

Villa's attack on Columbus, New Mexico, provoked widespread opposition to his position in Mexico by the United States. Once the darling of the United States press, Villa now received the characterization of assassin. In large measure, Villa acted impulsively. His sense of betrayal led him to irrational acts, for he did not calculate the long-term consequences of his raid. In all probability the attack on Columbus was a means of getting arms and ammunition. Reimposition of an arms embargo on Mexico made the supply of armaments difficult to obtain.

By now, Villa trusted no foreigners. Germany tried to influence him and to purchase his loyalty, and Villa, like a good negotiator, led them on in order to have some source of income for his forces. German citizens in Chihuahua felt the relief of pressure from Villa, but there is no direct evidence that Villa was in the pay of Germany.

Vanity if nothing else led Villa to Columbus. The idea of oblivion did not appeal to the man who had dominated the Mexican scene for so long. Villa struck Columbus forcefully. Setbacks later on in the year only allowed him to regroup his forces. Two seizures of Chihuahua City and then the takeover of Torreón proved to both Carranza and the United States that Pancho Villa still remained a force in northern Mexico. Any final settlement of Mexico's problems would require the acquiescence of Pancho Villa.

CHAPTER XI

Stalemate
and Peace

Nothing of the defeated general surrounded Villa's mien as he entered Chihuahua City with an escort of over fifty men in December 1920. The legendary leader of the División del Norte continued to possess the magnetism and courage of the preceding decade. Villa was now forty-two years old; a decade of fighting against the Huerta usurpation, the quarrel with Carranza, his invasion of the United States, and, finally, nearly four years of defensive and often frustrating action forced Villa to reach some accord with his enemies. But his entrance into Chihuahua City carried with it the implied threat that Villa could again take to the hills *(echarse al monte)* should the need ever arise.

Villa's entrance into Chihuahua two days before Christmas 1920 began as an inspection of mining properties in and around Guerrero. For about a week Villa remained in Chihuahua City. He visited Manuel Pereyra, a former member of Urbina's troops, and threatened and intimidated him. Believing that Pereyra knew of the location of monies taken by Urbina shortly before Villa apprehended his *compadre,* Villa had him summarily shot.

In large measure, Villa's boldness came from the continued support that the populace of Chihuahua extended to him. Defeats notwithstanding, Villa persisted as an autochthonous hero to the

chihuahuenses. His peaceful *entrée* into Chihuahua City came from
what the United States consul believed to be a "unique relationship" between Villa and Gen. Eugenio Martínez, commander of
the Federal División del Norte. Throughout Chihuahua there persisted the idea that Martínez proved "only too anxious to do Villa's
bidding. I have recently heard," continued the consul, ". . . that
General Martínez appears in the role of personal servant receiving
orders from Villa instead of giving them." Four years would pass
before Villa could enter Chihuahua City without soldiers scurrying
from their barracks and without the populace drawing the shutters
in order to avoid stray bullets that could easily eliminate the overly
curious and the foolhardy.

Disruption of Villa's forces by Pershing's misconceived expedition into Mexico in 1916 did not eliminate totally the threat that
Villa posited to both the United States and the bearded aristocrat
in Mexico City. Villa continued to rally support around his opposition to Carranza. Rumors abounded that German interests kept
Villa's movement viable and that German interests in Chihuahua
and in Mexico in general acted as advisors and directors of *villista*
opposition to the United States and Carranza.

Support for Villa caused a lack of enthusiasm in Chihuahua
for the constitutional convention that Carranza called in Querétaro
in December 1916. Chihuahua was woefully underrepresented.
Momentous decisions would be reached at Querétaro that affected
land reform, foreign ownership of property, education, the role of
the church, and political reform; but Chihuahua would have little
voice, for Villa controlled the countryside. No elections for delegates to the constitutional convention were held in most Chihuahua
districts. Thus, when a new constitution emerged on February 1,
1917 — probably the most sweeping constitutional document in the
world at the time — Chihuahua lacked input. Additionally, Carranza could not with good conscience claim that he controlled the
country, for the largest state of the republic still paid its first allegiance to its nearly mythical hero, Pancho Villa, and denied Carranza the unanimity that he publicly alleged. *Villista* organization,
though much reduced, remained viable.

Nine months after Villa struck Columbus, *villista* machinery in
El Paso regained strength and organization. More brazen than
ever, Villa's sympathizers openly solicited funds and found ways to

deliver ordnance to their leader. Active agents in El Paso continually worked with counterparts in Ciudad Juárez including, Cobb suspected, the *carrancista* commander of the Juárez garrison. "These Mexicans," reported Cobb, "whose mode of reasoning is different from ours, are assuming that they will not be interfered with by our government."

Villista organization in Juárez and El Paso, however, proved ephemeral. Consistent supplies did not reach Villa as they had in the past, and he was forced to resort to other means of acquiring ammunition for his men.

Villa's attractiveness to women was legendary in Mexico. From stately matrons in Saltillo to prostitutes along the border and in major cities of northern Mexico, the name of Francisco Villa brought about images and fantasies of the ruthless satyr, destroying feminine defenses and working his evil ways on their persons. In November 1916 the United States consul in Durango noted that Villa and his agents in that town successfully organized prostitutes as a means of acquiring much-needed ammunition. Federal soldiers, woefully arrears in their pay, could not afford cash money for a prostitute. Yet they had plenty of ammunition to pay for a bit of whorish ecstasy. Consequently, hookers who serviced federal soldiers charged an undetermined number of bullets for fleeting, momentary thrills.

Almost two years later, women continued to act as agents for *villista* arms procurement. Without having to prostitute themselves, female friends recruited by Villa's agents openly purchased ammunition from soldiers stationed in Juárez. Cautiously limiting their purchases to no more than ten rounds, the women quietly paid two cents apiece for the Mauser bullets. Carranza's soldiers continued without pay, and, as long as they could avoid detection, they willingly sold their ammunition to the *villistas*. One woman without too much difficulty acquired over one hundred rounds in three days of surreptitious activity.

While Villa attempted to acquire arms and ammunition in order to continue the struggle against the accursed Carranza, Constitutionalist officials who had taken over the administration of Ciudad Juárez seized the public slaughterhouse that Villa had refurbished and attempted to operate it. In a formal request in January 1917 to the United States, the *carrancistas* asked that an inspector be appointed so that fresh meat from Mexico could enter the

United States. Cobb, ever-vigilant, argued that the *carrancistas* wanted to exploit the cattle graft as had the *villistas*. Carranza and his commanders had learned, principally from Villa, that cattle served as an excellent source of revenue, and stolen cattle could be sold more readily as fresh meat than on the hoof. Too much pressure on United States officials and Carranza's generally bellicose attitude toward its northern neighbor kept Lansing and Wilson from granting the request.

Villa did not abandon cattle completely as a source of supply. While legal entry through Juárez became impossible, the ill-patrolled border provided more than one way to bring cows and buyers together. In late March 1917, approaches were made to Villa by Col. Charles Hunt, who would become a prosperous cattle broker in El Paso and a governor of Arizona. Cobb furiously recommended that such nefarious dealing with Villa by Americans had to stop. "By preventing such profits for Col. Hunt, or any one else," he spewed, "seeking commercial association with Villa, we can suppress Villista propaganda at the border." Hunt's original contact came in January 1917. He alluded to his connection with New Mexico Senator Albert B. Fall and stated that Fall wanted to meet with Villa. Hunt, in all probability, had exaggerated his connections with Fall, for the good senator would face an angry constituency had he met with Villa, the devastator of Columbus.

Initially, Villa repulsed Hunt's overtures but continued to sell Terrazas cattle to other brokers for ten dollars a head. Villa readily recognized an attempt by Fall to manipulate him for his own political ends. Fall, a staunch opponent of Woodrow Wilson, hoped that Villa would continue to embarrass Wilson and the Democrats. While Villa, desperate as he was, would probably have played Faust, cooperation with an anti-Mexican *gringo* like Fall would have been more than even a Centaur could endure.

Villista vitriol against the United States continued unabated. *Villista* sympathizers continually leveled their propagandistic cannonades at foreigners in general and *gringos* specifically. While showing little mercy for French, Chinese, and the God-cursed Spaniard, Villa and his people could not forget Woodrow Wilson's betrayal. In Villa's pronouncements and those issued in his name, German interests in Mexico received little notice.

The *villista* spark remained alive in Chihuahua. No doubt the humiliation of Pershing maintained Villa in reasonably good stead with the *chihuahuenses*, and *villista* activity continued throughout the capital of Chihuahua. But reprisal from Carranza came eventually and brutally. In early April 1917, Gen. Francisco Murguía, military commander of Chihuahua, reportedly hanged between 200 and 600 *villista* sympathizers. Desperate to crush the spectre of *villismo*, Carranza and Murguía capriciously struck out at Villa's alleged supporters, created more sympathy for Villa, and gave credence to Villa's charge that Carranza was in fact a despot in the Díaz mold.

Carranza's ill-timed hangings brought contributions to the *villista* cause. Gold and silver jewelry tinkled into the Villa coffers. In June, Hipólito Arango pawned some rings in order to convert them into cash. Cobb saw this as a move of desperation on the part of Villa and his followers, but it rather indicated the level of support that Villa enjoyed in Chihuahua. Unable to give money, convertible jewelry became the medium that the populace used to demonstrate their continued support of the cause.

Unanimity about Villa did not exist in Chihuahua. In the fall of 1917, an abortive attempt to assassinate Villa clearly showed the divisions that existed about Villa's continued activities. Political opportunists hoped to ingratiate themselves with Carranza through setting up Villa. Silvestre Terrazas, now in exile in El Paso, cautioned Villa about odious politicians. Terrazas advised Villa that his essentially good nature could get him killed because he trusted duplicitous political toadies.

Assassination attempts and venal politicians did not deter Villa. He continued to harass the *carrancista* officials in Chihuahua, much to the embarrassment of Carranza and his political cronies. Governor Ignacio Enríquez reaffirmed his vow to capture Villa and rejected an offer by Carranza to send an additional 2,000 men to Chihuahua. Enríquez declared that "Villa is reserved for me." Enríquez's rejection of Carrana's offer largely stemmed from the general low regard in which troops from southern Mexico were held in the more rugged and individualistic north. They were not the kind of soldiers to send after Villa, for the terrain and the people were alien.

More effective than Carranza's threats, however, were the *defensas sociales*, a sort of citizen militia established by Carranza as early as 1915 in areas that he controlled. These probably gained acceptance because they kept federal troops out of different towns and reduced tension. The *defensas sociales* were most effective in Chihuahua, for they were composed primarily of many middle-class elements who had reluctantly supported Villa when it looked as if he would win the struggle against Don Venus. The militia did undercut *villista* support in Chihuahua. Desperately, Villa addressed a proclamation to them asking their support in his defense of the sovereignty of Chihuahua. He thundered accusations at Carranza for plundering the riches of the state, of betraying the sanctified ideals of Francisco Madero, and of importing soldiers released from the jails of Mexico City to wreak havoc among the citizenry of Chihuahua.

Villa now appeared as the fully blown regionalist. He hammered away at Chihuahua's sovereignty, constantly emphasizing the inherent right of the state to handle its own affairs. Appeals to regional loyalties, however, also carried threats to those of the *defensas sociales* who continued their opposition to Villa. No longer, he declared, could he release prisoners captured from the militias. Instead, summary justice would be carried out since they had not repented their transgressions.

Villa's fortunes, while diminished, still kept him sufficiently viable to cause concern both in the United States and in Mexico City. Throughout the late winter and early spring of 1919, Villa's activities along the border included depredations of American-owned properties and the capture and holding for ransom of American citizens. Carranza had obviously failed to control the border and to guarantee the protection of American lives and properties. State Department officials pressed for increased Mexican protection along the border. Carranza refused, however, to respond. As a result, the United States sent seasoned cavalrymen recently returned from Europe to buttress existing forces along the border.

Instability along the border, prompted principally by *villista* raids, met with vigorous response from the United States. Not only were troop strengths increased, but major contingency plans came into effect. The United States, aggravated by Carranza's treatment of American interests and by his inability or refusal to control Villa, underwent a renewed push on the part of some United States interests to intervene actively in Mexico. In response to these pressures, the War Department began to plan for a possible invasion of Mexico. With broad pen, one member of the Army War College carefully mapped out possible points of supply and their logistical relationship to points of strong United States interest in Mexico. Tampico and Veracruz, key ports and oil depots, loomed paramount in war plans. Additionally, the protection of the recently opened Panama Canal occupied the concerns of the United States military establishment.

Constant rumor engendered by Mexican officials and by *villistas* in temporary exile in the United States fueled American preoccupation with Villa's activities and with generalized fear in Mexico of invasion from north of the Río Bravo. Mexican officials along the border reported rumors of *villistas, felicistas,* and other disaffected groups joining together against Carranza. Still, a hopeful note had sounded. Three Americans who supplied Villa with arms languished in El Paso jails for violation of United States neutrality laws.

Concern in Texas prompted the governor of that state to ask that the Texas National Guard be incorporated into federal service in order to patrol the border more effectively. Secretary of War Newton D. Baker refused the idea, stating that regular army troops in Texas could handle any contingency. Yet, when Texas was asked if Carranza could move Mexican troops across Texas soil, Governor William Hobby refused. To Hobby, Carranza and Villa were both bandits who had little if any respect for American rights and lives.

Secretary Baker spoke prematurely. In early June, increasingly frequent press reports noted the accelerated activity of *villista* forces along the border. By June 11, the commander of the Southern Department received orders that if *villistas* fired on Ciudad Juárez, "you will cross the border and disperse his [Villa's] troops but will on no account undertake an expedition into Mexico."

War Department orders proved a compromise. Secretary of War Baker wanted to serve notice on Villa that if a single shot should enter El Paso, United States soldiers would again enter Mexico. In part the compromise order resulted from the unpredictable consequences that could befall Americans living in Mexico if Villa proved vengeful.

Tension mounted. Villa's troops continued to move unhindered along the border areas of Chihuahua. Press reports, typically apocalyptic, saw a major effort by Villa and a vigorous response from the United States. Press speculation proved correct. By June 14, *villistas* moved in to attack Juárez. Without resistance from the *carrancista* garrison, the *villistas* took the American-owned racetrack south of the city and began an artillery barrage of the *carrancistas*.

Some shots fell into El Paso, occasionally killing and injuring citizens. Without a by-your-leave, Gen. James D. Erwin, commander of the El Paso District, led troops comprising cavalry, artillery, and infantry across the border and routed the *villistas* on the morning of July 16. Erwin's troops did not pursue the *villistas*.

On one level the Villa raid proved successful. Again Villa made the redundant point that Carranza could not control the country. Villa served notice that he could, with impunity, inflict damage on the United States and get away with it. This time Villa proved insensitive to where his artillery shells landed. No longer did he have to court the Puritan in the White House. He unleashed his wrath against his enemies, both foreign and domestic.

Reaction in both Mexico and the United States was quick and mixed. Initially, Carranza decried the invasion of Mexico's sovereign territory by the detested Yankees and demanded an apology. Rather quickly, Carranza did an about-face, for popular opinion in Mexico City supported the work of Erwin's troops. Mexican citizens feared that the United States would intervene in massive force if she were called on the limited action in Juárez.

United States congressional opinion lambasted Carranza. Villa, the perpetrator of the act, was virtually unmentioned. Instead, Carranza became the target of congressional splenetics. In the Senate, Albert Fall welcomed the Erwin action as a prelude to intervention. Representative C. B. Hudspeth of Texas lambasted Carranza for not protecting American lives. Carranza, argued Hudspeth, was "too busily engaged, or was sending felicitations to Kaiser Bill on the anniversary of his birth" to protect the border. Hudspeth concluded his diatribe by denouncing Carranza's initial demand for an apology from the United States. If he had anything to say in the matter, Hudspeth declared, "that flowing crop of whiskers [Carranza's] would grow to the ground and sweep out his tracks before Uncle Sam doffed his hat and apologized to that spineless cactus of Mexico."

Mexican expatriates, prompted by Villa's raid on Juárez, met in Washington, D.C., and formed a conservative *junta* that demanded the reinstatement of the Constitution of 1857. Carranza had failed to maintain order, live up to his revolutionary promises, and by his ineptitude practically invited wholesale American intervention in Mexico. In Chihuahua, Villa laughed.

Woodrow Wilson's irritation with Carranza compounded. By

mid-July, Wilson saw that Carranza either did not care or was incapable of controlling the *villista* elements along the border. As a consequence he made the control of the border even more difficult when he ordered an arms embargo on July 12. "I have found," Wilson wrote, "that there exist in Mexico . . . conditions of domestic violence promoted by the use of arms and munitions procured in the United States." Wilson reaffirmed the embargoes of 1912 and 1917 and promised stringent enforcement of these laws against those who violated American neutrality. Though philosophically noninterventionist, Wilson offered the threat of another American expedition into Mexico. United States diplomatic officials in Mexico would inform Mexican functionaries that "should the lives of American citizens continue to remain unsafe, and these murders continue by reason of the unwillingness or inability of the Mexican government to afford adequate protection, this Government may be forced to adopt a radical change in its policy with regard to Mexico."

American bellicosity and Mexican inability to control Villa in the north prompted some fancy sidestepping by Mexican Ambassador Ignacio Bonillas. In early August, Bonillas informed all Mexican consuls in the United States that "Mexico today has a stable government." He granted the existence of a few bandits, but general stability prevailed. Mexico would, moreover, meet all of her obligations, and he promised somewhat guardedly increased Mexican vigilance along the border. Mexican official action mouthed by Bonillas was seconded by Governor Enríquez of Chihuahua. With Carranza's permission, the state of Chihuahua placed a reward of 50,000 pesos on Pancho Villa. They hoped that greed would entice the stubborn Chihuahua peasant into betraying Villa, the quintessential *norteño*.

Villa's supporters kept alive the hope that Carranza could be overthrown or convinced to step down as an act of patriotism. Federico Cervantes, another of the coterie of intellectuals that surrounded Villa, found refuge in Leavenworth, Kansas. From there he kept in touch with Silvestre Terrazas, who had begun to achieve prominence in the Mexican-American community as a journalist. No doubt existed in Cervantes's mind about the possibility of an American invasion of Mexico. Carranza's truculence, his unofficial support of Germany during the struggle in Europe, and his inability to restore peace to Mexico increased the likelihood of United

States intervention. The removal of Carranza, thought Cervantes, would constitute a major step toward convincing the United States that intervention was unnecessary.

In large measure Cervantes, Terrazas, and other former *villista* officials saw the impossibility of bringing back some sort of pristine *villismo*. Instead they began to cast about for allies of various political stripes to form a multipartisan group for the restoration of Mexico. The creation of the Comité Mexicano de la Paz (Mexican Peace Committee) constituted such a response. Among its members appeared Elías L. Torres, who would become a leading Villa apologist. Torres, later a secretary to Villa, hoped that Terrazas would give sympathetic support to the group that sought to avoid personalist ambitions and achieve "intense Mexicanism" as a means of averting United States intervention. It was, reported Torres, a group that aimed to work among the nearly one million Mexican expatriates who wanted to restore peace to their fatherland and end the chaos in Mexico.

The nature of Mexican politics militated against the elimination of personalist ambitions. Among those groups that supported the Comité were *villistas,* former supporters of Emilio Vázquez Gómez, *huertistas, orozquistas,* and any variety of other disaffected Mexicans. There did, however, exist the possibility that the various groups would subsume their partisanism if Felipe Angeles took over leadership of a movement that might unseat Carranza.

Angeles, the brilliant artillery tactician who preferred active military service under Villa to bureaucratic indenture to Carranza, was reared in the military traditions of academy and army. Urbane and polished in word and manner, Angeles constituted the ideal presidential hopeful and potential leader against Carranza. He remained in the Madero mold politically, and his orientation aimed at political reform. In the light of the radicalism of the Mexican Constitution of 1917, Angeles appeared conservative and thus appealed to those individuals to whom the new document was anathema.

As early as January 1919, Angeles began to cause consternation in Mexico among the *carrancistas.* Rumors abounded about Angeles rallying dissident conservative elements, especially the *cientí- ficos* of the Díaz era. Oil interests, so went the rumors, preferred Angeles to any other Mexican leader because his orientation struck them as very much like either Díaz or Huerta. With Angeles organizing the political opposition and with Villa able to coordinate the military action, Carranza feared that he could be in serious trouble.

As a consequence, Carranza plotted to eliminate Angeles who, following the disastrous defeats of the División del Norte at Celaya and León, sought exile in the United States. He settled in El Paso, where he bought a ranch. Yet he remained uncomfortable as a non-participant in Mexican affairs and went to New York. There he formed the Alianza Liberal Mexicana, where he attempted to disengage the reactionary elements in the expatriate community from the traditionally liberal groups that sought refuge from Carranza. In Angeles's judgment, the conditions in Mexico were right for a move against Carranza. In 1918 he returned to Mexico surreptitiously and began to drill the *villista* forces and to weld them into what became the Ejército de Reconstrucción Nacional (Army of National Reconstruction). No member of that force was exempt from the rigorous training to which Angeles subjected it. Even Villa found himself undergoing extreme physical training. "Finally," puffed Villa the horseman, "someone has made me run!"

Carranza could not tolerate the existence of both Angeles and Villa in Mexico and began to plan carefully for the capture of Villa's *eminence grise*. As Angeles and his escort headed toward Parral, Chihuahua, on the way to join Villa in Durango, Gabino Sandoval, head of the *defensas sociales,* captured Angeles and sent him to Parral. From there Gen. Manuel Diéguez dispatched the prisoner to Chihuahua City to face a court-martial. No doubt existed about the outcome of the trial. The elimination of yet another prominent *villista* became an imperative of Carranza's megalomania.

Angeles's wife appealed to the Department of State asking that it intervene to save her husband's life. Coldly, Lansing responded that he had

> carefully considered your recent telegram and that of your children, and while deeply regretting your unfortunate situation, I am constrained to inform you that owing to your husband's being a Mexican citizen and for *reasons of state* [italics added] I am precluded from intervening on his behalf.

Appeals to President and Mrs. Wilson failed. The man who might salvage Mexico politically unfortunately remained allied with Villa, now one of Wilson's most ardent opponents.

On November 24, the trial of Felipe Angeles began. Diéguez wallowed in the glory of bringing Angeles to trial and claimed that with the elimination of Angeles, Villa would be finished. Angeles, he averred, constituted the brains behind the *villista* movement.

Diéguez also left no doubt that the court-martial merely existed to observe the legal niceties. Angeles would die.

The trial lasted for two days and was held in the Municipal Theater of Chihuahua City. Angeles steadfastly pleaded his innocence. Just as tenaciously, the prosecution insisted upon his guilt. On the morning of November 26, at 6:00 A.M., the court sentenced Angeles to die. Protests to save his life gained him a stay of execution from the Mexican Supreme Court. But the stay arrived too late in Chihuahua City. At 6:30 A.M., dum-dum bullets assured that Felipe Angeles's body would be devoid of life.

The news struck Villa like a well-placed kick in the chest. Impotent to help Angeles, Villa had suffered while Angeles courageously maintained the constancy of the *villista* position. Angeles, much like Madero, recognized in Villa the genius that lurked beneath the bandit exterior and respected the commander of the División del Norte. Genuine affection had existed between the two men. Now Angeles was dead, and Villa wept openly and passionately.

Again the old rages returned. Villa's spirit cried out for vengeance. In many ways it seemed that for the last year Villa had merely been going through the motions of opposition to Carranza. He could not make peace with the government, for Carranza would have him killed. Much of the heart had gone out of Villa. But on that chilly November morning when Angeles died, Villa found an outlet for his vengeance. No *carrancista* official was safe. Those recently captured were executed without the benefit of a trumped-up trial. Villa systematically began a renewed vendetta against Carranza.

Carranza also found that his position grew increasingly untenable throughout 1919 and into 1920. He had failed to pacify northern Mexico. Obregón now challenged Carranza's handpicked successor in the presidential contest. Truculent governors refused to listen to Carranza's orders. By April, open conflict between Adolfo De la Huerta, governor of Sonora, supported by Plutarco Elías Calles, and Carranza broke into the open. The Plan de Agua Prieta denounced Carranza and Sonoran recognition from Carranza.

By early May, Carranza saw that his tenure in Mexico City was at best limited. He prepared to escape once again to Veracruz. As news of Carranza's departure reached Villa, the Centaur of the North contacted De la Huerta and offered his services for the purpose of eliminating Carranza from the national panorama. De la Huerta, however, recognized that renewed activity by Villa could prove disastrous for Mexico. With care, but with success, he dissuaded Villa from declaring against Carranza. Instead, De la Huerta enjoined Villa to make peace with the government.

While Villa bided his time, Carranza saw himself increasingly bereft of support. Troops deserted him, schemers sought to exploit his political humiliation, and he was finally betrayed. On May 20, 1920, Venustiano Carranza suffered the fate of assassination at Tlaxcalantongo, Puebla. Mexico now remained without a president. Four days later, the Mexican Congress declared that Adolfo de la Huerta would serve as interim president until a new president was elected and then installed.

Probably the greatest coup for De la Huerta came in the pacification of Pancho Villa. During the short but intense fighting against Carranza, Ignacio Enríquez, now siding with De la Huerta, regained control of Chihuahua City and began to act as intermediary between De la Huerta and the suspicious *villistas*. Villa recognized that Enríquez still wanted revenge. In early discussions with Villa, Enríquez found out the number and locations of *villista* troops. He suggested that Villa go to Hermosillo with a small escort to continue talks with Calles and Obregón. Villa, however, countered with an offer to police the entire state of Chihuahua. Villa was no fool. He saw what Enríquez planned and moved his men and equipment. On schedule, Enríquez attacked the abandoned camp in late May. On June 2, Villa countered with an attack on Parral and routed the garrison there.

Elías Torres acted as Villa's envoy to De la Huerta. He traveled to Mexico City armed with a list of Villa's demands. Among those were that he would receive an *hacienda* in Chihuahua and would head a rural police force of no more than 500 men, whereby he could make Chihuahua a haven of safety and peace in Mexico. Calles rejected the conditions, for he saw any recognition of Villa by the interim government as a granting of legitimacy to a bandit. Obregón preferred to see Villa wiped out. Only De la Huerta saw the demands as merely a basis for negotiation.

Through representatives, Villa let it be known that if his conditions were not met he would unleash a reign of terror in northern Mexico. Initial silence met the new pronouncement. Villa proved good his threat. On July 26 he attacked Sabinas, Coahuila, captured the federal garrison, three freight trains, and tore up about fifty kilometers of track both north and south of the town.

Immediately after the attack, he entered into telegraphic conversations directly with De la Huerta. Villa proved his point. He still remained a potent force in northern Mexico. Now, he informed De la Huerta, he was ready to make peace with the government, and he would turn over all his arms to the government and release all of his men. Negotiations began at once. Obregón, campaigning for the presidency, publicly denounced the negotiations. He claimed that the United States would not give recognition to the Mexican government since it harbored a criminal.

De la Huerta, however, opted for peace with Villa. Too long had northern Mexico lived in insecurity. Only stability there could bring true peace to the entire nation. Again intense negotiations began, this time at Sabinas. Representatives from the government headed by Villa's antagonist Eugenio Martínez met with Villa, Elías Torres, and about sixty *villistas*. The agreement dated July 28 and signed at Sabinas, Coahuila, gave Villa the *hacienda* at Canutillo, on the border between Chihuahua and Durango. Additionally, any of Villa's men, who now numbered around 700, released by Villa would receive one year's wages plus land in any location he chose to reside. Those men who wanted to continue a military life would be incorporated into the regular army at their current ranks. Villa, however, did not completely trust the government. He insisted and received the right to hand-pick fifty of his *dorados* to act as guards for his *hacienda* and to serve as his personal bodyguards. Their salaries would come out of public funds.

The *hacienda* at Canutillo appealed to Villa. He had fought some battles in the area and had good memories about the place. More practically, De la Huerta saw Canutillo as a place where Villa could be kept out of the way, for it was far enough away from the capitals of Durango and Chihuahua to avoid trouble from Villa. Operating under the belief that Canutillo was government property, De la Huerta acquiesced. However, Canutillo had not been confiscated by the government. Consequently, De la Huerta authorized the expenditure of 60,000 pesos to pay for the property and thus pacify Villa.

Now at peace, Villa turned his attentions to agricultural pursuits. But the soul of a warrior continued vibrant in Francisco Villa. He had made peace with the government, but he still had a few *salvos* to loose at the United States. On August 10 he declared that he would "fight to the death" any *gringo* attempt to invade Mexico. Mexico's problems, Villa believed, lay squarely on the shoulders of the United States. Villa was loathe to let go of a grudge. With Carranza out of the way, he found opportunity to indulge in nationalist rhetoric and constantly remind Mexico of who fought for so long and so constantly in defense of national ideals.

Villa's last days as a bandit/revolutionary symbolized a desire to uphold personal honor in the face of calumny heaped upon him by Carranza and his supporters. To Villa, the honor of the nation was intrinsically wrapped up in personal perceptions that he had. He represented the *norteño* spirit: individualistic, buckling to no man or nation, desirous of finding a niche where deeds rather than status would earn deserved recognition.

Between 1916 and 1920, Villa proved to the nation that he could still command. Sufficient support came to the Centaur of the North. While no longer a major threat, he remained secure in regional influence, for Francisco Villa, a son of the north, never fell prey to the lure of Mexico City. His support came not from the upwardly mobile middle class but from the *campesinos*, from the *vaqueros*, from the prostitutes and street vendors, from all of those elements in the society that saw in Pancho the personification of abstract ideals.

The force of charisma as an instrument of leadership gave Villa a tremendous advantage in the north. Reduced militarily, his magnetism still attracted sufficient numbers to keep him viable. Once Carranza was removed from the national scene, Villa made peace. An assassin's bullet eliminated from Mexico a principal source of contention.

Villa created a myth and an image and a stereotype. Minstrels wrote *corridos* (a form of folk song) about him. He inspired novelists. In the popular mind, the revolution was Francisco Villa.

CHAPTER XII

Guerrilla,
Lover, Patriot

¡Pobre Pancho Villa!	Poor Pancho Villa!
Fue muy triste su destino	His destiny was sad
morir en una emboscada	to die in ambush
*a la orilla del camino.**	at the edge of the road.

Mexican *corridos* contributed to the spread and perpetuation of the folklore, myth, and fame of the mighty Centaur of the North. In a country that fought a revolution for a decade in order to achieve a new condition for the dispossessed, a generous estimate of the literacy rate for its citizens was about twenty percent. Oral tradition became the principal vehicle for the dissemination of information about the revolution, and the *corridos,* so much a part of Mexican popular culture, served as the primary means by which the masses and the members of huge revolutionary armies gained information as well as reinforcement about the course of the titanic struggle.

Pancho Villa, probably more than any of the other revolutionary leaders, garnered the bulk of *corridos.* Anonymous versifiers in the immediate afterglow of victory or the despondency of defeat

---

* All the *corridos* used in this chapter come from Armando de María y Campos, *La Revolución Mexicana a través de los Corridos Populares.*

plucked away at not very well-tuned guitars and began to recount events that they had observed or heard discussed. Often, for the sake of rhyme schemes, words were inserted that did not make sense or that exaggerated the impact of an individual or an event. Still, much of the popular conception about Villa grew out of the *corridos* that gained currency during the revolution and have become the stock in trade of *mariachi* bands throughout Mexico even today.

The death of Villa, assassinated in 1923 by cowardly political troglodytes, precipitated a rush of *corridos* that recounted his death and lay the blame squarely on the shoulders of Obregón and Calles, both of whom feared Villa's continued presence in the north. Villa again fanned the popular imagination, this time in death, and passions that had cooled superficially after Villa's retirement flickered once again.

Dicen que cayó diciendo:	They said that he fell saying:
"Ya Plutarco [Calles]	"Plutarco [Calles] has done
me amoló."	me in."

In another verse, the nature of Villa's assassins received full treatment.

En una casa alquilada	In a rented house
se apostaron los matones	the assassins waited
pues para matar a Villa	because to kill Villa
les faltaban . . . pantalones.	they lacked pants.

Obviously delicate and attuned to feminine sensibilities, the anonymous minstrel who wrote this *corrido* substituted the word *pants* for the more crude but equally effective rhyming word for testicles — *cojones.*

In large measure, Villa's impact on the popular imagination came from his exaggerated masculinity, from the whole Mexican idealization of the *macho.* For there exists no doubt that Villa possessed *cojones.* The whole macho conception revolves around courage, steadfastness in the face of adversity, and, of course, sexual prowess. Though sexuality is involved in the macho idea, it is not total. Assertiveness and total conviction underlie the macho ideal.

One joke that had some currency about Villa related that when Villa was going to attack Torreón the first time in October 1913, he was justifiably nervous and therefore was afflicted with a minor intestinal disorder. Around midnight Villa went behind the mesquite bushes to quiet his hyperactive innards. In a few minutes he began calling for his medical officer. The doctor responded immediately. "Doctor," groaned Villa, "every time that I try to get up I get this sharp pain in the pit of my stomach." Thoughtfully, the doctor told Villa to calm himself and grabbed a lantern. "All right, General," said the doctor, "move to the right a bit, now to the left . . . now just a shade to the right. Good, General, now stand up." Villa stood with no effort and readjusted his clothing. "Doctor," he asked, "what caused the pain in my stomach? Why couldn't I get up?" Pompously, the doctor responded: "General, I'm sorry, but we don't discuss such details with our patients." Angered Villa grabbed the doctor and shouted: "If you want to continue as the medical officer of this army and earn 25,000 pesos a year in gold, then you will tell me. If not, you son-of-a-bitch, I'll have you shot at sunrise." Shaken, the doctor gasped: "All right, General, if you insist, the reason you hurt so much was that every time you tried to get up, your testicles got caught on your spurs."

The story conveyed rather graphically the idea of the macho. The macho's *cojones* can occasionally cause him some trouble.

The emergence of Villa on the Mexican scene, especially after the death of Madero, catapulted the common man to prominence. *Corridos* sang his bravery and the fear that he instilled in the federal soldiers, often conscripts, that fought for Huerta.

Aquí está Francisco Villa	Here is Francisco Villa
con sus Jefes y Oficiales	with his officers and chiefs.
es el que viene a ensillar	He is the one who will saddle
a las mulas federales.	the federal mules.

Mexico's revolution became a vendetta for Villa. For years he had suffered; he had been forced into banditry; the authorities pursued him constantly, rarely allowing him the peace in which to build an established life. As such, Villa returned to banditry. His renown in Chihuahua before the revolution brought him to the attention of Madero and Abraham González. Villa, granted military command, engaged in a personal vendetta against those who had oppressed him and his beloved *norteños*.

Torreón marked his first major victory, though other less glorious battles prepared the way for the stunning siege of that vital town. Certainly, Villa approached the battle with a sense of purpose, of military strategy, but to the people whom he led and to the Mexican populace, he came into Torreón as an avenging angel, ready to smite the venal aristocrats who sought to keep the people suppressed.

La Justicia vencerá	Justice shall triumph
se arruinará la ambición	crass ambition shall be ruined.
a castigar a toditos,	Villa entered Torreón
Pancho Villa entró a Torreón.	to punish all [the oppressors].

Villa's *dorados,* the supreme fighting cavalry, also received a fair share of attention from the minstrels, for their bravery was second only to that of their commander. They had subsumed their personal ambitions to serve the Centaur of the North. Declared one *corrido:*

Yo soy soldado de Pancho Villa	I am one of Pancho Villa's soldiers.
de sus dorados soy el más fiel,	Of his *dorados* I am the most faithful.
nada me importa perder la vida,	I don't mind dying
si es cosa de hombres morir por el.	because it is a man's thing to die for him.

The almost slavish loyalty that Villa inculcated in his followers was only approximated by the *zapatistas* in the south. Even Obregón, probably the most skilled general to come out of the ranks of the revolution because of his innate grasp of modern warfare, did not inspire the same adulation that did Villa. Certainly, Obregón had his faithful supporters, but his strength came from his uncanny ability to gain alliances and to hold his allies rather than from the sheer magnetism of his personality.

As the División del Norte added to its list of victories, popular imagination swelled with the exploits of Villa and his followers. Torreón, Zacatecas, Chihuahua, Juárez, Ojinaga — all of Villa's triumphs received attention and added to the image of Francisco Villa. The consummate guerrilla leader commanded an army at one time numbering 60,000 men. In so doing, he became more than a hill fighter. He was a major military presence that often overshadowed his contemporaries.

Even in defeat and on the defensive, Pancho Villa retained his place in the popular mind. His invasion of Columbus, New Mexico, gave vent to Mexican frustration about the United States, and Villa's action sought to wreak symbolic vengeance on the *gringos.* Pershing's expedition into Mexico gave rise to a plethora of *corridos* that exalted Villa and denigrated the poor *gringos* that suffered in Chihuahua. One such song declared:

Los soldaditos que	The little soldiers that
vinieron de Téxas	came from Texas
los pobrecitos empezaron	Poor little things began
a temblar	to shake
muy fatigados de ocho	Tired from eight hours on
horas de camino	the road
los pobrecitos se	Poor little things wanted
querían ya regresar.	to return.

Contemptuously, the *corridistas* railed about the *gringos'* cowardice. *Corridos* centering on Pancho Villa exalted his *mexicanidad* (Mexicanness) in contrast to the weak and pallid *gringo*.

Villa the horseman, the Centaur, loved a good horse. Prime horseflesh caused him trouble with Huerta in 1912 and nearly removed him from the scene of the revolution. His favorite mare, Siete Leguas (Seven Leagues), also rated a *corrido* and gained a part in the Villa mythology. According to the story, the mare carried Villa as he escaped from *carrancistas*. Three soldiers fired at him; one shot the mare instead. Indomitably, the mare carried Villa for seven leagues (roughly twenty-one miles) so that he could make good his escape. The bullet passed through the mare cleanly, and Villa took her as his favorite horse. Supposedly, the mare had a better fate than her master, for she lived into the early 1930s.

Even when Villa decided to make peace with the government in 1920, no question was raised by the *corridistas* about Villa's loss of strength. Rather, the *corridos* praised the action as one of high patriotism.

¡Válgame Dios en los cielos!	God in heaven above
que contento estoy ahora,	how happy I am today
porque México está en paz	because Mexico is at peace
Pancho Villa no es malora.	Pancho Villa is not a destroyer.
Tiene un grande corazón	The great guerrilla
el famoso guerrillero	fighter has a great heart
todo el Norte lo quiere	All of the north loves him,
y lo cuida con esmero.	and guards him affectionately.

Villa as guerrilla fighter fell upon Mexico with the force of a thunderclap. His deeds reverberated throughout the country. There remained no doubt that Villa represented the essence of the

Mexican macho, leading his troops into battle, organizing raids, doing battle with the politicians who hoped to compromise the ideals he held for the people of his beloved nation.

Villa as consummate guerrilla fighter spread his fame throughout the Hispanic world. During the Spanish Civil War (1936-1939), Villa served as an inspiration to Republican forces. Villa became a Mexican Cid Campeador, the inspiration to battle, the invincible mountain fighter.

Héroe de la libertad	Hero of Liberty
su nombre copia y semeja	whose name is copied
que a México defendiera	who defended Mexico
Pancho Villa, Pancho Villa!	Pancho Villa, Pancho Villa!
Miliciano de la sierra.	Mountain fighter.

Yet the Mexican macho also had his domestic side, for throughout the revolution Villa acquired wives and children. His first wife, María Luz Corral, he married in 1911. Her frequent absences from Chihuahua necessitated by Villa's desire to protect her left him without feminine companionship. As a result he became essentially polygamous, marrying those who caught his fancy.

In this regard Villa seemed like a somewhat twisted moralist. Merely taking a mistress seemed to upset his sense of propriety. Instead, he chose to marry those women who appealed to him. At one time he had four "legal" wives — María Luz Corral, Soledad Seáñez, Austreberta Rentería, and Juanita Torres. The Muséo de la Revolución in Chihuahua estimates that Villa had a total of twenty-four wives. At the time of his death, five widows appeared on the scene to claim his estate.

The confusion was compounded for officials along the border. When Luz Corral, his first wife, attempted to cross into El Paso, she was informed that a Señora Villa was already across the border. Indignant, she accosted her husband, and he merely laughed and gave her a letter explaining that Luz Corral de Villa was his first and legal wife.

Though Luz Corral did survive the entire revolution at the hands of her capricious husband, there is no doubt that she suffered some extreme humiliations. The story circulated that when Villa married Austreberta Rentería, Luz Corral's dressmaker, the first Mrs. Villa was forced to serve the nuptial couple breakfast in bed. Since Villa's death there existed a fierce animosity between Austreberta Rentería and Luz Corral that ended only with Luz Corral's death in 1980.

Villa's major victory at Torreón not only covered him with military glory but also garnered him another wife, Juana Torres. It was Juana Torres who occupied Villa's traveling car and gave him solace as he led his troops to the north in an attempt to take Chihuahua City. But Juana Torres soon lost favor, for she and her venal relatives made the mistake of stealing from Pancho Villa.

Forty thousand pesos was missing. Villa questioned his brother Hipólito to see if he had spent the money for the army. Juana Torres denied any knowledge of the affair. Soon Villa and Hipólito began to investigate and found that Villa's mother-in-law and sister-in-law were the guilty parties. Luckily, because they were family, Villa did not have them summarily shot nor did he turn them over to his troops so they could have some fun and games. Instead, he threw them in prison until they made restitution.

Juana was desolated. Had she made a mistake in succumbing to the ardor of the noted revolutionary? Stupidly, she sent a letter to her incarcerated mother, and the letter reached Villa instead. "Mama," she lamented, "I suffer very much from what has happened to you. But what can I do with this bandit? My life with him is torture. I would rather die than endure it. I beg him, I weep, but he is heartless; he will never yield until he is paid." Villa launched into one of his classic rages. He railed that the only reason he did not kill the lot of them was because he loved Juana. Did being a revolutionary make him a bandit, he asked? He chose to humiliate Juana and made her read the ill-fated letter to him. Finally, after his rage had subsided, he set wretched Juana, her mama, and her darling sister free and gave them enough money to get to El Paso.

Villa's views on women were contradictory. Certainly he liked the ladies and obviously the ladies liked Villa. But he proved ferocious about his *dorados* hauling women along with them in battle. While the rest of his army could and certainly did bring their *soldaderas* (soldier women), Villa did not want his highly mobile cavalry unit — the *dorados* — encumbered by camp followers. While certainly Villa had no knowledge of the Thirty Years War, he avoided the problem that faced the Imperial Armies — too many camp followers. So many women trailed along after the armies of Wallenstein that he appointed a general with the title of Provost of the Harlots to keep the ladies in line.

Soldaderas proved to be quite effective. Many of them fought as well as the men, and in Villa's army some even held military rank. The *villista corrido* "Juana Gallo" extols the fighting qualities of these fierce women who often bore children while on the campaign trail, scrounged food, provided first aid, and gave solace to Villa's army at night. But the *dorados* did not need the encumbrance.

Villa claimed that the success of his campaign against Ciudad Juárez in 1913 came from an absence of women. His *dorados* were not tied down. "We had no tail," he averred. While Villa realized that "laying hands on a woman once in awhile" was absolutely necessary to good health, his men could search out "*las viejas*" (the old ladies) when there was little danger of being surprised by the enemy. He did not want any battle or maneuver to fail because the *dorados* were more worried about the women than about the coming conflict. Strangely moralistic, Villa warned his men about rape though he himself had abducted a French receptionist in Mexico City when he took the town in December 1914. Villa claimed that she was merely being shy; she called it abduction. Anyway, Villa told his *dorados:* "Who is to stop you from getting married? When a wedding is needed, it will be arranged. There is no judge nor priest who can resist the reason of a carbine."

Villa's amatory escapades provided much of the mythology that surrounded his image. His peasant beginnings, his constant struggle against a social system that oppressed him, and his relentless pursuit of the cause of his *muchachitos* impressed as crusty an old soldier as Hugh L. Scott. In his memoirs Scott wrote:

> He always impressed me as a man of great force and energy and willing to do right when directed by those he respected. After all, he was a poor peon without any advantages in his youth, persecuted and pursued through the mountains, his life always in danger; but he had the cause of the peon at heart. He was fully aware of his own deficiencies and even at the height of his power had no desire for the presidency.

The total charisma of the man underscored the role of personality in the Mexican Revolution. Men fought for Villa when they could have stayed home and continued to derive a wretched existence from the parched soil of Chihuahua and Durango. Villa represented for many of his men the absolute personification of Mexican manhood. He released in them a sense of freedom that had been subsumed by the peonage under which they toiled. To the novelist Rafael F. Muñoz, the Villa charisma led to the men sacrificing their families and possessions in order to fight under the command of the brilliant Centaur. In his ¡Vamanos con Pancho Villa!, Muñoz's principal character, Tiburcio Maya, returned to his home, his wife, his child, his land. Villa rode up and demanded that Maya ride with him, for it was time to go into battle again. Maya tried to excuse himself because he now had responsibilities. Villa grabbed his pistol, shot the wife and child, and informed Maya that now he had no responsibilities: he could ride into battle again. Without a word, Maya joined with Villa.

Such charismatic control was certainly exaggerated by the novelist, but it remained very real. Roberto Blanco Moheno talked to an old villista in Torreón. The old man, probably senile, claimed that Villa had not been killed in Parral; rather, he had passed through Torreón shortly after Lázaro Cárdenas did in 1934. Such a fertile grip on the imagination of a people in both culture and the general mind was probably not enjoyed by any other hero of the Mexican Revolution. Zapata is best remembered for his constancy, his unswerving dedication to the cause of the landless in Morelos. But Villa's impact was total. While the same general mythology persisted in Morelos that Zapata had not died at Chinameca, the villista hold on literature, on music, on the minds of the people could not be matched.

Villa's deeds elevated him to secular saint. In the popular culture he was the Mexican Übermensch, Superman, who took the cause of his people and against overwhelming odds successfully led his armies against the oppressors of the Mexican peones.

For many people on both sides of the Río Grande, Villa personified the revolution. "He was," wrote Richard and Florence Lister, "a violent contradiction of good and evil, kindness and sadism, ignorance and crafty intelligence. . . . His violence was the very symbol of the revolt." The villista phenomenon could only be understood on the basis of the exceptional man emerging from conditions that oppressed lesser men and eventually overcoming them through the sheer force of his will and personality. This inspired men to follow him into the cannon fire of the enemy.

Villa committed atrocity after atrocity against both his enemies and his own men when they betrayed him. In the context of
the social upheaval of the revolution, however, normal mores had
dropped. Military necessity, the sense of rightness that Villa felt
about his cause, forced him to use extreme measures in dealing
with those who would deflect him from his course. While Villa is
often remembered as the most violent of the revolutionary leaders,
all of the great men of the revolution had blood on their hands. Political venality often led to political assassination. To Villa, the execution of a traitor or an enemy merely advanced the cause of his
people. Villa, however, did have some brutal subordinates. Rodolfo
Fierro frightened even Villa, for Fierro's homicidal instinct could
only be controlled by Rodolfo himself and by no one else. Yet
Fierro remained slavishly loyal to Villa.

Villa's confiscation of properties involved restitution to his
men for their participation in the fight against Huerta and then
against Carranza. What he attempted to do was to establish a stable government at least in Chihuahua. He did not have personal
ambition to be president but rather hoped to create a situation
where a president sensitive to the needs of Villa's *norteños* would be
selected for the presidential chair in the Palacio Nacional. Villa declared to Gen. Hugh L. Scott that Angeles should be president, for
he would have "changed the whole history of Mexico. I heard Villa
declare several times, 'There have been too many dictators in Mexico and there never shall be another as long as I am alive.' " General Scott too was impressed with Villa's use of confiscated properties when he wrote:

> All the generals of the revolution confiscated property wherever
> they found it, just as Villa did, but many were far more selfish
> about it, building up a private fortune for themselves. I was told
> by the banker who handled [Villa's] money that Villa had no for-
> tune put away; that whatever he got he spent right away on food,
> clothing, and ammunition for his men, whom he took care of to
> the best of his ability. I never heard that Villa took part in the
> looting of Mexico City, but I did hear that Carranza did, sending
> trainloads of furniture to his home in Coahuila.

Villa personified the northern temperament. Fiercely individualistic, he resented the communitarianism of the *zapatistas*. An
ardent though nonideological populist, Villa did not possess a set of
clearly articulated principles as did Zapata, for the *villista* impulse

came from northern Mexico, the more pragmatic part of the country. Men were tough in the north; the environment demanded fortitude. Practical application triumphed over ideology, and as a result Villa constantly faced *ad hoc* decisions, both civil and military.

Villa possessed a winning charm when he wanted to be charming. He felt uncomfortable in the presence of the city-raised, educated people who surrounded Carranza and other Mexican leaders. The Mexican peasant, suddenly catapulted to fame and prominence, could not bring himself to trust Carranza, for Don Venustiano personified the type of individual who had manipulated the peasantry for so long. "The tragedy of the Mexican Revolution is," wrote Blanco Moheno, "[that] neither Villa, the armed might, nor Zapata, the saving ideology, were capable of vanquishing their inferiority complexes before the 'perfumados.' "

Tragedy ended Villa. His impact on the revolution was monumental. He inspired love and hate, fear and adulation, respect and disgust. For many, Villa brought blood and tears to the people of Mexico. In equal numbers, however, Villa came to represent the very best that Mexico could produce in its leaders: fearless, a complete macho, unswerving in his pursuit of his ideals. Villa, the Centaur of the North, stamped his personality on the revolution and ultimately forced the leaders to recognize that here was a true man.

Bibliography

Bibliographies present a constant problem to the historian and biographer. They can be nothing more than a simple listing of works and thus fail to indicate whether or not these tomes actually were consulted. They can comprise long, erudite essays that demonstrate the author's depth of knowledge as he comments on the sources at his disposal. Often, padded bibliographies add flesh to otherwise slim volumes. Hopefully, this compendium of works on Villa will avoid some of those pitfalls.

The basic ingredient that nurtures historical and biographical research lies in the primary sources — both unpublished and published — available to the writer. These open the door to the time about which he/she writes and allows both the writer and the reader an opportunity to share, vicariously to be sure, the historical epoch that has drawn their interest. Like most other things in this life, primary sources vary as to quality and thus must be used with an appreciable amount of care.

The preparation of a biography of Francisco Villa adds an additional problem in terms of sources. Villa left very few papers that allow the biographer to delve into his mind. Some Villa papers exist in other collections, but a biographer is forced to view Villa often through the eyes of his enemies or some of his sycophants. Consequently, the difficulty becomes compounded when one tries to arrive at some reasonable approximation of actual events and their causes.

While all of this may sound like *caveat*, its only purpose lies in crying on the reader's shoulder about the difficulties involved in preparing a biography of Pancho Villa. Villa deserves more than one biography. He was and is controversial. Biographers will perceive him in different ways. Even today, Villa contributes to polemics in Mexico. Sources that are not used carefully can often lead to distortion and lend themselves more to the polemicist than to the historian and biographer.

Primary Materials

Unpublished sources
Archivo General de la Nación. Papeles de la Secretaría de la Presidencia. Alvaro Obregón.

181

Centro de Estudios de Historia de México (CONDUMEX). Papers of:
Venustiano Carranza
Francisco León de la Barra
Emiliano Zapata
Secretaría de Relaciones Exteriores (México). Archivo Histórico de Relaciones Exteriores.
United States National Archives (Washington, D.C.):
Papers of the Department of Agriculture. Bureau of Animal Industry.
Records of the Adjutant General's Office.
Records of the Army War College.
Records of the Department of State relating to the Internal Affairs of Mexico, 1910–1929. (This listing includes subsidiary files not listed.)
Records of the Department of State relating to Political Relations with Mexico, 1910–1929.
University of California, Berkeley, Bancroft Library:
Silvestre Terrazas Papers.
University of Texas, Austin. Papers of:
William F. Buckley, Sr.
Lázaro De la Garza

Published Primary Materials
Comisión de Investigaciones Históricas de la Revolución Mexicana. Isidro Fabela, ed. *Documentos Históricos de la Revolución Mexicana.* México, D. F.: Editorial Jus, various publication dates. This multivolume set constitutes a prime source of information on Villa and the revolution in general.
Corral de Villa, Luz. *Pancho Villa en la Intimidad.* Chihuahua, Chih.: Centro Librero de Prensa, S. A., 1977.
Guzmán, Martín Luis. *Memorias de Pancho Villa.* México, D. F.: Cia. General de Ediciones, S. A., 1963.
Guzmán, Martín Luis. *Memoirs of Pancho Villa.* Translated and abridged by Virginia Taylor. Austin: University of Texas Press, 1965.
María y Campos, Armando de. *La Revolución Mexicana a través de los Corridos Populares.* 2 volumes. Mexico, D. F.: Biblioteca del Instituto Nacional de Estudios Históricos de la Revolución Mexicana, 1962.
Obregón, Alvaro. *Ocho Mil Kilómetros en Campaña.* México, D. F.: Fondo de Cultura Económica, 1960.
Scott, Hugh L. *Some Memories of a Soldier.* New York: The Century Company, 1928.

Newspapers
El Demócrata (Mexico, D. F.)
El Heraldo del Norte (Ciudad Juárez)
El Paso Herald
El Paso Morning Times

New York Times
El Universal (México, D. F.)
Vida Nueva (Chihuahua, Chih.)

Books and Articles

Almada, Francisco R. *La Revolución en el Estado de Chihuahua.* 2 vols. México, D. F.: Biblioteca del Instituto Nacional de Estudios Históricos de la Revolución Mexicana, 1964.

Atkin, Ronald. *Revolution: Mexico, 1910–1920.* New York: John Day and Company, 1970.

Beezley, William. *Insurgent Governor: Abraham González of Chihuahua.* Lincoln: University of Nebraska Press, 1973.

Blanco Moheno, Roberto. *Pancho Villa. Que es su padre.* México, D. F.: Editorial Diana, 1969.

Boletín de la Sociedad Chihuahuense de Estudios Históricos. This journal contained a series of articles by Silvestre Terrazas, published in 1953 and 1954, that gave a better view of Villa than much of the material in the Terrazas papers at the University of California, Berkeley.

Braddy, Haldeen. *Cock of the Walk. Qui-qui-ri-qui. The Legend of Pancho Villa.* Albuquerque: University of New Mexico Press, 1965.

Clendenen, C. C. *The United States and Pancho Villa: A Study in Unconventional Diplomacy.* Ithaca: Cornell University Press, 1961.

Cumberland, Charles C. *The Mexican Revolution: The Constitutionalist Years.* Austin: University of Texas Press, 1972.

―――. *The Mexican Revolution: Genesis under Madero.* Austin: University of Texas Press, 1952.

Dulles, J. W. F. *Yesterday in Mexico: A Chronicle of the Mexican Revolution, 1919–1935.* Austin: University of Texas Press, 1963.

Gilderhus, Mark T. *Diplomacy and Revolution: U.S.-Mexican Relations under Wilson and Carranza.* Tucson: University of Arizona Press, 1977.

Gómez, Marte R. *La Reforma Agraria en la Filas Villistas, Años 1913 a 1915 y 1920.* México, D. F.: Biblioteca del Instituto Nacional de Estudios de la Revolución Mexicana, 1966.

González Ramírez, Manuel. *La Revolución Social de México.* 3 vols. México, D. F.: Fondo de Cultura Económica, 1960, 1965, 1966.

Hall, Linda B. *Alvaro Obregón: Power and Revolution in Mexico, 1911–1920.* College Station, TX: Texas A&M University Press, 1981.

Johnson, William Weber. *Heroic Mexico: The Narrative History of a Twentieth-Century Revolution.* New York: Doubleday, 1968.

Katz, Friedrich. "Agrarian Changes in Northern Mexico in the Period of Villista Rule, 1913–1915," in James W. Wilkie, Michael C. Meyer, and Edna Monzón de Wilkie, eds. *Contemporary Mexico. Papers of the IV Inter-*

national Congress of Mexican History. Los Angeles: University of California Press, 1976.

————. "Pancho Villa and the Attack on Columbus, New Mexico." *American Historical Review* 83 (February 1978).

————. *The Secret War in Mexico. Europe, the United States, and the Mexican Revolution.* Chicago: University of Chicago Press, 1981.

Langle Ramírez, Arturo. *El ejército villista.* México, D. F.: Instituto Nacional de Antropología e História, 1961.

Lister, Florence C., and Robert H. Lister. *Chihuahua: Storehouse of Storms.* Albuquerque: University of New Mexico Press, 1966.

Machado, Manuel A., Jr. *The North Mexican Cattle Industry, 1910–1975: Ideology, Conflict, and Change.* College Station, TX: Texas A&M University Press, 1981.

————, and James T. Judge. "Tempest in a Teapot?: The Mexican-United States Intervention Crisis of 1919." *Southwest Historical Quarterly,* July 1970.

Martínez, Oscar J. *Border Boom Town: Ciudad Juárez Since 1848.* Austin: University of Texas Press, 1978.

Meyer, Michael C. *Huerta: A Political Portrait.* Lincoln: University of Nebraska Press, 1972.

————. *Mexican Rebel: Pascual Orozco and the Mexican Revolution, 1910–1915.* Lincoln: University of Nebraska Press, 1967.

Quirk, Robert E. *The Mexican Revolution, 1914–1915: The Convention at Aguascalientes.* Bloomington: Indiana University Press, 1960.

Romero Flores, Jesús. *Anales Históricos de la Revolución Mexicana.* Various volumes.

Taracena, Alfonso. *História Extraoficial de la Revolución Mexicana.* México, D. F.: Editorial Jus, S. A., 1972.

Tuchman, Barbara W. *The Zimmerman Telegram.* New York: Bantam Books, 1966.

Womack, John J. *Zapata and the Mexican Revolution.* New York: Alfred A. Knopf, 1969.

Villa's mausoleum in the Parque de la Revolución in Chihuahua City. Villa ordered this built for his remains but it was never used. He was interred in Parral and·later reinterred in the Monument of the Revolution in Mexico City.

— Photo by the author

A list of villista officials who lived with Villa at Canutillo. The monument was constructed on the 100th anniversary of Villa's birth (1878).

— Photo by the author

Monument to Villa in Parral, Chihuahua.
— Photo by the author

The main house at Canutillo, Durango, where Villa spent the last years of his life.
— Photo by the author

A field piece, typical of those used by the villistas, *at the Muséo de la Revolución en Chihuahua, formerly Villa's home, "Quinta Luz."*

— Photo by the author

Villa was vain about his tack and his horses. Note the intricately worked silver saddle horn on this saddle.

— Muséo de la Revolución en Chihuahua,
Photo by the author

This interesting piece of artillery was built onto a packsaddle frame and could be fired from the back of a pack mule.

— Muséo de la Revolución en Chihuahua,
Photo by the author

The dining room at Quinta Luz.

— Muséo de la Revolución en Chihuahua,
Photo by the author

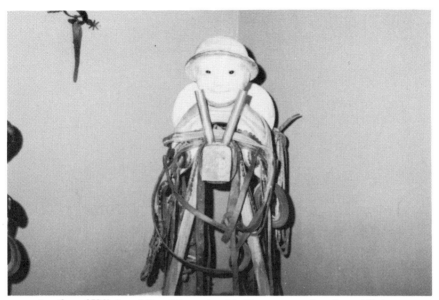

Another of Villa's saddles, this one has his likeness carved on the saddle horn.
— Muséo de la Revolución en Chihuahua,
Photo by the author

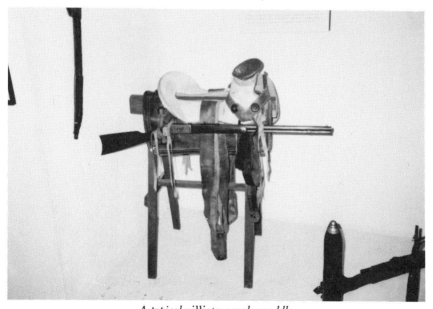

A typical villista *cavalry saddle.*
— Muséo de la Revolución en Chihuahua,
Photo by the author

A photo of Villa in uniform inscribed "to my esteemed friend, Rodolfo Fierro."
— Muséo de la Revolución en Chihuahua,
Photo by the author

Facsimile of a "wanted" poster issued for Villa by the sheriff of Columbus, New Mexico, on the day that villistas hit that border town (March 9, 1916).

The 1923 Dodge in which Villa was shot. Note the bullet holes that ventilated the vehicle.

— Muséo de la Revolución en Chihuahua,
Photo by the author

Villa seated on presidential throne, flanked on the right by Zapata and Urbina and on the left by Fierro.

Villa weeping at Madero's tomb, December 1914.

Villa leading the charge. Purportedly, this was taken on the way to the first battle of Torreón (October 1914).

— Muséo de la Revolución en Chihuahua

Villa dressed in one of his favorite field uniforms, replete with pith helmet.

Generals Obregón, Villa, and John J. Pershing at the customshouse in Ciudad Juárez in 1914. Over Pershing's left shoulder is Lt. George S. Patton.

Trains provided the principal means of transportation for the growing revolutionary armies.

Gen. Francisco Villa and his wife, Sra. Luz Corral de Villa.

Villa in camp, sometime in 1915. Villa is kneeling and his face is shaded.
— Courtesy of James Shideler

The Villa monument in Chihuahua. Taken from a postcard.

A ten-peso note issued by the Constitutionalist government in Chihuahua. These notes were called dos caras *or two faces. They had likenesses of Abraham González and Francisco Madero, two of Villa's idols.*

Villa in retirement at Canutillo. The saddle horn is a sculpted likeness of Villa.
— Muséo de la Revolución en Chihuahua

Villa (center, seated) and some of his supporters.
— Muséo de la Revolución en Chihuahua

Convention President Eulalio Gutiérrez (center) flanked by Villa (his right) and Emiliano Zapata (left).

— Muséo de la Revolución en Chihuahua

Villa with Fierro on his right and Toribio Ortega and Juan Medina on his left.

— Muséo de la Revolución en Chihuahua

VIVA VILLA CABRONES

LA REVOLUCION NO HA TERMINADO.

A postcard, issued in 1977 by what would become a left-wing political group in Chihuahua, calls up the spirit of Pancho Villa to unite the north of Mexico against the impositions of Mexico City. The postcard denounces aristocrats and political leaders who disparage the north and refer to that area merely as "the provinces." A long message printed on the reverse calls for the northerner to "defend himself! . . . Fight! . . . Prepare for the long and hard battle that awaits us!" The pictorial part of the card states: "Viva Villa, you bastards! The Revolution isn't over."

Villa as an officer in Madero's army, 1911. Taken from a postcard.

Villa on horseback.
— O. T. Aultman Collection,
El Paso Public Library

Villa and some of his officers.
— O. T. Aultman Collection,
El Paso Public Library

Villa in formal military garb.
— El Paso Public Library

United States troops crossing the Río Grande in pursuit of Villa, June 1919.
— O. T. Aultman Collection, El Paso Public Library

Villa loved adult mechanical toys — airplanes, cars, motorcycles. Here Villa poses with a new Indian motorcycle.

— O. T. Aultman Collection, El Paso Public Library

Villa with Edwardo Hay and Emilio Madero
— O. T. Aultman Collection, El Paso Public Library

Gen. Felipe Angeles.
— O. T. Aultman Collection,
El Paso Public Library

Pancho Villa loved ice cream among other things. Here he and some friends are in the Elite Confectionery, El Paso, sometime in early 1913 before Villa returned to Mexico following the death of Madero.
— O. T. Aultman Collection, El Paso Public Library.

Luis Terrazas's coach following the retreat of the federales *from Chihuahua in December 1913. The photo was taken near Ojinaga. Chihuahua.*
— O. T. Aultman Collection, El Paso Public Library.

Villa and Gen. Hugh L. Scott conferring at the racetrack in Ciudad Juárez, spring 1914. Note Fierro's fierce look with a cigar in his mouth.
— O. T. Aultman Collection, El Paso Public Library.

Index